IMPLEMENTING COGNITIVE STRATEGY INSTRUCTION ACROSS THE SCHOOL

The Benchmark Manual for Teachers

IRENE GASKINS AND THORNE T. ELLIOT
Benchmark School

With the assistance of:
Susan Audley, James Benedict, Marjorie Downer, Anne Gutman,
Penny Moldofsky, Joyce Ostertag, Ferdows Poosti, Sharon Rauch,
Heidi Robinowitz, Susan Soja, Debra Wile
who allowed us to use transcripts of their lessons

And:
Richard C. Anderson, Jonathan Baron, Michael Pressley
*who shared their expertise regarding the design
of the research and development project*

Brookline Books

Library of Congress Cataloging-in-Publication Data

Gaskin, Irene West.
    Implementing cognitive strategy training across the school :
a Benchmark manual for teachers / by Irene Gaskin.
       p.   cm.
    Includes bibliographical references and index.
    ISBN 0-914797-75-1 : $24.95
    1. Benchmarks School (Media, Pa.) 2. Thought and thinking — Study
and teaching (Elementary) — Pennsylvania — Media — Case studies.
3. Cognitive learning — Pennsylvania — Media — Case studies.
4. Reading — Pennsylvania — Media — Remedial teaching — Case studies.
I. Title.
LD7501.M43722G39   1991
372.13 — dc20   90-28461
                                            CIP

This book is dedicated to the senior author's husband, Richard C. Gaskins.

Table of Contents

SECTION 4: Implementing A Strategy Program

Foreword

At the June 3, 1990 celebration of Benchmark School's Twentieth Anniversary, Drs. Richard C. Anderson and Ralph C. Preston were honored as the two people who have had the greatest impact on the intellectual life of the school during the past 20 years. These two individuals have guided us to understand how children learn and inspired us to translate that understanding into better academic programs for students. In addition, they have supported and encouraged us every step of the way. Without these two extraordinary men, Benchmark would not be nearly so successful in meeting the needs of bright underachievers. Because of the important roles each has played in the life of Benchmark School, both were asked to write a few words to help us introduce this book. The Foreword begins with Richard Anderson's acceptance remarks upon receiving the 20th Anniversary Award. Dr. Anderson's remarks are followed by Dr. Preston's introduction to this volume about strategy teaching.

Dr. Richard C. Anderson

I am deeply honored to be recognized at this celebration as someone who has contributed to Benchmark School. When Irene Gaskins called me to break the news, I must say that I was astonished. Sure, I've tried to make myself useful so that I'll be invited back. But there has never been any doubt in my mind that Benchmark gives more to me than I give to Benchmark.

Benchmark is a remarkable school. As students, or parents of students who have failed in other schools, I know you already believe strongly in Benchmark: here is where most of you, or your children, learned to read. As an outsider who specializes in reading and language education, I can confirm for you that your evaluation of Benchmark is widely shared. Benchmark is famous in reading, special education, and elementary education more broadly. Successful approaches to teaching created at Benchmark in 1990 will be emulated in other forward looking schools in the year 2000. Benchmark is in education what a first-rate teaching and research hospital is in medicine.

Benchmark is an extraordinary school because of its excellent teaching. At one time or another I think I have observed in the classrooms of the majority of the teachers at Benchmark. I have always seen excellent teaching. There are features common to all Benchmark teachers attributable to a shared understanding of goals and means for achieving those goals. But within this shared framework I see a wide variation in personal styles.

Benchmark is not a school for the teacher who could be satisfied doing an adequate job using conventional methods. No matter how well the school may seem to be doing, at Benchmark there is a relentless determination to do even better. It is a place where teachers read and discuss educational research, initiate their own research and development projects, and try to improve their instruction based on what they learn. It is a place where teachers are expected to be self-critical and where they are constantly subjected to the scrutiny of others. This regimen may be tiring, and occasionally uncomfortable, but I believe it's one of the major sources of the school's strength.

And, why is Benchmark notable for excellent teaching? That traces directly to the vision, intelligence, and competence of its exemplary founder and director, Irene Gaskins.

Richard C. Anderson
Professor and Director
Center for the Study of Reading
University of Illinois

Dr. Ralph C. Preston

Irene Gaskins and Thorne Elliot have performed a valuable service for all teachers and school administrators in writing this book. It describes in detail the principles and practices which account for the stunning success of Benchmark School, and it cites and summarizes the research on which its practices rest. Although Benchmark is a school for children of elementary-school and middle-school age who started there as poor readers, many of its procedures, I believe, are probably also applicable for teaching students in secondary school and even college who may be able to read but who must struggle to keep their heads above water.

When Benchmark opened its doors twenty years ago, a confusing array of vigorously promoted proposals for curriculum reorganization were swirling about in the educational world. They ranged widely in type and purpose. Among them were a renewed cry for a back-to-basics curriculum; a proposal for non-graded schools; an insistence that students learn generalizations through "discovery" rather than through traditional presentations by teacher or textbook; and a widely touted plan for dividing a classroom into a phalanx of learning centers. The now almost forgotten Right-to-Read movement, initiated by the U.S. Commissioner of Education, with its noble if quixotic aim to make universal literacy a reality by 1980, added to the medley of reform. Such a mind-boggling mixture of signals for change, each with some degree of merit, seemed to perplex some school administrators I knew, causing them to shy away from any fundamental change and to fall back on conducting school business as usual.

During this period of floundering, some schools, in turning away from panaceas, searched for more promising ground. Benchmark, for example, began building a research-based curriculum with the support of Title 1 grants, generous encouragement from foundations, and the counsel of well-known specialists in learning theory and language. Each of the latter was invited to visit the school and see its classrooms in action, and then to conduct faculty seminars. This book records Benchmark's efforts, successes, and challenges as it proceeded over the subsequent years to fashion a new kind of curriculum—a curriculum in which the students simultaneously acquired both knowledge of the subject and knowledge of the process (the latter prompted on a given day by one or more of the 40-plus "thinking strategies" compiled by the faculty).

The day-by-day work of the school is admirably illustrated by numerous transcripts of teacher-led discussions. They include the work of a variety of teachers, students of varying ages, and several different subjects and strategies. As a teacher, I had learned that there is probably no task calling for greater skill than conducting a discussion. The participating teachers deserve high grades for their recorded performances. Student participation appears spontaneous and eager. At times, a teacher may lecture when sensing that a class needs more information on the spot.

The book branches out into matters that surprised and pleased me. There is an absorbing chapter telling of the collaboration in the teaching of a history course between a professional historian and an advocate of process knowledge, and what each learned as a result of the collaboration. Another chapter describes a pioneering mini-course in psychology taught to four middle-school classes by Dr. Gaskins, focusing upon how the mind works. There are briefer treatments of firmly held commitments. For example, Benchmark seeks to conserve schooltime for academic purposes. Hence, workbooks, so-called educational games, and learning centers are ruled out as legitimate seatwork activities; such unscheduled time is considered better used by having a student read from a book and make a written response to the reading.

We learn through this "Manual for Teachers" of the attitudes and practices that transformed students who had experienced two or three years of frustration and failure in their early school experience. When they arrived at Benchmark as battered students, as Dr. Gaskins once described them, they began to develop self-assurance and independence as learners and as people.

Ralph C. Preston
Professor Emeritus
University of Pennsylvania
Fall 1990

Preface

This book is about thinking. It will describe a program to guide young people to be goal oriented, planful, strategic, and self-assessing. The intended audience for this book is anyone who is interested in the application of cognitive science to classroom instruction. We have tried to make the book understandable and interesting to a wide range of readers, from undergraduates to researchers and from primary school teachers to secondary teachers.

Our book is the result of twenty years of research-based curriculum development as we have searched for ways to help bright underachievers in reading meet with success in school that is commensurate with their ability. It has been, and continues to be, an exciting project. Each year as we learn more, we fine-tune the program; thus it is ever evolving. Our last three years have been particularly productive and rewarding as a result of our James S. McDonnell research and development grant to teach thinking strategies across the curriculum. This book tells the story of that project, as well as how we came to realize that teaching strategies was one of the crucial links in our program to return successful students to the mainstream.

We owe a debt of gratitude to many people for their encouragement and support. During our first decade Ralph Preston headed our Curriculum Advisory Committee which met annually with the Benchmark Staff for many years beginning in the spring of 1971. Those on the committee were: Richard Bocchini, Morton Botel, Bartell Cardon, William Carey, Rachel Cox, Roy Kress, Laura Murphy, Margaret Rawson, Janet Rogers, Nicholas Spennato, and Mary Gray Stoner. In addition, the Benchmark Staff has had the privilege of interacting with and learning from many researchers who have had a significant impact on the Benchmark curriculum that we describe in this book. These include, in addition to those mentioned above: Richard Allington, Donna Alvermann, Richard Anderson, Eunice Askov, Isabel Beck, John Borkowski, Mary Bryson, Jack Cassidy, Mary Coleman, James Cunningham, Patricia Cunningham, Beth Davey, Donald Deshler, Gerald Duffy, William Durr, Dolores Durkin, Joan Finucci, Philip Gough, Donald Graves, John Guthrie, Jane Hansen, Albert Harris, Roselmina Indrisano, Dale Johnson, Doris Johnson, Marjorie Johnson, Peter Johnston, Nancy Larrick, Marjorie Lipson, Anthony Manzo, Anne McDourt-Lewis, Jana Mason, William Nagy, Donna Ogle, Jean Osborn, Annemarie Palincsar, Scott Paris, David Pearson, Charles Perfetti, John Pikulski, Gay Su Pinnell, Michael Pressley, Taffy Raphael, Laura Roehler, Barak Rosenshine, Jay Samuels, Jennye Schultz, Jean Schumaker, William Sheldon,

Mary Seifert, Kenneth Smith, Trika Smith-Burke, Rand Spiro, Steven Stahl, Sandra Stotsky, Dorothy Strickland, Robert Tierney, Joanna Williams, Karen Wixson, and Peter Winograd.

Probably our greatest leaps forward in developing curriculum for bright underachievers have resulted from our various curriculum development projects described in this book which were undertaken with Richard Anderson, Jonathan Baron, Patricia Cunningham, Donald Graves, and Michael Pressley. In particular, the influence of the research emanating from the Center for the Study of Reading under the leadership of Richard Anderson cannot be overstated. The knowledge we gained from their Technical Reports provided the structure for our curriculum development.

Benchmark staff members who have graciously allowed us to tape record their lessons and use the transcripts of those lessons as examples in this book are: Susan Audley, James Benedict, Marjorie Downer, Anne Gutman, Penny Moldofsky, Joyce Ostertag, Ferdows Poosti, Sharon Rauch, Heidi Robinowitz, Susan Soja, and Debra Wile. Those staff members and good friends who have read and reread drafts of various chapters and given us helpful feedback are: Nancy Alvarez, Richard Anderson, Susan Audley, Mary Lee Bass, Francis Boehnlein, Milton Budoff, Ruth Gail Cohen, Betsy Cunicelli, Marjorie Downer, Diane Eyer, Robert Gaskins, Jennifer Gaskins, Eleanor Gensemer, Nancy Helm, Tom Hurster, Deborah Lee, Eric MacDonald, Margo Matt, Joyce Ostertag, Nancy Powell, Michael Pressley, Ralph Preston, Taffy Raphael, Sally Laird, Colette Sabatina, Heidi Robinowitz, Linda Six, Susan Soja, Debra Wile, Judie Young, and Warren Young.

We are especially grateful to the James S. McDonnell Foundation, both for their support and for the opportunity they provided for our working with and learning from McDonnell personnel and the other grant recipients: John Bransford, Ann Brown, John Bruer, Robbie Case, Glynda Hull, Dana Kay, Jill Larkin, Alan Lesgold, Jim Minstrell, Kathryn Spoehr, Robert Sternberg, and Marianne Wiser. Each one has had an impact on our thinking about cognition and strategy instruction.

And, finally, we would like to acknowledge the patience, understanding, and encouragement of our husbands Dick and John. Without their whole-hearted support throughout Benchmark School's twenty-year history, we would not have been able to have spent the hours and days wrapped up in the exciting adventures in curriculum development described in this book.

Section 1:
Background

CHAPTER 1

Benchmark — A School for Poor Readers

An Introduction

For twenty years Benchmark School has been developing programs to prepare bright underachievers in reading to be successful students in the mainstream of education (Gaskins, 1980; Gaskins & Elliot, 1983; Gaskins, 1988). The school was started because of the first author's growing dissatisfaction with the instructional options and prognosis for poor readers during the 1960's. Tutoring programs and pull-out programs, such as special education and remedial reading, were producing dismal results. With few exceptions, these programs did not produce students who eventually returned to regular classes and functioned academically on a level commensurate with their abilities or even on a level equal to average students at their grade placement. As we entered the seventies, it was clear to many parents and the author that the programs for remediating reading problems and preparing poor readers for successful school experiences were not working. There had to be a better way and Benchmark's mission, as it opened its doors in a damp church basement in September 1970, was to find that way. That better way would be based on the realization that there is no best or right way to teach children to read, to learn, or to think. Instead, we found a few research-based principles to guide us in making program decisions at each juncture in achieving our mission.

Recommendations for dealing with poor readers during the sixties and into the next decade were discouraging, suggesting that the fault for poor reading and lack of success in school was to be found in the child. For example, during the early years of the school, Benchmark parents often reported that, prior to their Benchmark experience, they had been given one of three recommendations for dealing with their child's lack of success: 1) convince your child to try harder, 2) accept that your child is immature and will outgrow the problem, or 3) realize that your child has either an emotional or neurological problem and needs special therapy or training which addresses the symptoms he or she is demonstrating (i.e., acting out behavior, depression, letter reversals, etc.).

At Benchmark we did not subscribe to any of these prescriptions. We believed that providing students with success often would prove to be an antidote for acting-out behavior and depression, and that teaching students heuristics (informal methods to learn by themselves) and strategies for dealing with such problems as making letter reversals, miscalling words, and misunderstanding selections would lead to increasingly better reading and to an improved sense of self-worth.

Most of the children who attended Benchmark in the early years of the school had experienced their first reading instruction in schools where all students were taught to read using the one program the school or district had adopted as "the way" to teach reading. In some districts this was a synthetic phonics program, while in others "the way" might have been a specific basal reader series, linguistic reading program, or the language experience approach. These programs led to adequate reading proficiency for most of the students in suburban schools. This fact often led administrators and teachers to believe that, if most children were successful with one of these programs, then those children who failed to make satisfactory progress using the same program must in some way be deficient. In other words, the problem lay with the child, not with the instructional approach.

The first author had a different hypothesis. She believed that most successful readers learn to read in spite of teachers and programs. She believed that this happened either because successful students adjusted their way of learning to match the way a particular reading program was taught or they ignored the specific cues used in a program (e.g., rules for applying sounds to symbols) and learned to read using cues of their own choice (e.g., context clues). If it was true that many successful readers learned to read in spite of teachers and programs, then it appeared that the very students who needed specific instruction to learn to read were being ignored. The easy-to-teach students were in the majority in suburban schools and many teachers (including the first author in her early years of teaching) were able to delude themselves into thinking they were teaching, when the very students who needed teaching were judged to be unteachable.

With the view that every student is teachable, Benchmark teachers throughout our 20-year history have used diagnostic teaching to ascertain the best match between the way a child learns and the method for teaching him or her to read. To do this, teachers use a variety of approaches to teaching reading. As diagnostic teaching proceeds, teachers eliminate from each student's program those approaches that do not seem beneficial and emphasize those which seem to foster each student's progress. As a result, we have learned that some of our students respond well to a traditional directed-thinking-activity approach, while others need more specialized techniques such as repeated reading or tracing, saying, and writing each new word as they learn it. All seem to benefit from the addition of decoding instruction to their individually designed programs. All of our students have learned to read using this flexible approach to differences in learning style. However, in our early years, these same students did not necessarily become successful students when they returned to their regular schools.

This book tells how we at Benchmark came to our present (but still evolving) conclusions about how to teach our poor readers. These conclusions derive from some of our failures — students we taught to read, who were not successful students. They exhibited a variety of maladaptive behaviors. Some were disorganized, frequently misplacing completed papers and/or neglecting to gather the necessary materials to complete assignments. Others, despite above-average intelligence, read and reread their texts or took copious notes, yet could not discuss the major ideas being studied. Still others passively flipped pages and rarely participated in classroom discussions. As we followed our early students' progress after they left Benchmark it was becoming increasingly obvious that there was more to helping poor readers become successful students than merely teaching them how to read.

And so our vision of the student who would leave Benchmark and meet with success in each subsequent school setting broadened to include far more than competence in reading. We recognized the need to provide our students with the tools for actively acquiring and processing information. Our vision became students who would be motivated, have the knowledge of content and strategies to take charge of their own learning, and would put forth the effort to set goals, plan, self-assess, and implement strategies.

As the reader will see, not everything we have tried has been as effective as we would have liked, but we feel we are well on our way to creating readers, learners, thinkers, and problem solvers. The follow-up reports from receiving schools have been increasingly encouraging since our shift in focus from teaching reading to addressing the needs of the whole student. These positive reports propel our continuing efforts. We are still investigating, experimenting, and revising, as is apparent as this story of Benchmark unfolds.

This first chapter describes the philosophy which led to the founding of Benchmark School, as well as the students and the setting of the school. To fully set the context for the reader, we also describe the structure and staffing of the school, the curriculum, and staff development.

A Philosophy of Instruction

Benchmark School was founded in 1970 with the goal of guiding poor readers in grades one through eight to succeed in school on a par with their potential. Recognizing that each person is different, it made sense that each student learns differently and that a one-program-fits-all approach to teaching would be neither appropriate for, nor fair to, students. Our firm belief was that students who had not experienced success in learning to read had been victims of instruction that did not match the way they learned. Benchmark's teachers would have to know how to teach using numerous approaches and / or methods and to adjust these, as well as the skills and strategies they would teach, to the needs of individual students.

Benchmark's faculty believes that every child with average or above potential can be taught to read. Although Benchmark opened as a school for poor readers, the school's interest from the start has been in the total child. Our goal is to provide each student with the experience of success that will develop a sense of self-worth and self-confidence, for these are the prerequisites for the motivation and the willingness to take risks that are so necessary to academic success. We believe it is not only our charge to provide each child we accept with a successful academic experience during the child's stay at Benchmark, but also to equip the student with the heuristics (informal methods to learn independently), strategies, and skills needed to cope with the demands of educational settings after Benchmark.

As early as the school's first year, progress was made toward achieving these goals by teachers who were able to love those who rejected their love, to see positive attributes in every child, and to persist in finding a way to reach each child. Benchmark teachers plan extensively, work as a team, and continue to grow professionally. They find their rewards in every smile, every step forward, every head held high, and every "Yes, I can" behavior.

Benchmark's Early Students and Setting

Benchmark's first students were drawn primarily from the first author's tutoring practice. These founding students were 17 bright, poor readers who attended classes from 8:45 A.M. until 11:15 A.M. each day in a dingy Sunday school classroom to receive instruction in reading. At the conclusion of the morning reading program, the students returned to their regular schools for the remainder of the school day. The second year, there were 32 students enrolled in the half-day, released-time program at Benchmark School. We expanded into a second church basement room. The students ranged from 6-14 years, and all had primary reading problems.

During the third year a full-day program was added. Children could then attend Benchmark for either a half day or a full day. The full-day program was state approved for children referred by school districts as either socially and emotionally disturbed or learning disabled/brain damaged. The children in the full-day, state-funded program needed to meet the Benchmark criterion of average or above intelligence with primary reading problems, and the state criterion of having been labeled as emotionally disturbed or neurologically impaired. In our view, the students we accepted who were labeled "emotionally disturbed" had mild emotional overlays, seemingly due to the difficulties they had experienced in school. With one or two exceptions, the students referred as "neurologically impaired" were so diagnosed based on "soft signs," such as letter, word, and figure-drawing reversals.

A few of the full-day students were privately funded, but most attended Benchmark at no cost to their parents and were from homes of limited means. Our enrollment began to grow at an increased rate. We outgrew the church basement and added classes in rented space in a nearby public school. As we entered our sixth year, we moved into our own newly constructed building, a building with ten classrooms and a large library at its center into which all the classrooms opened.

The pattern of accepting primarily state-funded, full-day students continued through 1978. Then, due to PL 94-142, we began receiving state-funded referrals that were inappropriate candidates. Only the most serious special education cases were referred to private schools after 1978. In the Philadelphia area this seemed to mean students who were approaching or in adolescence and who were difficult to handle in regular schools. Because Benchmark was an elementary school with expertise in teaching reading for learning-disabled children who demonstrated no primary emotional problems, we did not feel qualified to continue to accept state-funded students. Many of the state-funded students referred in 1978 or before remained at Benchmark School through the eighth grade, well into the mid-eighties.

Students and Setting Today

From 1978 until the present, we have accepted more and more privately-funded and scholarship students. Today the student population of 167 is entirely composed of full-day, privately funded students whose primary referring problem is poor reading despite average or better intelligence. The school is housed in a modern complex of buildings located on 19 acres of woods and playing fields. Since 1975 the school has added a gymnasium, as well as a middle-school addition which houses four classrooms, an art room, a conference room, and a psychological services suite. The original building, with two stories plus a mezzanine, houses the library and ten classrooms on the main floor, four math classrooms, a science room on the lower level, and numerous offices on the main level and mezzanine.

During the most recent five years, Benchmark students have tended to be predominantly white, middle-class boys with an average WISC-R full-scale IQ of 115; about one-quarter of the 167 students are girls. A few students each year are African-Americans, Orientals, Iranians, Indians, etc. The vast majority of the students have higher Verbal WISC-R scores than Performance scores and tend to have low Information, Arithmetic, Digit Span, and Coding scores, as compared to their other subtest scaled scores on the WISC-R.

Most students enter Benchmark when they are between seven and ten years old; the vast majority enter as virtual nonreaders. Some students remain through the age of 14, though no new students are accepted who are older than 11. All students accepted for admission to Benchmark exhibit a significant discrepancy between reading level and potential as measured by the WISC-R. Maladaptive cognitive styles and temperaments are not uncommon entering the school. A few of the characteristics most often mentioned in reference to entering Benchmark students are: inattentive, disorganized, passive, impulsive, rigid, nonpersistent, intellectually curious, verbal, and charming.

During the last five years the average length of stay has been four years, after which 99% of the students enter a full-time, regular-school setting reading at or above the mean reading level of the receiving school's student body.

THE STRUCTURE OF THE SCHOOL

An Elementary School

For many years the school operated as a grades 1-8 elementary school. The organization of each of the 14 classes was very similar. For example, $2^3/4$ hours each morning were devoted to reading and language arts, with the afternoon divided into four periods of forty minutes each for: 1) lunch and recess, 2) science or social studies, 3) mathematics, 4) art, physical education, music, or health. The language arts time included process writing and sharing, word identification, reading group, seatwork and literature, with bits of time for individual conferences and goal checks, etc. squeezed in.

More recently, the school has been divided into a *Lower School* composed of ten classes of children in grades 1-5 and a *Middle School* composed of four classes of children in grades 6-8. The *Lower School* continues to have a schedule like that outlined above.

The Middle School operates like most middle schools with more changes of class, a different composition of teachers and students for each course, and all classes sharing a common lunch break. The school day runs from 8:30 until 2:30. Language arts (reading 80 minutes, writing 40 minutes, and word identification 20 minutes) still commands the lion's share of the day. Mini-courses such as Psych 101, grammar, Latin, and literature occupy approximately 20 minutes a day. Social studies and science meet each day for 40 minutes each. Health, music, and art are taught once a week and physical education meets twice a week.

Class size varies throughout the Lower School and Middle School from 11 students per head teacher and teaching assistant to 13 students per head teacher and co-teacher. Students are grouped according to age and reader level for all of their classes except mathematics, where they are grouped by age and math level.

Faculty

The administration of the school is composed of the school's director, the head of the Lower School, the head of the Middle School, and supervisors of the mathematics department, the psychological services department, special subjects, speech and language, research and development, and supervisors who assist the Lower and Middle School heads. A placement director is responsible for the placement and follow-up of all Benchmark graduates. Follow-up is an ongoing process, with follow-up data formally collected about Benchmark graduates for five years after they leave Benchmark. In addition, informal data have been collected recently about students who graduated as many as 18 or 19 years ago.

The teaching faculty is composed of 14 head teachers, 8 co-teachers, and 7 teaching assistants who are responsible for the instruction of reading and language arts. The administrative staff and head teachers tend to have master's degrees, most often in reading. Co-teachers and teaching assistants tend to be certified teachers who are in training for a full-time position at Benchmark and teach only half days.

The 14 head teachers are responsible for their students for the entire day, though many of the subject-matter areas are taught by specialists. Among the specialists, there are 5 mathematics teachers, 1 social studies teacher, 2 science teachers, 1 health teacher, 3 speech and language therapists, 1 art teacher, 1 music teacher, and 1 physical education teacher and a librarian. There is also a psychological services staff composed of 6 psychologists and social workers with one member of the staff assigned to each classroom. Additional staff members are employed as research assistants and assistants to the placement counselor.

THE CURRICULUM

Reading

In the early seventies our primary efforts were concentrated on developing methods that would facilitate improved reading ability among our poor readers. In fact, only reading was taught during the school's first two years. Instruction in mathematics, writing, social studies, science, and the other curriculum areas typical of elementary schools was added to the program by the third year when we added a full-day elementary-school program to the half-day, released-time remedial program.

The heart of the school by the third year was our rapidly expanding library of color-coded books which helped students select books at their independent levels. With each successful reading experience, students seemed to gain in the satisfaction they derived from reading. The highlight of the day for many students was the individual book conference with a teacher or teaching assistant about a book read at the student's independent level.

> *Doing a great deal of easy reading,* rather than struggling in books that were too challenging, *seemed to be one key to the increased reading proficiency of our students.* We discovered that *it was the number of words read that correlated with progress in reading, not the difficulty of the text.*

Another key to our students' success was the daily reading instruction they received in small groups which emphasized explicit instruction in strategies such as using background knowledge, reading for a purpose, and making inferences. Students were also introduced to a variety of strategies for decoding unknown words, with the suggestion that each student choose the strategy that worked best for him or her.

A psychological services department was added in the school's fourth year to support teachers in dealing with the emotional overlay that was characteristic of many of these students who had known only failure in school prior to entering Benchmark. Class meetings were held for students and evening programs were conducted for parents. Teachers met regularly with members of the psychological services staff to brainstorm ways of better dealing with their students.

It was clear by the school's fifth year, based on the follow-up work of school placement counselor Joan Davidson, that Benchmark students who returned to the mainstream were successful readers. Most had found ways of learning to read that allowed them to compensate for their individual learning differences. In addition to reading well, many had taken with them, or devised on their own, strategies for succeeding in school. For example, one former Benchmark student supplied a classmate with carbon paper to use when taking notes or writing assignments so that a correct copy of the notes or assignments was passed on to him. This student had learned that, due to poor spelling that often was not even phonetic, he frequently was unable to read the notes or assignments he had written. Another former Benchmark student compensated for his slow reading pace by having an adult tape record each chapter that was covered in social studies and science. This enabled him to complete his assignments on time, by not having to laboriously work his way through reading the text before answering the questions assigned for homework. Several other students learned that in order to pass weekly spelling tests, they had to use a procedure learned at Benchmark called Say, Cover, Write, and Check.

Mathematics, Science, and Physical Education

During the middle seventies we concentrated on bringing other areas of the curriculum up to the level of expertise demonstrated in reading instruction. We received a grant to develop a mathematics program for learning-disabled students. Four teachers were hired to teach all the math classes. The goal was to create math specialists, just as we had reading specialists. The reading specialists were responsible for teaching reading and language arts, and the application of reading to the content areas. The reading specialists would no longer, however, teach math.

In the second year of our grant we were allowed to expand the grant to develop not only the mathematics program, but our science and physical education programs. We hired a science specialist who worked with classroom teachers to create special science units. Later, a science teacher was hired who took on the responsibility of teaching science to 12 of the school's 14 classes. Presently one science teacher teaches science to eight of the lower-school classes twice a week. The classroom teachers of the two youngest lower-school classes teach science to their own classes. The four middle-school classes have science four times a week taught by two science teachers.

As a result of the grant, our physical education teacher was able to add an Outward Bound component to the physical education program. The physical education program already comprised a traditional physical education program taught twice a week to each of the 14 classes, plus "Little Gym," a five-day-a-week class for the two youngest classes, and an after-school program which featured, among other activities, a soccer clinic, a junior varsity soccer team, and a varsity soccer team. The latter two teams compete very successfully each fall against other private-school soccer teams. Benchmark's winning record clearly lends status to attending Benchmark.

Writing

Our approach to teaching writing is a process approach. In 1978 we were introduced to a process approach to writing. This approach was adopted throughout the school as one way of assisting students to develop skills in written composition (Gaskins, 1982; Gaskins, in press). Students who enter the school as nonreaders, and who may know as few as five or six sound/symbol relationships, write stories about what they know using invented spellings and lines. (Lines are used when a student has no idea of what letters to use for a word.) Content is valued and spelling and punctuation are de-emphasized, except in cases when a student chooses to take a piece through the writing process to a final draft. Students write every day for approximately a half hour. They also have a daily time for sharing what they have written. As students increase in proficiency as writers, they are introduced to more formal types of writing including reports, letters, essays, summaries, character sketches, etc. However, no matter how advanced the students' writing, there is always time for writing on topics of one's choice, with the opportunity to work through the writing process to publication and the presentation of one's book to the library.

Content-Area Reading

Another area of emphasis in the late seventies was reading in the content areas, with the first author experimenting with various approaches to guiding Benchmark students to success in handling difficult social studies and science textbooks (Gaskins, 1981). Students were directly taught such strategies as surveying, setting purposes, discerning main ideas, outlining, predicting test questions, self-testing, etc.

In the past several years, and especially since our immersion in a funded program to teach strategies across the curriculum with the goal of creating better learners, thinkers and problem solvers, content-area reading has come to the fore. Students are learning that, more than in any other form of reading, successful reading in informational texts requires active involvement. They are also learning which reading strategies work best for them. They are assuming ever-increasing responsibility for selecting and applying those strategies independently.

Special Projects

Taped-repeated reading. Despite the success of our program in creating readers, we still had students whose progress in learning to read was incredibly slow—so slow that we often wondered if we were making any progress at all. Among other instructional innovations, we experimented in 1976-77 with the Impress Technique, a technique we piloted with three students who were having the most difficulty obtaining a sight vocabulary. Over the years, as we adapted this technique, it became a taped-repeated reading program that continues to prove helpful for some students who have the most difficulty acquiring a sight vocabulary. Using Benchmark's version of the Impress Technique, a student follows in a book a passage that has been taped. The listening/following procedure is repeated until the student feels he or she can read the passage aloud smoothly, with expression, and without error. The passage is most often taped by a parent and practiced at home with the parent. The student then reads aloud a portion of the passage selected by the teacher and the teacher keeps a record of the student's progress.

Language-through-literature. In 1976-77, we added a language-through-literature program for each class, in which a language therapist reads aloud to a class a selection from children's literature. The selection provides listening practice and a basis for class discussion. The language-through-literature program has proven particularly beneficial for students with both receptive and expressive language problems. The success of this program seems to result both from the weekly lessons presented in the classrooms by the language therapist and from the knowledge about developing language skills the classroom teachers gain from observing the therapist's language lessons, knowledge they apply in their work with their students throughout the week.

Academic-engaged time during seatwork. In the mid-seventies, we became increasingly committed to structuring our students' time in class so that they spent a high proportion of their time academically engaged, as opposed to time in such activities as playing games and moving between learning centers. We became very focussed on how our students used their time. Teachers were encouraged to ask themselves the purpose of each assignment or task they were considering for their students. If they could not justify the value of the assignment as leading to academic progress on a valued objective, they were encouraged to have their student read rather than complete the proposed assignment or task. We were convinced that consistent engagement in meaningful tasks was what would maximize academic progress.

Many heated debates were held among staff members, as well as with experts who visited the school, regarding criteria for selecting meaningful activities for students. For example, we had difficulty justifying the value of phonics workbooks and worksheets, finding them to be exercises in encoding, rather than providing meaningful decoding practice. We ceased using them. Most reading skill sheets and workbooks were rejected as fragmenting the process of reading, rather than strengthening skills which would transfer to real reading. Basal reader workbooks were discarded as being busywork and providing little opportunity for real reading. Once aware of the inadequacies of published seatwork, the staff was left with no prepackaged materials to occupy the students who were at their desks while reading groups were being conducted. Learning centers were tried, but these too often turned out to be workbook-like, with the added disadvantage of reducing academically engaged time as the students moved from center to center and needed time to refocus on each new center.

The solution to this dilemma was to allow students to do *lots of easy reading* during their seatwork time. Students began to read two or three stories or chapters at their independent level during each forty-minute seatwork period. They were allowed to progress at their own rate; thus students often were all reading different stories or books on any one day. There was usually some kind of written response required after the completion of each story or chapter. Our guideline: 80% of the seatwork time should be spent reading and no more than 20% of the time on writing a response to what was read. These responses were not intended to be inquisition-like. Rather they were to provide the student with an opportunity to reflect on what was read and make a judgment or interpretation. A further guideline was that students were to be given feedback regarding their written responses sometime during the morning language arts period on the day the response was completed.

Research and development. The development of programs for bright underachievers continues to be a priority at Benchmark. For example, follow-up of Benchmark students as they entered the mainstream revealed that teaching students to read well was not the only ingredient necessary for our students to be successful after they left Benchmark School. We discovered that, though most of our graduates read well and generally understood what they read, they were not always able to convey this understanding in writing. This discovery was the impetus for a curriculum development program to improve our writing program.

We were successful in improving the writing ability of our students, and some even won local writing contests; yet some ingredient (or ingredients) was still missing from our program. Despite improved writing ability, too many of our students still were not able to experience success equal to their ability when they returned to the mainstream. This was particularly true in the content areas where there was a heavy reading and study load and a great deal of independence expected of students.

We began to realize that we needed to teach our students strategies for coping with the maladaptive habits, styles, and temperaments that contributed to and resulted from their initial difficulties in school, and to teach them those strategies needed for school success in all areas of the curriculum that many bright students figure out on their own. As a result, eight months were spent working with Jonathan Baron to develop a program of strategy instruction that would help students successfully cope with maladaptive cognitive styles such as impulsivity, rigidity, and nonpersistence (Gaskins & Baron, 1985). In addition, various programs were developed and piloted to teach our students how to cope more successfully with the study demands of a regular school (Gaskins, 1981; Gaskins and Elliot, 1983).

Decoding problems among our students were another area of concern. This resulted in a five-year research and development project with Richard Anderson of the Center for the Study of Reading and Patricia Cunningham of Wake Forest University. The purpose of this project was to develop a word identification program that would provide our students with several strategies to use when they encountered unknown words (Gaskins, Downer, Anderson, Cunningham, Gaskins, Schommer, and The Teachers of Benchmark School, 1988). Currently a three-year research and development project, funded by the James S. McDonnell Foundation, is underway to teach students to use strategies across the curriculum for becoming better learners, thinkers, and problem solvers. This project gave impetus to this book.

STAFF DEVELOPMENT

The rich opportunities for professional development tend to be one of the primary reasons teachers join the Benchmark staff. Sources of professional growth are available both within and outside the school. The staff contributes to and consults with outside experts to guide research-based change for improvement. As a result, the Benchmark program is always evolving, never static.

During the school's first year we learned the importance of the infusion of new ideas into the system. As a founding member of the school's Board of Directors, Ralph Preston formed the Benchmark Curriculum Advisory Committee, a group of well-known educators and psychologists in the Philadelphia area who agreed to meet with the Benchmark staff one day a year. The stimulating meetings with this group served both as the impetus for our better meeting the needs of our students and as evidence of the value of hearing, considering, and accepting ideas from outside the confines of Benchmark.

Since the school opened, the staff has met weekly to discuss professional literature and to exchange ideas; informal discussions go on daily. The academic and behavioral problems exhibited by our early students presented a considerable challenge, and staff development projects, then, focused exclusively on ways to meet the reading *and* behavioral needs of the students. The teachers adopted the motto, "All I can change is me!"

A formal weekly research seminar was initiated during our eighth year, replacing the less formal weekly discussions of professional literature which were attended by a core group of eight or ten staff members. Current professional articles that relate to instructional concerns at Benchmark are selected from Benchmark's extensive professional library and distributed for review. During the weekly seminars, teachers briefly summarize the articles, then lead a discussion on the relevance of each article for instruction at Benchmark.

Weekly meetings also take place among groups of teachers, between each classroom teacher and the teacher's supervisor, and each teacher and the director.

In addition to the members of the Curriculum Advisory Committee, Benchmark has invited well-known experts in fields related to our program to present all-day workshops at Benchmark. For example, in 1977 Barak Rosenshine presented a workshop on direct instruction and time on task. The following year Robert Ruddell, Donald Graves, Robert Hillerich, and John Guthrie shared their expertise and guided us to make research-based decisions about our methods in teaching reading, writing, and spelling. During the intervening years our monthly inservice meetings have continued to feature well-known experts who have helped us grow in our understanding of research and pedagogy.

The development of the Benchmark curriculum was also greatly influenced by the research generated by the Center for the Study of Reading at the University of Illinois. Faculty members attended conferences where this research was presented and read Center publications. Meetings were held at Benchmark to report and brainstorm applications. Experts from the Center visited Benchmark to present workshops and several collaborative projects were undertaken.

As this text vividly indicates, staff development at Benchmark is a major and ongoing enterprise. It is central to our beliefs about achieving school change and professional growth. It is the major focus of the final chapter.

SUMMARY

The curriculum of Benchmark School has developed over a period of 20 years. Improving reading instruction has been the primary focus of the school, although strategies for coping with unique learning and cognitive styles, as well as specific temperaments, have also been stressed across the curriculum. The school emphasizes the importance of students doing a great deal of easy reading, and teachers plan each student's program to maximize academic-engaged time. Traditional elementary-school and middle-school subjects are part of the Benchmark curriculum. Much of the curriculum has been developed as a result of specific research and development projects, and all instruction is research-based.

Despite the fact that our programs are continually being developed and improved based on our own experience and current research, we are never satisfied that we have it right. We are continually striving to make our programs better. Program development is never ending, a process we will share with you in this book.

OVERVIEW OF THE BOOK

In this book we describe the various phases of Benchmark's development of a program to create **strategic learners, thinkers, and problem solvers across the curriculum**. Our goal is to provide teachers and administrators with a handbook that can be used as a reference while they are developing a program to combine the teaching of content and strategies.

We begin in Chapter 2 by sharing our rationale for teaching both content and strategies. Also in Chapter 2 we discuss the issues that impact on the implementation of such a program. In Chapter 3, we summarize our present understandings about how the mind works to learn, think, and problem solve.

Section 2, which begins with Chapter 4, describes the strategies presently being taught at Benchmark. Chapter 5 presents our most recent model for teaching strategies. (The reader may want to skip Chapters 2-5 for now and move right into Chapter 6 to get a feel for the program in action.)

Section 3 is composed of five chapters (Chapters 6 - 10) which describe practices at Benchmark School. Chapter 6 tells of a pilot project for joining the teaching of process and content. Chapter 7, about Psych 101, describes a course for learning about learning, a course developed for the Middle School to teach students a rationale for using learning strategies. Chapters 8 and 9 describe strategy instruction in the Lower School and Middle School respectively, while Chapter 10 is a case study of eight months of strategy instruction in one class.

The last chapter of the book describes principles and practices for engaging, training, and supporting teachers in the implementation of a strategy program across the curriculum.

CHAPTER 2

Rationale and Issues: Teaching Content and Thinking Strategies

In this chapter we develop the rationale for Benchmark School's twofold mission: to teach thinking skills and to impart knowledge. This is a mission endorsed by most educational institutions, from elementary to graduate and professional schools (Frederiksen, 1984; Nickerson, Perkins, & Smith, 1985; Resnick & Klopfer, 1989). However, despite widespread agreement regarding the need to integrate the teaching of strategies (thinking skills) and content (knowledge), researchers and educators have translated this mission into vastly different beliefs and practices. We review our struggle with these beliefs and practices as we endeavored to develop a rationale that would make sense to faculty, students, and parents. Issues that impact on the implementation of such a program are also reviewed.

OVERVIEW

We begin by tracing the development of Benchmark's rationale for combining the teaching of content and thinking strategies. The rationale grew out of our attempt to resolve three issues of concern to the staff related to students' difficulties in the content areas: *why* every teacher should teach both thinking skills and subject matter, *which* strategies students should be taught, and *how* strategies should be taught.

Why Teach Both Content and Strategies?

The first issue involved a controversy regarding whether it was necessary for every teacher to teach both knowledge of thinking processes and knowledge of subject matter, indeed whether every teacher was even competent to or had the time to teach both. Our attempt to resolve this first issue focuses on research regarding the differences between good and poor students, the necessity for acquiring different kinds of knowledge in order to learn more knowledge, and the differentiation between usable knowledge and inert knowledge. We conclude the discussion of why teachers should teach both strategies and content with Benchmark's current resolution of the content-versus-process debate, including answers to questions about content coverage, motivation, and age appropriateness of a combined strategy-content program.

What Strategies Should Be Taught?

The second issue that faced us as we tried to implement a program of strategies across the curriculum was, if we teach strategies, which strategies should we teach? This question relates to the degree of specificity of thinking. Our faculty wondered about the benefit of teaching the same strategies across the curriculum, if in fact some or all strategies may be either content-specific or unique to specific situations. Realizing that some teachers and researchers believe that higher-order thinking processes are specific to domains of knowledge or situations, while others believe that there are both content-specific and general thinking processes, we set out to resolve the issue of the specificity of thinking strategies in terms of Benchmark's program and purposes. Questions about usefulness and number of strategies also needed to be addressed. We were able to arrive at research-based conclusions that also agreed with what we had learned from experience.

How Should Strategies Be Taught?

The third and last issue concerned how strategies should be taught, and whether there is merit in teaching a separate, or stand-alone, course in how to process information (how to use strategies). The suggestion for a separate course, taught by a strategy teacher, seemed sensible to some of our content teachers who felt they did not have the background or the experience to teach strategies. Related issues concerned how long to teach strategies and the social mediation of learning strategies (i.e., student interactions and teacher-student interactions). The chapter concludes with a summary of our current thinking about the teaching of strategies and content.

WHY TEACH BOTH CONTENT AND STRATEGIES: KNOWLEDGE OF CONTENT VERSUS THINKING PROCESSES

Our proposal was for teachers not only to teach students content, but also to teach students how to think about the content knowledge they were learning. This proposal raised a number of questions: Why should content-area teachers be the ones to teach thinking skills? How can content teachers cover all the content they are expected to cover and still find time to teach strategies? Might strategy teaching take the fun out of content-area subjects, thus reducing student motivation? Is a combination of teaching strategies and content equally appropriate for all age levels?

Three Practices

As we initiated our focus on strategies across the curriculum almost five years ago, we identified three practices among our faculty regarding the content-process debate. These differences in practice existed despite the fact that Benchmark teachers agreed that knowledge of both content and thinking skills are necessary for successful intellectual performance.

1. Some content-area teachers focussed almost exclusively on content. They felt the content of academic subject matter was the only knowledge they were responsible for teaching. They either believed that bright students develop good thinking strategies without instruction, or that it was not their responsibility to teach students strategies for thinking about the content they were teaching. These conscientious and caring teachers often appeared to regard students "as receptacles for knowledge that teachers transmit" (Stodolsky, 1988, p. 135). Such practice is not surprising, for undoubtedly it was the way these teachers had themselves been taught and trained.

2. Some teachers did teach skills and strategies for processing information, but rarely shared with students knowledge about how the mind works or why the skills and strategies they were teaching were worth learning. It is our experience that it is these kinds of knowledge that motivate students to want to learn and use strategies. As the students' understanding increases about how the mind works, they seem to grasp the need to take some kind of action to help the mind organize information through the use of strategies.

3. The occasional teacher who believed in the value of teaching skills and strategies taught isolated skills without connecting them to an understanding of content. When skills were taught in this manner, there was little evidence that students applied these skills independently when it would have been appropriate to do so. It appeared that the students were unable to understand how the parts (the skills) fit into the whole.

Each of the three groups of teachers seemed to assume their students would discover the ingredients missing from their instruction and successfully integrate process and content on their own. Our experience and the research literature suggest otherwise (Beyer, 1988a).

Three strands of research provide insights into why teachers should teach both content and strategies: research comparing good and poor students, research regarding different kinds of knowledge, and research describing usable versus inert knowledge.

Differences Between Good and Poor Students

The research comparing students like those entering Benchmark to good students consistently demonstrates that the difference between successful and less successful students of similar intellectual ability is the use of strategies to learn, think, and problem solve (Chan & Cole, 1986; Wong, 1985). Good students, we have discovered and as confirmed by the research, are *aware* of factors that affect learning and of how to implement an array of strategies. They also take *control* of factors affecting learning and thinking by actively managing the strategies that are needed to succeed. A review of the literature suggests that, similar to Benchmark students, poor students do not demonstrate these traits; however, they do profit from explicit training regarding awareness and control of variables affecting learning. In fact, *all* students who are taught strategies for taking charge of their learning, thinking, and problem solving tend to perform better than their counterparts who receive no training (Duffy & Roehler, 1986; Paris & Oka, 1989; Pressley, Goodchild, Fleet, Zajchowski, & Evans, 1989). It is clear that, like our Benchmark students, many potentially adequate to superior students do not discover how to be learners who are goal-driven, planful, self-assessing, and strategic (i.e., putting information processing plans into action). Thus, it is the responsibility of teachers to become thinking/learning coaches (Gaskins, 1988c; Shuell, 1986) in order to help students develop thinking skills. To accomplish this, both teachers and students need knowledge.

Three Kinds of Knowledge

When teachers in educational institutions speak of knowledge, they are usually referring to one kind of knowledge, knowledge of an academic subject. Yet the research has established that it is not content knowledge alone that sets the competent student apart from his peers. There are other kinds of knowledge the good student commands. When students encounter difficulties, a teacher needs to be familiar with these other bodies of knowledge and be able to evaluate the awareness and application of these kinds of knowledge in a student. At Benchmark we stress three bodies of knowledge:

1. Real-world knowledge (*what* one thinks about, or the content)

2. Strategy knowledge (knowing *how* to think)

3. Metacognitive knowledge (knowledge *about* thinking)

Content knowledge. Sometimes a student's difficulties may result from lack of background knowledge about the content being studied. This point was vividly illustrated by Manolakes (1988) in his account of his own distress in reading an article in *Popular Mechanics*. He, like many students, experienced difficulty understanding what he was reading. His lack of understanding was not due to a problem of knowing how to apply the appropriate skills and strategies, rather it was due to a lack of knowledge about the topic. Each day in working with students we witness the fact that what a student knows or believes influences what he or she can learn or understand about that subject (Anderson & Pearson, 1984; Nickerson, 1988). For example, it would be difficult to learn to add fractions without first knowing about the addition of whole numbers, just as it would be difficult to understand the Boston Tea Party without an understanding of the issue of "taxation without representation."

Strategy knowledge. Lack of success in the content areas may be due to not knowing how to process the information. The knowledge that is missing may be strategy knowledge. We find that students have a difficult time writing a book summary or finding a main idea if they have not been taught the strategy knowledge necessary to complete these tasks.

Researchers support our conclusion that at least two kinds of knowledge are necessary to succeed in school. For example, Day (1985) spoke of two kinds of knowledge: knowledge of content, such as math, science, social studies, etc., and knowledge of skills and strategies for learning content. Palincsar and Brown (1989) also discussed two types of knowledge and added a third. They called the three types of knowledge: real-world knowledge, strategy knowledge, and metacognitive knowledge. Though researchers may disagree as to the number of different kinds of knowledge, they do agree that, in addition to teaching specific content or real-world knowledge, teachers also need to share with students knowledge about how to employ strategies, as well as knowledge about how their minds work, or metacognitive knowledge, (Brown, 1985; Flavell, 1985).

Metacognitive knowledge. Based on our own experience and confirmed by the professional literature, we became convinced that teachers need to be aware of and to teach students about two aspects of metacognition, or how their minds work.

1. An *awareness* of how task, person, strategy, and environmental variables affect learning

2. Executive processing or *control*, the processes which carry out the work of the mind, the planning, implementing, monitoring, and assessing.

Thus, in addition to content knowledge, we need to provide students with an awareness of the variables that affect learning and the skills and strategies that would put them in control of their learning. Three different kinds of knowledge are needed as a foundation for learning more knowledge: *content knowledge, strategy knowledge, and metacognitive knowledge.*

Usable Knowledge vs. Inert Knowledge

Given the importance of possessing knowledge as a foundation for acquiring more knowledge, it is easy to understand how some of our teachers were seduced into believing that the focus of their energies should be on teaching the content of their subject areas. In addition, about the time we were launching our strategy program, content teaching gained new momentum from the publication of Hirsch's (1987) book, *Cultural Literacy.* Hirsch makes an impassioned plea for schools to emphasize the teaching of specific content knowledge he feels is basic to our culture. Needless to say, Hirsch's views led to many stimulating discussions among the Benchmark faculty!

Many faculty were concerned about the wisdom of encouraging students to stockpile facts. They worried that students would not see the relationships among the individual bits of information—relationships so necessary to conceptual understanding and transfer. Some recalled that Bereiter and Scardamalia (1985) had warned that if teachers are encouraged to be "knowledge tellers," the result may be that students acquire inert knowledge, knowledge that is unusable because it is not represented in one's long-term memory in a way that facilitates retrieval, since it is not connected to other information in one's fund of knowledge.

There was also concern about whether or not students of knowledge-telling teachers would ever be able to use what they were taught. These students often were able to perform well, for example, on tests and quizzes that required the recognition or regurgitation of information. However, because they seemed to have processed the information in the superficial manner characteristic of rote memorization, the transformations (changes in the form of the information to fit into one's idea framework or background of information) necessary for deep understanding appeared not to have taken place. Thus, the facts seemed to be of little value in problem solving and in understanding other information. Our conclusion, like that of Resnick and Klopfer (1989), was that, for knowledge to be used to interpret new situations, solve problems, think, reason, and learn, "students must elaborate and question what they are told, examine the new information in relation to other information, and build new knowledge structures" (p. 5). Time and again parents and teachers have shared examples of superficial student knowledge that could not be accessed or applied because it was acquired by simply memorizing facts. Even telling students the key principles and concepts seemed not to provide usable, truly generative knowledge—knowledge that could be used to produce other knowledge.

Rote learning, whether of minute facts or key concepts, circumvents the deep processing necessary to form connections between the new information and previously acquired knowledge. The result is inert knowledge (Bereiter & Scardamalia, 1985; Nickerson, 1988). What we have observed among our students is that deep processing occurs when students transform or change knowledge into their own language and fit it into their existing schema or knowledge framework for that topic. This deep processing and real understanding are the result of using such strategies as elaborating, questioning, examining, and building knowledge structures. These are the processes we must foster.

Resolution of the Knowledge-Versus-Process Debate

Interdependency of content and strategies. Clearly, what one is able to think about is constrained by one's knowledge of content. Knowledge about a subject is crucial to thinking about it. Because knowledge of the content (the what) and thinking strategies (the how) are interdependent and necessary for efficient learning, we decided that both should be part of the curriculum taught by every teacher.

Support for our belief in the interdependency of knowledge and thinking comes through clearly in two recent books about curriculum development *What's Worth Teaching?* (Brady, 1989) and *The Subject Matters* (Stodolsky, 1988). Brady (1989) suggests that instruction should be aimed at creating and clarifying ideas or the relationships between ideas within a conceptual (meaning) framework by using the thinking processes of construction, organization, and elaboration (p. 10). Like Brady (1989), we ask teachers to organize the curriculum so that new information is part of an all-encompassing meaning structure. The teacher's primary responsibility is to help students understand this organization.

For example, one of the authors, in introducing information about the Georgia Cherokees who took part in the Cherokee Removal, provided a superordinate idea as a framework for the new information. In this case, it was that the Cherokees who lived in Georgia had for several generations been adapting to the white man's way of life. With this framework, it was relatively easy for students to learn information about the Cherokees by constructing, organizing, and/or elaborating ideas based on what they already had learned about how the white man lived in that time period. Knowing that the Cherokees were doing what white men were doing, the students had the framework within which to construct images of the way the Cherokees dressed, lived, learned, and worked. Thus, the concept of Cherokee adaptation provided the conceptual framework for integrating a great deal of information about the Cherokees. In addition, the concept of Cherokee adaptation provided a framework for constructing a point of view regarding the white man's dealings with the Cherokee.

Stodolsky (1988), in her study of fifth grade mathematics and social studies instruction, also became convinced that integrating instruction about knowledge of subject matter and thinking is in the best interest of students. She concluded that student success results from knowing both content and process: knowing about the subject content, and the set of skills that involve knowing how to do the content tasks.

Content coverage vs. strategies. Even the teachers who were convinced of the need to combine the teaching of content and thinking processes were concerned about covering the content they had covered in previous years. At the same time, they acknowledged that, beyond the date of a test, students seemed to recall only a small portion of what had been covered in class and were able to use even less in thinking about related issues and problems. This suggested that teachers should aim to cover less content and to cover it in a way that teaches students how to use the content for thinking about issues and problems, a conclusion supported by Brophy (1990)'s review of the literature on teaching social studies. Students also need to learn strategies for generating knowledge from what they already know, rather than relying on rote recall which too often lets them down. Our belief is that it is a more profitable learning experience for students if teachers are extremely selective in terms of the concepts they present. These concepts should be ones that have the potential for developing rich connections and relationships among various areas of knowledge.

Fun and motivation. Another concern expressed by the faculty was that strategy teaching would take the fun out of learning the content usually taught in their classes. The faculty was accustomed to presenting content in a manner that students found interesting and motivating. They feared that adding a "skills" component would make their classes less fun, negatively affecting motivation for learning the content.

Motivation is one of the most powerful factors affecting the success of instruction at Benchmark. Many of our students appear to be "school battered" when they first enter Benchmark. They are bright students who have tried and failed. Often they are not so sure they want to risk trying again. Some seem to feel that it is better not to try, than to try again and fail.

To circumvent these feelings, we strive both to make the content interesting and to scaffold instruction in bite-sized bits, beginning at levels where success can be guaranteed. As students experience success, many of them begin to feel that school is fun. Achieving success in reading seems to occur before success in other areas of the curriculum, and, with that success, comes the motivation to read. Success with writing usually takes place more slowly. Holding thoughts in mind while also struggling with the physical act of writing continues to take extra effort for a good number of our students for many years. Perhaps because writing is a part of so many of the strategies we teach, motivation to exert the extra effort is always an issue we must confront if strategy teaching is to be effective.

Traditionally, the teaching of skills and strategies has not fostered the motivation to use them. Initially, when strategies were introduced to our students, they claimed to see no reason for using the strategies they were taught. In fact, they saw using strategies as taking too much effort, which, when one is learning a new strategy, may be an accurate perception. We set ourselves the task of discovering how to convince them that the use of strategies is worth the effort.

Techniques to make strategies meaningful and motivating:

1. When introducing a strategy, teach how to use the strategy, why the strategy is beneficial and *when* it can be used.

2. Develop an informal experiment. Students are asked to do an assignment covering content in their usual manner. Then, they are taught a strategy that, correctly employed, should produce improved understanding and remembering. Next, students are asked to compare their understanding and remembering on the two assignments. The result is almost always a new awareness by the students of the benefits of strategy use plus an increase in motivation for strategy use. In addition, students think the experiments are fun. (See Gaskins, 1988c, for further examples of informal experiments.)

3. Discuss with them why a strategy is being introduced, practiced, or reviewed.

   Benchmark teachers remind students each day of *what* the strategy is that is being featured, *why* it is important, *when* it can be used, and *how* it is implemented. For example, a teacher might say to a group of young children reading at the primer level, "Today we will continue working on finding the central story problem. Does anyone remember why it might be helpful to think about the central story problem when you are reading?" ... "Yes, finding the central story problem lets us focus on the main happenings of the story which lead to the solution of the problem. If we wanted to summarize the story for someone, we could tell a little about the story problem and its solution and that would be a good summary of what we read—almost like the book reports some of the older children write."

4. Tell a personal story about what happened when one of us (or our children) did or did not use a particular strategy. The students seem to love hearing these personal experiences and appear to use them as "hooks" for understanding how a strategy can be beneficial as well as when to use it.

We see motivation as closely related to metacognition, as apparently do Marzano, Brandt, Hughes, Jones, Presseisen, Rankin, and Suhor (1988) who define metacognition as "awareness and control of one's thinking, including commitment, attitudes, and attention" (p. 146). Paris, Lipson, and Wixson (1983) refer to metacognition and motivation as *skill* and *will*, believing as we do that both the skill to facilitate the processes of learning and the will, or motivation, to apply what one knows how to do are necessary for success in school.

In summary, one important aspect of motivation requires helping students understand the rationale for the strategies that are taught. They need to know they will gain practical benefit for their efforts. This instruction seeks to foster the beliefs that strategies are important, worth some extra effort, and instrumental in enhancing performance. Guiding students to discover for themselves the value of specific strategies has also proved motivational, as has sharing personal experiences related to strategy use. For additional suggestions regarding the relationship of motivation and thinking strategies, see the work of Borkowski and his colleagues (e.g., Borkowski, Estrada, Milstead, & Hale, 1989).

Is a combination of teaching strategies and content equally appropriate for all age levels? Although we are continually evaluating the efficacy of teaching strategies to our younger children, we have tended to pilot most of our general, across-the-curriculum strategy instruction with the 11-14-year-olds. Notable exceptions to this trend are the strategies we emphasize in both reading and writing with all age groups.

For example, the first thing we teach our youngest students is that reading and writing must make sense. If what you read or write does not make sense, you need to go back and fix it. This strategy seems to be understood by our youngest students for they demonstrate its application by self-monitoring and self-correcting when reading stories or books for pleasure. However, these same young children do have more difficulty noting when their own writing does not make sense. They often do not apply the reading-must-make-sense strategy to reading in the content areas.

Our observations seem to confirm what other researchers have found, that is, with young children, strategies are more tightly "welded" to the specific contexts in which they are learned and that, developmentally, children seem to move from the specific to the general. It is our conviction that a combination of strategies and content instruction is appropriate for all age groups. If children are to be expected to use the same strategy in various contexts, it is important to reteach and cue the strategy for the child and to the new situations.

Undoubtedly, many aspects of an ideal thinking program differ based on the age, intellectual level, and expertise of the students. Good and Brophy (1989), for example, speak of different developmental states regarding strategy teaching. They point out that what is good instruction for six- to eight-year-olds may not be good instruction for the nine- to thirteen-year-old. What constitutes effective instruction varies with the subject matter, students, and other factors. Bruner (1985) notes that ability to reflect on one's own performance increases with age, suggesting, as has Brown (1978),that it is not until the mid-to-late adolescent years that children spontaneously self-monitor and self-manage. Glaser (1989), on the other hand, feels that experience or expertise, more than maturation, determines cognitive proficiency. In other words, spending several years studying about and gaining proficiency in a domain or area of knowledge may be more important than developmental age. This appears to be true of young chess experts, for example; and work with our poor readers at Benchmark also suggests that expertise may be more crucial than developmental age.

After a discussion of strategies in a Benchmark inservice meeting or at a research seminar, it is not unusual for a faculty member to question whether something introduced to students of one age would be appropriate for another age group. We have not discovered the answers to questions of this nature, but we continue to pilot strategies with various age groups and are often surprised at the benefit of strategy teaching for children in our Lower School—an age group for whom some researchers believe strategy instruction may not be beneficial due to insufficient maturation of thinking skills (Thomas, Strange, & Curley, 1988).

WHAT STRATEGIES SHOULD WE TEACH: THE ISSUE OF GENERAL AND DOMAIN-SPECIFIC THINKING

Core List of Strategies

A starting point in developing a core list of strategies is to look at the strategies that good students independently use to process information successfully. Today, as we observe our successful students, we discover that they are actively and strategically involved in accomplishing four broad tasks: constructing meaning, monitoring understanding, remembering concepts, and taking control of task, person, strategy, and environmental variables.

During the 20-year history of the school our recommended list of strategies has been constantly evolving as we discover through practice which strategies appear to be the most beneficial to our students. In Chapter 4 we discuss Benchmark School's current core list of strategies. The strategies are all cognitive strategies, the strategies which are employed to do the actual work of thinking. The metacognitive strategies we teach are those which focus on awareness and control of task, person, strategy, and environmental variables that affect thinking, including planning, monitoring, checking, and revising.

Though we have worked hard to pare down the core list to a manageable set of strategies, the question always arises, "Are all the strategies equally useful?" We wonder, with time so precious, which strategies will produce the biggest pay-offs for our students. Should we invest more time in strategies for general, domain-specific, or situated thinking?

General Thinking

General thinking strategies or skills are those thinking processes which can be used effectively to process information regardless of the specific content or domain. Our experience suggests there are some basic strategies that students should be encouraged to learn and apply across the curriculum. We encourage teachers to teach and reinforce these strategies in all areas of the curriculum.

Some examples:

1. We consider categorization to be an example of a general thinking strategy. We encourage students to process information by organizing concepts under superordinate categories. For example, in thinking about the Spanish American War, students might categorize information as related either to the war in Cuba or the war in the Philippines. Categorization could be used in science to organize information about different types of vertebrates and invertebrates.

2. Strategies for managing maladaptive cognitive styles seem to be general. There are certain styles that interfere with students' successful processing of knowledge, regardless of the domain. These styles include the tendencies to be impulsive, rigid, and nonpersistent. Strategies can be taught that are applicable across the curriculum to control the negative effects of these styles. For example, Gaskins and Baron (1985) taught impulsive students to "take time to think" before answering a question, handing in a test, writing down an answer, etc. This simple strategy (others call

it a heuristic) favorably affected a student's success across the curriculum.

3. We have found numerous aspects of metacognition (awareness and control of thinking) equally applicable to various domains. For example, on most occasions, regardless of the content, it is a good idea to analyze a task before beginning to complete it, to monitor progress as one completes a task, and to take remedial action when the strategy being used is not providing a satisfactory result.

Domain-Specific and Situated Thinking

Domain-specific thinking processes are believed to facilitate thinking in only one domain or area of subject matter. For example, the strategy for checking a subtraction problem has little application except for checking the correctness of subtraction problems. Some also would argue that a strategy for completing and summarizing a science experiment has limited application beyond the science class.

In addition, some cognitive psychologists speak of thinking as "situated." Brown, Collins, and Duguid (1989), for example, state that learning and cognition are "fundamentally situated" (p. 128), meaning that thinking strategies are useful for specific situations, rather than a strategy being equally usable in numerous situations. They would contend that a basic problem-solving strategy must be adapted for use in mathematics, science, history, etc., believing that each situation requires a slightly different strategy for solving a problem. Psychologists who believe that thinking is basically domain-specific or situated, also believe that for strategies to become well developed, they must be in continued, situated use.

Chance (1986), elaborating on Glaser's (1984) argument for situated strategies, stated that "learning to use a thinking skill inevitably means learning to use it in a particular context" (p. 119). Chance (1986) also argues that students do not learn "to solve problems." Rather, they learn specific strategies for solving different kinds of math problems, science problems, decoding problems, history problems, etc.

Likewise, they believe that recognizing important ideas (e.g., in novels, science lectures, social studies, etc.) is a different strategy in each domain or situation. Those who believe that cognition is situated usually believe, as Benchmark teachers do, that the teaching and cuing of thinking strategies should be deeply embedded in all instruction across the curriculum.

In debating the issue of general versus domain-specific thinking at Benchmark, we find ourselves asking the question, "Does it really matter whether we designate a strategy as a general or domain-specific strategy?" There is certainly a great deal of similarity among the strategies used in various areas of the curriculum and in real-world situations, suggesting they are general thinking strategies, but that they function in specific ways to fit the situation.

Both Domain-Specific and General Thinking Skills

Some researchers have begun to shift from viewing thinking as completely domain-specific to conceding there may be some general thinking skills. Being in control, for example, is a strategy which we promote across the curriculum at Benchmark. It is also one supported by Resnick, who cited the sense of being in control as an example of a general thinking process — a perception of oneself as being in control of organizing one's attentional resources (Brandt, 1988-89). Nickerson (1988) also concluded that "while there are indeed domain-specific aspects of thinking, there are also certain processes, skills, strategies, principles, attitudes, dispositions, and beliefs that are applicable to thinking in many domains" (p. 29). Nickerson and his colleagues (1985) suggested that cognitive style traits might be "reasonable candidates for an important component of skilled thinking that cuts across fields" (p. 57). We conclude from this that it might be reasonable to expect a reflective person (a person who takes time to think) to exhibit reflectivity in a variety of domains and situations.

Perkins and Salomon (1989) also provide support: "there are general cognitive skills; but they always function in contextualized ways" (p. 19); that is, a general strategy or style (e.g., reflectivity) will be adapted to the demands of the context or setting. For example, when the context is not challenging, the reflective person may have no need to take time to think.

The conclusion we have reached from our experience teaching strategies across the curriculum is that for students to transfer strategy knowledge from one subject or situation to a different subject or situation, teachers should teach knowledge of specific content plus three aspects of thinking:

1. general principles of reasoning (e.g., take time to think, consider the possibilities),

2. skills for monitoring progress towards one's goals (e.g., putting ideas in one's own words, visualizing concepts being presented), and

3. the potential application of the skills and strategies (i.e., recognizing that the strategy being taught could be used in other situations). We, like Prawat (1989), believe that problem solving is the application of known concepts to new situations. The key is to analyze the problem, which we view as a general strategy.

We believe there are some thinking processes that are general and some that are domain-specific. The distinction is not easy to delineate, but it appears that general thinking processes are the more abstract processes; thus, they are less tied to specific domains. These general thinking processes include cognitive style traits, such as reflectivity, flexibility, and persistence, as well as dispositions and attitudes. The strategies of reasoning, planning, questioning, monitoring, assessing, clarifying, attending, inferring, imaging, summarizing, elaborating, and seeing patterns/analogies appear to have both general and situated aspects.

Usefulness and Number of Various Strategies

It is our belief that only the most useful strategies should be taught, the ones for which there will be the most occasions for use, both across the curriculum and in real-world situations. This seems crucial because we cannot anticipate every domain or situation that students will encounter. Even if we could, there is not time in a student's school career to teach all the knowledge of content and thinking processes that a student might need. Thus, our job is to teach students the thinking processes that will have the most application. In most cases, these will be general thinking strategies. Teachers will need to coach students on how to adjust these strategies to specific situations. By teaching the same strategies across the curriculum, we are able to provide our students with the constant practice and reinforcement that we have found so beneficial to our population. Clearly, however, there are also domain-specific strategies that need to be taught.

What we must stress, however, is that students acquire and apply their knowledge of strategies if teachers teach and reinforce a few strategies in depth, rather than introduce students to many strategies during a school year. This topic will be explored further in Chapter 4.

HOW SHOULD STRATEGIES BE TAUGHT: EMBEDDED AND STAND-ALONE TEACHING

Before we developed The Benchmark Model of strategy instruction, which will be discussed in Chapter 5, we needed to address a number of concerns. These included:

1. Could strategy teaching be accomplished as a separate (stand-alone) course and infused in regular classes, rather than taught and embedded in regular classes? That is, could strategies be taught as a separate course and then presented in the language

arts and content-area classrooms to be reviewed, adapted and applied to new situations? Or should each strategy be introduced, taught, practiced and reviewed only as an integral part of the regular content instruction?

2. How many weeks or months should a strategy be taught before teachers should expect students to apply the strategy independently?

3. How was a teacher to handle the social issues that mediate learning strategies?

4. Should instruction in reading, writing, and the content areas include *only* domain-specific strategies or *both* domain-specific and general thinking strategies.

5. If general thinking strategies were taught, should they be embedded in courses across the curriculum? Other possibilities exisit, of course, such as teaching both concepts about general and domain-specific strategies in a stand-alone course and infusing these concepts into content-area courses.

A Three-Pronged Approach

After experimenting with a number of possibilities, we decided on a three-pronged approach:

1. All teachers teach a core-group of 17 cognitive strategies for achieving meaning and remembering, 13 strategies for knowledge production, and 8 metacognitive strategies across the curriculum. These strategies are discussed in Chapter 4.

2. Teachers teach strategies specific to domains and situations as the need arises.

3. Our third prong is composed of two stand-alone courses taught by the senior author. The Middle School course is called Psych 101 and the Lower School course is Learning and Thinking (LAT). The objective of both courses is to share with students how the mind works in order to provide them with a rationale for learning the strategies that are being taught in their other classes. Psych 101 is described in Chapter 7. LAT is presently a twelve-session course taught to the eight oldest Lower School classes. Students in LAT take part in three informal experiments which serve to illustrate the gains one can achieve in learning and remembering by being actively involved.

The research literature provides no clear-cut answer to the question of whether one manner of teaching thinking strategies is better than another. There are probably as many opinions as there are possibilities. For example, Pogrow (1988) suggested that instruction in thinking skills should be a separate course for one or two years taught by specially trained teachers, and content teaching should be left to the remainder of the staff. Chambers (1988), Deery and Murphy (1986), Joyce (1985), and Presseisen (1988) all recommended that thinking should be taught as part of the content-area curriculum. Chambers (1988), believing that thinking is domain-specific, recommended that teachers teach strategies specifically adapted to the content they are teaching. Presseisen (1988), however, noted that there are across-the-curriculum dispositions; thus, by teachers cuing strategy use, students could gain transfer from subject to subject and situation to situation.

Several experts have suggested combining either infused or embedded thinking skills instruction with separate courses in thinking as we have done at Benchmark. When infusion is recommended, the primary responsibility for teaching the thinking processes falls to the teacher of the stand-alone course, with the regular classroom teacher responsible for cuing transfer and helping students adapt the strategy to their situation. At Benchmark the classroom teacher observes and/or participates in the Psych 101 or LAT instruction presented by the senior author, then "infuses" concepts from the courses into his/her instruction throughout the day.

Embedded courses are those where the content-area teacher integrates the teaching of content with the teaching of thinking strategies to facilitate processing the information. These strategies may be general thinking strategies or domain-specific strategies. The teacher of embedded thinking skills takes responsibility for teaching thinking strategies as well as the subject matter of the course (i.e., mathematics, science, social studies, etc.). This approach is also practiced at Benchmark. In the case of embedded instruction, a stand-alone course may or may not be part of the curriculum. At Benchmark we have chosen to have both embedded instruction and a separate course about thinking, which hopefully leads to infusion. The research literature supports each of these practices. The verdict is still out on which, if any, of the approaches is best. Clearly, teaching thinking skills in either stand-alone or embedded courses is superior to not teaching thinking skills at all.

Developing Control Takes More Than One Year

Teaching students to use a general or domain-specific strategy when they are under the teacher's supervision is relatively simple. More difficult is guiding students in the development of control. The goal is for students independently to take control of factors affecting learning and thinking by actively managing the strategies that are needed for success. This includes setting goals, planning, monitoring, and orchestrating strategies for acquiring and producing knowledge. Deery and Murphy (1986) suggest that control, sometimes referred to as "executive control," must be developed gradually and automated over an extended period of time.

Our experience suggests the ability and the will to take control of a strategy and apply it independently is a process that takes many weeks of continuing and consistent instruction characterized by explicit instruction, modeling, scaffolding, and teacher feedback, followed by months and years of teacher cuing, reinforcement, and reteaching before students take full control of a strategy.

Duffy and Roehler (1987) and their colleagues confirm our experience, concluding from their research that the development of control requires a gradual restructuring of a student's understanding over time. Johnston (1985) also notes that becoming strategic (i.e., independently orchestrating strategies) takes time because considerable repeated exposure is necessary. Benchmark teachers have discovered that from the time a strategy is introduced until a student can and will use it independently is often a matter of years.

In summary, both the dispositions and strategies for higher-order thinking require sustained and long-term cultivation. In the words of Resnick (1987), "They do not emerge from short-term, quick-fix interventions" (p. 42); they need to be developed over time. Our belief is that, beginning in the early grades, students need to be informed about factors that affect learning and explicitly taught strategies for controlling these factors. These strategies must be reinforced, re-explained, and cued over a number of years. Such instruction through the school years will provide students with the support they need to develop control.

Social Factors Influence Thinking

Learning is a social process. Establishing a social climate where learning, thinking, and problem solving are valued is a cornerstone for building a successful program that combines the teaching of knowledge and thinking.

Our teachers play a crucial role in establishing a classroom social climate where students and teacher are involved in a continual and joint process of learning, thinking, and problem solving. A classroom with such a social climate is a place where each contributes to the class's learning and profits individually from the understanding that arises from the process of sharing. It is a place where questioning and wondering are valued and working together on school tasks is encouraged. It is a place where the teacher reinforces the dispositions to be goal-directed, planful, self-assessing, and strategic, and where the teacher models and mediates these characteristics of a thinking approach to knowledge acquisition and production.

Both the Benchmark program and many of the current programs designed to teach thinking skills rely on the social setting and social interaction. Students may work in pairs or small groups for discussion or practice, employing various cooperative learning models suggested by Slavin (1983, 1989) or reciprocal teaching as studied by Palincsar and Brown (1989). For example, our teachers often think aloud while processing information. Then, using the process modeled by the teacher, students work in dyads to justify ideas to one another and to evaluate each other's ideas.

We find that it is in the process of explaining an idea to others that students develop both understanding and an awareness of what they do and do not know. Dialogue creates in students an awareness of the struggle to make meaning. Without dialogue, students too often delude themselves into thinking they understand, when in fact they may not. Social interaction provides the support that enables students to rework ideas.

Social settings play several roles in the development of thinking. The social setting:

1. provides occasions for *modeling* effective thinking strategies. Modeling opens normally hidden mental activities to inspection and allows others—peers or a teacher—to critique and shape one's performance.

2. provides a kind of scaffolding or support for a learner's initially limited performance. Those in the group give other learners guidance when they encounter a task that they are unable to complete on their own, but can complete with some cues or instruction from others.

3. functions to motivate students, lending social status and validation to the disposition or inclination to higher-order thinking. The social community establishes norms of behavior where dispositions for higher-order thinking can be cultivated by participation in social settings that value thinking and independent judgment (Resnick, 1987).

SUMMARY

Knowledge, without an understanding of how to process that knowledge, is of limited value in creating students who are lifelong learners, thinkers, and problem solvers. One of the striking differences between successful and less successful students of similar intellectual ability is the use of *strategies*. However, a program of teaching only the knowledge of processing is not sufficient. Students need content-specific knowledge to be able to learn more knowledge.

Clearly, both the content and thinking skills need to be taught.

Whether thinking skills are situation-specific or general, and when subject matter and thinking skills should be taught, are addressed in this chapter. Our current thinking is that there are both general and domain-specific thinking skills. We believe there are processes, strategies, principles, attitudes, and beliefs that are applicable to thinking in many domains. These can be profitably taught in stand-alone courses or by embedding them in courses across the curriculum. The option we have chosen is to combine stand-alone and embedded instruction, with the concepts taught in the stand-alone course being infused into courses across the curriculum.

Another issue addressed in this chapter is what students need to learn about thinking. We have presented the Benchmark rationale for guiding students to an *awareness* of the variables affecting their success and for explicitly teaching *strategies* that will enable students to take *control* of those variables. In addition, we feel that strategy instruction must focus on fostering the *motivation* to be strategic. Motivation to use strategies is enhanced when students know the rationale for using them and believe that they are worth the effort. Additional factors that we feel should be considered in developing a combined content-strategy curriculum are student age and time constraints, as well as the social climate and setting.

CHAPTER 3

Mental Processes: Background Knowledge for Teaching Thinking Strategies

Although convinced of the value of developing a curriculum which combined content and process, the Benchmark faculty had concerns about their preparedness to accomplish this task. Before trying to integrate concepts about process into their lessons, the faculty felt a need to learn more about how the mind works. Thus, numerous seminars over several years were devoted to discussing articles and books about learning and thinking. In addition, experts in the fields of cognitive psychology, strategy teaching, and reading instruction presented workshops at Benchmark, interacted with the staff in roundtable discussions, and some even presented demonstration lessons. We also gained experience and knowledge from our collaborative research and development projects, as well as from our informal experiments. As the faculty became comfortable with various concepts and principles about how the mind works, they began integrating these ideas into their teaching.

This chapter presents a summary of our present understanding about how the mind works to learn, think, and problem solve, based on our study and discussion, and our own experience adapting these ideas to the realities of classroom instruction. It is our belief that an understanding of these concepts related to how the mind works provides a foundation upon which others can begin to build a program for teaching students how to learn and think.

We began our search for understanding how the mind works by reviewing definitions of learning and thinking in order to become aware of how other researchers and educators use the terms and to develop definitions for these terms to use in our project. In the process, we found that we also needed to establish our own definitions for the terms "skills" and "strategies," as these terms have no universally accepted meaning among researchers and educators. The four overlapping concepts of learning, thinking, skills, and strategies are discussed in this chapter.

LEARNING

Learning, which has as its basic ingredients knowledge and thinking skills, begins the minute we are born. Almost immediately, for example, we learn to distinguish mother's voice from the voice of others. And, as we grow older and interact with family and teachers, we learn to talk, to build with blocks, to recite nursery rhymes, to distinguish and name colors, and to predict correctly the ending of a story that is being read to us. All of these are socially mediated learning experiences and all involve the individual in using thinking skills to actively construct knowledge.

The definition of learning that we currently use is that *learning is a socially mediated, knowledge-based process that requires active involvement on the part of the learner and which results in a change in understanding.* Learning, therefore, is both process and product. As a result of learning experiences, novice learners become competent individuals.

We concluded that the characteristics of learning involved in the acquisition of knowledge and the characteristics of competence or expertise are fairly well known. Less, however, is known about the factors that turn novice learners into increasingly competent individuals. It is this process of moving the novice learner to competence that is of the greatest interest to us. Schmeck's (1988a) definition of learning is not atypical of how the research community describes this process. Learning is "a by-product of thinking, the tracks left by our thoughts. We learn by thinking, and the quality of the learning outcome is determined by the quality of our thoughts" (Schmeck, 1988a, p. 171). Such statements do not give us much guidance for building a program to teach students how to develop the characteristics demonstrated by good learners. That guidance, most likely, will come from looking at what happens in classrooms where children are learning. Our focus first, though, will be on studying what psychologists and researchers can teach us about how the mind works. Based on those understandings, we can develop classroom applications.

Learning: A Knowledge-Based Process

It is a given that learning requires knowledge. Further, to be useful in learning, knowledge must be understood. Thus, it seems unlikely that attempting to give knowledge to students by merely telling, lecturing, or having students copy notes from the chalkboard will be the best approach to helping students learn. One of the Benchmark faculty's first convictions as we read about the learning process was that, if learning is to occur, students must construct knowledge for themselves. They must do something with the knowledge being presented to them.

Students bring thoughts and ideas about a topic to the learning situation. This knowledge serves as a basis for their theories (internal models) which are tested in each new learning experience. Using their theories as a starting point, students hypothesize and develop new relationships and predictions which they test by comparing their theories and models with their observations based on the newly presented knowledge. If their theories or models fail to account for certain aspects of their observations, the theories or models are rejected, modified, replaced, or given only temporary acceptance. This process of modifying theories to arrive at a new understanding is learning (Glaser, 1987b, p. 398).

Teachers attempt to facilitate this process by asking students to share what they know about a topic and by suggesting that they use what they know to make predictions which are tested and modified as they study and interact with the teacher and other students. In addition, teachers foster learning by requiring that students do something with the new knowledge to integrate it with their background knowledge. For example, teachers can encourage students to elaborate what has been presented or to compare new information to other information. The goal is for students to build new theories and frameworks for their ideas.

Knowledge that is processed in this manner becomes generative, meaning it can be used to learn new knowledge (Resnick & Klopfer, 1989, p. 5). For example, when students know the characteristics of mammals, and they read that a whale is a mammal, they can use their background knowledge about mammals to make hypotheses about what the specific characteristics of a whale might be. As students use the new knowledge to interpret new situations, to solve problems, to think and reason, and to learn, there is a change from the relatively undeveloped theories of beginners to more sophisticated theories and concepts (Glaser, 1987b).

New understanding, as any teacher will tell you, does not occur for all those who were present in the same instructional setting where new knowledge was introduced. There are a number of possible reasons for this. One reason understanding may not occur is that the necessary knowledge base is missing. Another is that the necessary skills and strategies are not known, or it could even be that the teacher and the student have interpreted the task differently (Newman, Griffin, & Cole, 1989). Equally likely is that motivation is the issue, that students may not choose to use the knowledge of content and/or strategies they possess (Resnick & Klopfer, 1989). Another possible reason for lack of learning is students' poor general attitude about themselves as learners (Bransford & Vye, 1989).

In summary, learning is knowledge based. It is a complex process which uses thinking as its basic tool to modify theories about knowledge. The result is a change in the form of a person's knowledge. Two kinds of knowledge are involved in learning: knowledge of content (the what) and knowledge of how to learn. What is learned (or mislearned) is affected by one's understanding of the task. Learning also requires the motivation to learn and is influenced by the learner's self-concept. The other major characteristic of learning, in addition to knowledge, is active involvement, which is discussed below.

Learning: An Active Thinking Process

The characteristic of learning about which we have the most difficulty convincing many of our students is the need for the learner to be actively involved. In fact, there seems to be no way of avoiding active participation if one wants to gain the product of learning. If the student chooses not to participate, learning does not occur. As obvious as this may seem to an adult, it is far from obvious to students. When we discuss what active involvement means with our students, we too often hear superficial responses such as, "Keep your eyes on the teacher" or "Pay attention."

We are presently trying to convince students that keeping one's eyes on the teacher and paying attention to the content being discussed are great ways of getting *ready to learn*. However, participation in learning necessitates the orchestration and regulation of many additional factors, such as motivation, beliefs, prior knowledge, interactions (with teachers, family, and peers), new information, skills, and strategies. In addition, the students must make plans, monitor progress, and employ skills and strategies, as well as other mental resources, to keep on track toward achieving their goals. Learning, as our students are discovering, takes effort and requires much more of the student than showing up for class and occupying a desk. Not even keeping one's eyes on the teacher or paying attention is sufficient. Learning requires that the learner mentally manipulate knowledge. (See Bransford & Vye, 1989; Shuell, 1986; Weinert & Kluwe, 1987; and Wittrock, 1988, for further elaboration of the concept of active involvement in learning.)

Not a day goes by that a teacher's experience does not substantiate the vital role played by active involvement. The students who regularly are not actively involved tend to stagnate at the novice level, responding to tasks and problems based on visible, concrete features rather than responding by making inferences and identifying principles, which is more typical of proficient individuals (Glaser, 1987a). Without active involvement, a meaningful learning experience does not take place. Several components of active involvement that we have found important to discuss with students are setting goals, organizing knowledge, constructing meaning, and using strategies. These components of active involvement are discussed in the next four sections.

Setting Goals. For learning to take place, a student must have a goal, such as understanding or completing an assignment, and be actively engaged in trying to reach that goal (Shuell, 1986). Proficient learners know that the learning process involves analyzing the learning task, which includes the goal and the conditions for achieving it (Newman, Griffin, & Cole, 1989), breaking the goal into manageable subgoals (if necessary), and devising a plan (or solution path) appropriate for the goal or each subgoal (Derry, 1988-89).

Goals determine which stimuli the learner will respond to and which will be ignored. Relevant prior knowledge is accessed and used as a point of reference in evaluating and/or assimilating the new information. The learners receive the new information in a spirit of anticipation, guessing and predicting what is yet to come. Finally, they evaluate what has been learned to determine whether they successfully achieved their goals. One's goals determine whether or not learning will occur, as well as the kind of mental activity needed to learn.

Organizing. Learning requires organization, a characteristic we often find lacking in our poor readers, yet a characteristic of those who become proficient learners. One of the keys to proficient learning is the development of organizations of knowledge that enable learners to perceive meaning and patterns (Glaser, 1987a, ix). Our experience suggests, and research confirms, that learners need to take an active role in recognizing structure or imposing structure on information. All of us have experienced, but it sometimes is hard to get students to realize, how difficult and extremely inefficient it is to try to learn unorganized information. When learners try to learn bits of information as separate entities, rather than recognizing or imposing patterns of organization, they soon experience a disheartening phenomenon which psychologists call displacement, that is, the most recently encountered information takes the place of (displaces) the earlier information in short-term memory. The limited number of slots in short-term memory (approximately seven, plus or minus two), having been filled to capacity, can hold no more; therefore, some of the information is lost.

A way to avoid this loss of information is to organize the incoming information. It is important to convince students that to maximize learning efficiency, they need to organize the information they are trying to learn. One way for them to do this is by chunking or grouping related information. To convince her students of the value of chunking information, the senior author told her students that she wanted them to be able to name four major professional sports teams in each of three major cities (New York, Boston, and Philadelphia). On a pretest, none could. She then told them the names of the 12 teams and retested the students. Still none could name all 12 teams. Next, she suggested that to learn the names of the professional sports teams in New York, Boston, and Philadelphia, they should group the teams either by sport or by city. Using sport as the superordinate category, one slot would be given to basketball teams and those teams were listed (Knicks, Celtics, and Sixers), another to the baseball teams, another to the football teams, and another to the hockey teams, with all the 12 teams listed by sport. A similar classification was done by city. The result was that the bits of information (the names of the teams) now could be handled despite the limited number of slots in short-term memory. Many of the students were able to list the 12 teams on the next trial. In analyzing their success, the students claimed that organizing the information was the key. Only information that is organized is meaningful and usable in learning (Shuell, 1986).

Constructing Meaning. Learning is a process of construction. In other words, what is learned is put together by the learner. The basis for the new construction of knowledge is what is already known (Anderson & Pearson, 1984). Psychologists think of knowledge as being stored in the learner's head as networks of concepts or schemata. As one learns, connections are made between new information and the learner's existing network of knowledge. Connecting requires mental activity, activity that is facilitated by social-mediation (the input of teachers, family, and peers) that stretches learners just beyond what they can handle alone, but is not too challenging to be beyond their understanding. It is in this "zone" that learning is constructed, an interaction between what was known and the interpretations of others. (For additional information on the construction of knowledge see Newman, Griffin, & Cole, 1989; Nickerson, 1988; Peterson, Fennema, & Carpenter, 1988-89; Vosniadou & Brewer, 1987; and Wittrock, 1986.)

To illustrate for her students the concept of learning as construction, one of the authors shared this example: When you hear me talk about China, you relate what you hear to what you already know about China—information and beliefs stored in your brain in your China schema. As a result of the new information I tell you and ideas raised by other students, each of you modifies your China schema or conceptual map, constructing a new China schema, one that will also be different from mine and those of the other students in the class. Thus, your current theories about China are modified on the basis of the new information and a new idea map or schema is developed that facilitates more advanced thinking and problem solving regarding topics related to China.

Construction, rather than the gradual accumulation or stockpiling of information, is clearly what learning is all about. It is a process of change, of rearranging old ideas and making changes in one's conceptual model.

Using Strategies. Learning requires the use of various processing skills and strategies. These skills and strategies facilitate both the self-management component of learning and the thinking component. Learners orchestrate such general strategies (or mental processes) as organizing, analyzing, elaborating, rehearsing, remembering, monitoring, and evaluating to take charge of task, person, and environmental variables which affect success in learning. An in-depth discussion of skills and strategies can be found later in this chapter.

Strategies are crucial to efficient learning. When either the skills or the strategies required for a task are not sufficiently developed (or are developed, but are not used), learning is jeopardized. A common illustration of this phenomenon seen at Benchmark is the student with a poor sight vocabulary. When word recognition is not at the level of automaticity and a student must focus an inordinate amount of attention on decoding words, as in a difficult social studies book, there is little attention or short-term memory remaining to focus on the higher level task of comprehending the concepts. Likewise, if students are not aware of how to implement the organizational strategies needed to compensate for the limits of short-term memory, learning will be inefficient at best. Students may even perform satisfactorily in situations where decoding strategies or strategies for organizing information are the goals of the lesson. However, the development of these strategies may not be sufficiently automatic for the strategies to operate together or the strategies may not be accompanied by the knowledge of why and when to use them that is crucial for transfer.

In summary, learning is a socially mediated process of change that involves the active construction of meaning, using both old and new content knowledge as well as knowledge of how to learn. Learning requires motivation to learn and is influenced by the learner's self-concept. It involves thinking that is goal-driven, organized, constructive, and strategic. Because learning is active, it requires effort.

Learning Produces New Understanding

The product of learning is a change in the form of one's knowledge, a new and deeper understanding. Thus, rote recall is not an example of learning. Using the vocabulary and knowing enough information to earn a satisfactory grade on an objective academic test is not equivalent to understanding a body of knowledge. When there is understanding, one can think with and about the knowledge, suggesting that the real test of learning is understanding, demonstrated by the ability to use the knowledge.

It is, therefore, a sad commentary on today's schools that some create achievers (i.e., students who earn good grades), yet they have not created learners, because the students are not able to translate what they achieved into effective use. These students have not seen the connecting themes and key ideas between the isolated bits of knowledge they have learned. They have missed the connectors that serve as the glue in forming cognitive structures.

New understanding that is usable results from socially-mediated interactions that strengthen connections between related knowledge and allow the learner to see relationships. Good teaching fosters discourse and dialogue which facilitate seeing these relationships. New understanding is the result. (See Newman, Griffin, & Cole, 1989; Nickerson, 1988; Prawat, 1989; Schmeck, 1988a; and Sheull, 1986 for further discussion on this topic.)

Not only does learning require change, but it also requires that the change be an enduring one. Learning, therefore, is both a process and a product. One of the key components of learning is thinking, which is discussed in the following section.

THINKING

Our current view is that thinking is a mental process which is determined by knowledge, mental activity, and dispositions (habitual inclinations to behave in a certain way). Thinking is the process basic to learning and intelligent behavior.

Problem solving and reasoning are two of the terms that sometimes are used synonymously with thinking, though they probably do not have as broad a meaning as thinking. Thinking can be described as cognitive behavior, a mental process, and the manipulation of concepts and precepts (Wolman, 1989). Researchers agree that thinking involves mental activity and that it is the process that undergirds intelligent behavior. It is used when one solves a problem, composes a passage, or learns. Thinking includes critical and creative thinking, though these probably are not processes in themselves, rather are ways of describing different aspects of thinking.

Although researchers tend to disagree as to the number of discrete elements of thinking and to the labels for each (e.g., components, dimensions, aspects, etc.), all include, as we do, knowledge, mental activity, and habitual inclinations in their definitions of thinking. (For further discussion of the definitions of thinking see, Beyer, 1988b; Marzano, et al. 1988; and Nickerson, 1988.) In the next three sections we discuss the concepts of disposition, knowledge, and mental operations as they relate to thinking.

Dispositions

All of us are well aware of the tremendous impact beliefs or attitudes can have on the way our students think. The product of beliefs, values, attitudes, and styles is one's disposition, a habitual inclination to behave in a certain way.

Beliefs, values, and attitudes provide the filter through which reality is perceived and thoughts are processed. Over time, responses to perceptions and thoughts become habitual styles and dispositions which determine how critical and analytical one's thinking will be. As one would predict, the beliefs, values, and attitudes of students who demonstrate good thinking tend to result in dispositions characterized by active fair-mindedness in seeking and using evidence, while students demonstrating poor thinking are often more inflexible, holding on to their original views. Good thinkers also seem more reflective, inquisitive, and eager to understand their world. In addition, they seem to have a better understanding of human cognition and how to manage their dispositions effectively.

Cognitive style, an aspect of one's disposition, is "the mode in which a person organizes and classifies his or her perceptions of the environment" (Wolman, 1989, p. 64). Examples of characteristics we associate with cognitive style are reflectivity, persistence, and flexibility (Baron, Badgio, & Gaskins, 1986). On the other hand, there are some researchers who do not use the term cognitive style, referring to all habits of the mind as dispositions.

Further, while we call reflectivity a style, others such as Dewey (1933), think of reflectivity as synonymous with thinking, for it certainly is synonymous with *good* thinking. Discipline, flexibility and persistence are, in our view, also desired traits or habits of the mind we associate with a disposition inclined to good thinking. Brandt (1988) notes that good thinkers are frequently persistent (persevere and check answers) and flexible. Costa (1987) listed other styles or dispositions that we agree affect thinking. We feel they are not separate styles, but are related to the three styles we have already discussed. Costa's (1987) styles include striving for precision and accuracy (necessitating, we believe, reflectivity, flexibility, and persistence), considering another's point of view (requires flexibility), supporting conclusions with evidence (seems to require reflectivity and persistence), taking risks (requires flexibility), and feeling empathy (necessitates the flexibility to walk in the shoes of someone else). While it is dispositions that affect the effectiveness of thinking, it is knowledge that is the content of thinking.

Knowledge

As was true of learning, knowledge is necessary for thinking. In order to think in a specific domain, a person needs knowledge about that domain. The connections among knowing, thinking, and learning are "deep and unbreakable" (Nickerson, 1988, p. 35). One cannot learn or think without knowledge to think about. One also cannot think without being mentally active.

Mental Activity

Tools are necessary for any operation and mental operations are no different. When one uses tools, there is activity; without the tools of thought the activity necessary for thinking is absent. Some of these tools of thought are skills and strategies, which are discussed in the next section of this chapter. Another category of mental operations is metacognition, which is thinking about thinking, the awareness and control one has over his or her thinking.

Thinking depends on a small number of general mental processes such as focusing attention, gathering information, and remembering. We have broken these general processes down into more specific processes, which we call *strategies*, because their specificity makes them clearer to our students and easier for teachers to teach. These include, among others, comparing, summarizing, classifying, interpreting, criticizing, looking for assumptions, making images, organizing data, recalling, hypothesizing, applying facts and principles in new situations, and decision making (Raths, Wassermann, Jonas, & Rothstein, 1986). Other general mental processes that have been suggested by researchers and theorists are resolving conflicts, evaluating, proving, using fix-up processes, analyzing, generalizing, analogizing, seriating, deducing, and inducing.

It is clear that good thinkers have an extensive repertoire of these processes or tools of thought, and know how and when to use them. Cognitive psychologists generally include the use of skills and/or strategies to process information as part of their definition of thinking, believing that thinking is an interaction between processes and knowledge. Pressley, et al. (1989), for example, describe competent thinking as a combination of strategies, metacognition, and knowledge.

In summary, we believe that thinking is a mental process determined by dispositions, knowledge, and the use of cognitive and metacognitive strategies. Good thinking results from such mental operations as focusing, information-gathering, remembering, organizing, analyzing, generating, integrating, and evaluating.

STRATEGIES

Successful learners, thinkers, and problem solvers are strategic. They employ strategies to accomplish their goals, whether those goals are to learn about the concept of erosion, solve the problem of how to prepare for two major exams and write a report during the next week, or think about how to express their ideas in an essay. Strategies are essential to success as a learner, thinker, or problem solver.

Despite our effort in this chapter to delineate skills and strategies, we do not feel that labeling the thinking processes as strategies, skills, or something else is of primary importance to teachers. What is important is assuring that students acquire an understanding of the thoughts and behaviors that facilitate the processing of knowledge. Regardless of the label one chooses, the tools of mental processing should be explicitly taught to students.

Thoughts and Behaviors

Strategies are the learners' actions and thoughts that occur during learning and that influence both motivation and the acquisition, retention, and transfer of knowledge. When learners are strategic, they are in control. They plan, evaluate, and regulate their own mental processes. Their actions are deliberate, involving choice and decision making, and are affected by dispositions, intentions, and efforts. Strategies are the means of selecting, combining, and redesigning cognitive routines.

Strategies are goal-directed resources. To facilitate performance, learners flexibly and adaptively match strategies to their styles and needs, as well as to the requirements of situations. Because strategies facilitate performance, they have been called "enabling skills" (Paris & Oka, 1989). Strategies can be specific to a particular task or more general, applying to the pursuit of almost any goal. A strategy can appear as a single event, but more often is a sequence of activities; thus, students must learn both the component processes and a routine for organizing the processes.

There are two categories of strategies: cognitive strategies and metacognitive strategies. While cognitive strategies help learners achieve the goals of their cognitive enterprise, metacognitive strategies provide the learners with information about progress toward their goals. As Flavell (1985) succinctly states it, cognitive strategies are employed to "*make* progress" and metacognitive strategies "to *monitor* it" (p. 106). Other researchers have also divided strategies into two (or more) categories, yet their categories differ from ours, such as differentiating between major and basic thinking strategies. (See, for example, Beyer, 1988b.) However, we do not see this distinction as helpful to teachers.

Although theoretically we believe that two main categories of cognitive processes exist (strategies and skills), we admit that the distinction is not always clear, nor meaningful. For example, some researchers include heuristics as strategies, as we do, while others think of heuristics (any method someone invents or uses to make progress toward a goal) as merely informal thinking routines. Others speak of three categories: strategies, tactics, and skills. We do not see the usefulness of a third category of thinking processes; thus we do not use the term "tactics," nor do we separate heuristics from strategies. (If the reader is interested in a more detailed discussion of the rationale for the strategy/tactic distinction, which will not be discussed in this book, see Deery & Murphy, 1986; Kirby, 1988; Schmeck, 1988a, 1988b).

The definition of strategy that we use in our work is one of the more commonly accepted definitions of the term "strategy." Nevertheless, the diversity of definitions for strategy among researchers and educators can be confusing.

For example, contrary to our point of view, there are those who define strategies by focusing only on thoughts or plans. Actions are not part of their definition of strategies, rather the actions or behaviors are considered a separate part of mental processing. For example Deery & Murphy (1986, cited in Deery, 1988-89) believe that a learning strategy is "a complete plan one formulates for accomplishing a learning goal" (p. 5). Snowman (1986) defined a learning strategy as "a general plan one formulates for determining how to best achieve a set of academic objectives *prior* to dealing with the learning task itself" (p. 244). Researchers who define strategies as thoughts or plans, thus not including behaviors in their definitions, are often those who use a term such as "tactic" to describe the behavior or high-level mental processing, and a third term "skills" for low-level, automated processing.

In contrast, we use skills to mean the learned procedures which become automated in proficient learners, and thus are unconsciously applied. Skills are existing cognitive routines used to facilitate knowledge acquisition and production. They are overlearned through repetition so that speed and accuracy are assured every time the response is called for. The confusion regarding the differences between categories of mental processing is discussed in the next section

Strategy/Skill Confusion and Resolution

"Strategy," "skill," "tactic," "heuristic," "cognitive operation," "cognitive tool," "cognitive activity," and "process" are some of the terms that are used interchangeably in the literature on learning and thinking. In our work we have chosen not to use the term "tactic." We believe that the terms "strategy" and "skill" are sufficient to define categories of mental operations, when such a delineation is necessary or meaningful. We occasionally use the term "heuristic" to mean a general conscious mental procedure. We do use the more general terms "cognitive operation," "cognitive tool," "cognitive activity," and "process" when we are speaking of activities of the mind that could be either strategy or skill, for often that distinction is not clear. Marzano, et al. (1988) have handled this fuzziness by using the terms "processes" and "core thinking skills" as the two categories of cognitive strategies. We do not see how this makes the distinction any less fuzzy, though we agree with their feeling that various situations and materials determine whether a procedure is in one category or another.

That there is lack of clarity between categories of cognitive activity seems to be a given (Kirby, 1988; Marzano, et al., 1988). "What might be a strategy early in one's reading career must often become a skill, and then an automatized skill, if one is to progress beyond that level" (Kirby, 1988, p. 264). An example of this progression from strategy to skill is usually seen in decoding. First, as children are acquiring the skill to decode words, they use decoding strategies, but as decoding ability becomes automatic, decoding becomes a skill.

Others suggest that situations and materials will determine whether a procedure such as summarizing or identifying a main idea are strategies or skills. We agree. To our way of thinking, though, it is not of concern what teachers call decoding, summarizing, finding the main idea, etc., as long as they teach students why they are important, when to use them, and how to do them.

Though we do not belabor the "correct" labeling of the mental processes that we encourage students to develop, we have established our own operational definitions. We believe that strategies are the thoughts and behaviors that influence how one processes information, and skills are automated, unconscious mental processes.

Important Strategies

Our list of important strategies includes both cognitive and metacognitive strategies, strategies for helping the learner both make and monitor progress. For examples of strategies suggested by several other researchers see Figures 1 and 2. Below is a summary of the general mental processes discussed in this chapter and a few related specific strategies which researchers suggest facilitate each. The next chapter, Chapter 4, describes the strategies that are currently considered to be priority strategies at Benchmark School.

Examples of mental processes and related strategies are:

1. Focusing attention: set purposes, allocate attention, define problems, and set goals.

2. Information-gathering: observe and form questions.

3. Rehearsing: underline, highlight, invent mnemonics.

4. Remembering: activate background knowledge, store, and recall.

5. Analyzing: identify attributes and components, relationships and patterns, main ideas.

6. Elaborating/generating: make mental images, paraphrase, summarize, describe, infer, and predict.

7. Organizing/integrating: represent graphically, compare, classify, put in order, and change the form.

Figure 3-1
Basic Thinking Process

Focusing Skills — attending to selected pieces of information and ignoring others.
  1. Defining problems: clarifying needs, discrepancies, or puzzling situations.
  2. Setting goals: establishing direction and purpose.

Information-Gathering Skills — bringing to consciousness the relevant data needed for cognitive processing.
  3. Observing: obtaining information through one or more senses.
  4. Formulating questions: seeking new information through inquiry.

Remembering Skills — storing and retrieving information.
  5. Encoding: storing information in long-term memory.
  6. Recalling: retrieving information from long-term memory.

Organizing Skills — arranging information so it can be used more effectively.
  7. Comparing: noting similarities and differences between or among entities.
  8. Classifying: grouping and labeling entities on the basis of their attributes.
  9. Ordering: sequencing entities according to a given criterion.
  10. Representing: changing the form but not the substance of information.

Analyzing Skills — clarifying existing information by examining parts and relationships.
  11. Identifying attributes and components: determining characteristics or parts of something.
  12. Identifying relationships and patterns: recognizing ways elements are related.
  13. Identifying main ideas: identifying the central element; for example, the hierarchy of key ideas in a message or line of reasoning.
  14. Identifying errors: recognizing logical fallacies and other mistakes and, where possible, correcting them.

Generating Skills — producing new information, meaning, or ideas.
  15. Inferring: going beyond available information to identify what reasonably may be true.
  16. Predicting: anticipating next events, or the outcome of a situation.
  17. Elaborating: explaining by adding details, examples, or other relevant information.

Integrating Skills — connecting and combining information.
  18. Summarizing: combining information efficiently into a cohesive statement.
  19. Restructuring: changing existing knowledge structures to incorporate new information.

Evaluating Skills — assessing the reasonableness and quality of ideas.
  20. Establishing criteria: setting standards for making judgements.
  21. Verifying: confirming the accuracy of claims.

(Marzano, et al., 1988, pp. 147 & 148)

Figure 3-2
Basic Strategies

1. Basic rehersal strategies: repeating the names of items in an ordered list.
2. Complex rehearsal strategies: copying, underlining or shadowing material.
3. Basic elaboration strategies: forming a mental image or sentence relating the items in each pair, such as a state to a product it produces.
4. Complex elaboration strategies: forming a mental image or sentence relating the items in each pair, such as a state to a product it produces.
5. Basic organizational strategies: grouping or ordering to-be-learned items from a list or a section of prose.
6. Complex organizational strategies: outlining a passage or creating a hierarchy.
7. Comprehension monitoring strategies: checking for comprehension failures, such as self-questioning.
8. Affective and motivational strategies: being alert and relaxed to help overcome test anxiety, reducing external distractions, using thought stopping to prevent thoughts from directing attention away from the task at hand.

Weinstein & Mayer, 1986

8. Evaluating: evaluate critically for consistency and compatibility, set standards, and verify.

9. Monitoring: self-question and paraphrase.

10. Taking charge of affective and motivational factors.

(See Brown, Palincsar, & Armbruster, 1984; Chance, 1986; Jones, Palincsar, Ogle, & Carr, 1987; Marzano, et al., 1988; and Weinstein & Mayer, 1986 for comparison lists of mental processes and strategies.)

SUMMARY

Learning is a socially mediated process of change that involves the active construction of meaning. This construction uses both old and new content knowledge, as well as knowledge of how to learn. Learning is facilitated by motivation and a positive self-concept and involves thinking that is goal-driven, planful, organized, and strategic. Learning is active and effortful. When learning has occurred, there is an enduring change. Thus, learning is both process and product. The mental process used in learning is thinking.

Thinking is affected by dispositions, knowledge, and the use of cognitive and metacognitive skills and strategies. Thinking depends on the basic mental processes of attention, observation, and discrimination. Additional mental operations of thinking include elaborating/generating, organizing/integrating, evaluating, and monitoring. These processes have been called skills, tactics, and strategies by various researchers. The authors of this book use strategy to mean thoughts and behaviors that influence how one processes information and skill as the term for automated, unconscious mental processes.

Although the terminology used in discussing learning, thinking, skills, and strategies may vary, researchers and educators do agree on the basic facts about learning and thinking. It is these basic facts or cognitive knowledge that teachers need to share with students.

Section 2:
Thinking Strategies for Schools

CHAPTER 4

Cognitive and Metacognitive Strategies

The literature related to thinking processes and strategies seems to be in agreement regarding a "core" list of important strategies. The "core" strategies are those that good students independently know how to implement in order to process information successfully. These are strategies that require active involvement by the student to construct meaning, monitor understanding, and remember concepts, as well as to take control of task, person, and environmental variables. Both cognitive and metacognitive strategies compose the "core" list.

The cognitive component is the thinking processes that one employs to do the actual work of thinking. The metacognitive component includes awareness of the factors that affect thinking and the control one has over those factors. Metacognition is the executive or boss who has control over cognition, the worker, whose tools are strategies.

During the time since strategy instruction began at Benchmark, teachers have experimented with and revised various lists of strategies. Surely more additions and revisions will be made as we continue to experiment. The lists in this chapter comprise both those strategies most widely taught and used at Benchmark as of the present writing and those which we realize need to receive more emphasis. We have included both cognitive and metacognitive strategies for processing information and for managing task, person, strategy, and environmental variables.

COGNITIVE STRATEGIES

Strategies for Achieving Meaning and Remembering

In this section we list the cognitive strategies for processing information with the goal of achieving meaning and/or remembering. In this discussion of cognitive strategies there is some overlap with the control aspect of metacognition (i.e., monitoring), to be discussed later in this chapter. The meaning-acquisition-and-remembering strategies which are emphasized at Benchmark are:

1. Survey. Look over the assigned material to make a mental framework or outline. Surveying may include as little as reading the title and looking at pictures or it may entail those activities plus reading the introductory section, bold-face headings, and chapter summary, and studying any maps or other graphics.

2. Access background knowledge. Think about (call to mind) what is known about the items in the mental framework developed while surveying. The background information and the framework from surveying are integrated and become each student's schema or mental construct with which new information will be integrated, compared, etc.

3. Predict, hypothesize, and/or set purposes. Guess what information will be presented, based on the mental framework developed while surveying and on background knowledge, and establish reasons for processing the information, such as "I want to find out...."

4. Compare. Relate new information to what is known, as well as note similarities and differences within the new information.

5. Create mental images. Make a mental picture in order to be able to "see" what is being processed. Students should be able to see something similar to a television program in their minds and know that when the picture becomes fuzzy there is a breakdown in understanding.

6. Make inferences. Gather facts about a situation from the information being presented and combine the facts with information or beliefs already possessed to draw conclusions, such as why someone responded in a particular way or how an event occurred.

7. Generate questions and ask for clarification. Pose questions regarding the information presented. These questions may be questions that students hope will be answered as they proceed through the presentation; questions that are answered in the text and which the students want to jot down as a means of study later; or the questions may be about points on which they lack clarity and for which they plan to ask for clarification during class discussion.

8. Select important ideas, including story elements in fiction and main ideas in nonfiction. Identify the problem around which the action in a story revolves, as well as the major characters and the character traits of each, the setting, and the resolution of the problem. Identify topics of paragraphs in nonfiction and state in one's own words the most important idea that was presented about the topic.

9. Elaborate by thinking of examples, nonexamples, analogies, comparisons, etc. Self-talk or visualize examples or nonexamples of the ideas being presented, especially when it seems important to understanding and/or remembering, think of how the information is similar to known information (situations), or note how it is different from a similar situation.

10. Evaluate ideas presented in the text, lecture, movie, etc. Develop a mental set to think critically about the author's/speaker's purpose and point of view, including whether or not statements and findings are supported by evidence.

11. Paraphrase or summarize to represent the substance of information. State the gist of what was presented in one's own words, omitting repetitious ideas and using superordinate categories to group similar concepts.

12. Monitor progress/achievement of purpose. Confirm predictions, identify gaps in knowledge or understanding, extend learning to new questions, fill in gaps, etc., and take remedial action, if necessary.

13. Classify information on the basis of attributes. Group ideas that are related in some way and label the ideas. For example, in social studies, students might list important events, names, dates, and places as information is presented. Then these notes could be classified for easier retention under several topics according to related ideas (e.g., Cuba and Philippines, if the topic was The Spanish American War).

14. Identify relationships and patterns. Note cause/effect, time order, whole/part, superordinate/ordinate, etc. relationships and patterns, such as those found in history, which repeat themselves.

15. Organize key ideas. Make graphics, outlines, sequential lists, etc. as a way of organizing information.

16. Transfer or apply concepts to new situations. Demonstrate understanding by being able to transfer knowledge learned in one situation to a similar, but new, situation and by analogy correctly predict what the new situation will be like.

17. Rehearse and study. Review notes, homework, and quizzes; integrate notes into one outline; recite major ideas; compose and answer essay questions; predict and answer objective questions; develop mnemonics, etc.

Strategies for Knowledge Production

In the model presented by Marzano, et al. (1988) knowledge production or application includes composing, problem solving, decision making, and research. Composing will be dealt with in greater depth later in this chapter. Strategies for problem solving and decision making include:

1. Recognize, identify, or admit a problem.

2. Define or analyze the problem.

3. Decide on a plan.

4. Implement the plan.

5. Evaluate both progress toward the solution and the solution.

Research or scientific inquiry uses both problem solving and decision making and is "primarily directed toward understanding how something works and how to use this understanding to predict phenomena" (Marzano, et al., 1988, p. 52). Strategies for scientific inquiry, in addition to the five above, include:

1. Access what you already know about the problem.

2. Generate hypotheses.

3. Test hypotheses.

4. State conclusions.

As can be seen, the strategies of problem solving, decision making, and research are similar to those already discussed in the section on achieving meaning and remembering. However, it is unlikely that students will automatically transfer their knowledge of these strategies when occasions arise for problem solving, decision making, and research. Therefore, teacher cuing of both cognitive and metacognitive strategies will be crucial to the transfer or satisfactory implementation of these thinking processes when knowledge production is called for.

Composing

Though composing is basic to dance, music, painting, and other arts, we speak of it here in relation to writing. As with strategies for achieving meaning and remembering, we have for some time been experimenting with and learning from experts about strategies for teaching writing. As we have experimented and learned from our experience, our strategy lists for composing have also changed and, undoubtedly, will continue to do so.

Though strategies are of necessity presented in lists, we do not view composing as a series of linear steps. We see writing strategies/ processes as interactive and recursive (reflecting a writer's tendency to interrupt forward progress momentarily to go back and rework sections of text written earlier). As in acquiring knowledge, the metacognitive and motivational strategies related to task, person, strategy, and environmental variables are key factors in composing. We see writing as a problem-solving activity that is purposeful, takes place over time—rather than in discrete lessons—and is socially constructed (the result of asking for and receiving feedback from peers and teachers). The strategies for composing are:

1. *Access knowledge*
    a) Brainstorm ideas for possible topics.
    b) Identify the audience.
    c) Call to mind plans, patterns, and other guides for writing, such as known story grammars or text structures.
2. *Plan*
    a) Gather necessary information by recalling relevant informa- tion and/or doing research.
    b) Organize by categorizing, outlining, generating new ideas based on relationships, and picturing how the information will be integrated.
    c) Set procedural and substantive goals such as determining the pattern of organization to be used and determining main points to be made.
3. *Draft*
    a) Focus initially on capturing ideas in rough form.
    b) Keep audience in mind.
4. *Review*
    a) Evaluate and re-work during writing and at the conclusion of each draft.
    b) Solicit feedback from others which encourages refinement of thinking processes.
    c) Revise based on self-evaluation or the reactions of others by organizing, clarifying, and elaborating.

As the writers proceed through the four components above, they monitor their progress, as well as make decisions as to when to move from one component to another.

It is always our goal, in implementing all the strategies for processing information, that students monitor progress in light of their goals and plans and are aware of and in control of related task, person, strategy, and environmental variables.

METACOGNITIVE STRATEGIES

Most frequently in the strategy literature, as in actual practice, there are three recommended strategies for the preparation phase of processing information (in which goals are set and plans made): surveying, accessing background knowledge, and hypothesizing/ predicting/purpose setting. The lists of "core" strategies compiled by cognitive scientists and educators (discussed in Chapter 2) rarely include the metacognitive processes which prepare students to take *control* of task, person, strategy, and environmental variables (see Chapter 7)—the very preparation that so often seems to be lacking in poor students. Instead, the strategies most often featured and taught, if any are taught, are those for "how to" process information, the acquiring-meaning-and-remembering and knowledge-production strategies. What is missing in such cases is the rationale, motivation, awareness, and control regarding the "how to."

This lopsided emphasis has also been characteristic of the Benchmark curriculum. We are just becoming aware that we have tended to conscientiously teach the cognitive strategies listed earlier in this chapter while doing all the metacognitive work for the students—then we wonder why the students are not taking charge. Too often we have analyzed tasks *for* students and told them the results of our analysis and what the students will need to do to cope with the task. Modeling this process would be commendable; however, telling and modeling are not the same. Further, we have told students what personal characteristics they need to modify to be successful, and even how we would like the characteristics modified. The prognosis for implementation, however, is not good when students are not part of the decision about the whats and hows of modifying unproductive personal characteristics. We have also made suggestions about environmental factors, such as studying in a quiet place or writing assignments in an assignment book, while the student's role was too often passive. And, finally, we have "recom-mended" the strategies that we want them to use for each assign-ment, rather than guided students to select and orchestrate the appropriate strategies.

Our resolve is to be more conscientious in teaching students to be aware of and take control of task, person, strategy, and environ-mental variables. This emphasis is reflected in the list of strategies below, most of which are metacognitive strategies.

Control Strategies for Task Variables

1. Analyze the task.
    a) Identify the task. Set a goal: ask yourself what you hope to ac-complish/learn by performing the task. Ask yourself with what level/quality of performance you will be satisfied.

Determine how much time the task will require. Determine the materials that will be needed. Decide whether the task is one task or a task comprised of subtasks.

b) Express your understanding of the task. Using self-talk (write down in your own words or dictate to someone), tell yourself your understanding of the task.

c) Check your understanding of the task by discussing it with others.

d) Activate/access prior knowledge. If there is material to be read, survey the material to note the content focus, organizational pattern, and graphic aids and brainstorm ideas about the topic to assess the adequacy of background knowledge, and whether or not compensatory strategies (e.g., reading an easier book to gain background knowledge or discussing the topic with a parent) are necessary.

e) Determine whether the reading level of the materials is appropriate or whether compensatory strategies are necessary.

f) Determine criteria for success.

g) Organize, categorize, outline, or represent graphically ideas from your background knowledge.

2. Select appropriate task-related strategies. For example:

a) Write down or dictate to someone the steps you will need to go through to accomplish the task.

b) Make a schedule for completing the task.

c) Write or dictate to someone a list of materials that are needed.

d) Use compensatory strategies, if necessary.

1. Ask someone to make an audio tape recording for you of the material to be read.

2. Ask someone to read the assignment aloud to you.

3. Check out and read a library book on the task topic that is written at an easy level.

4. Request to view a video tape, filmstrip, or movie related to the topic.

5. Listen to an audio tape about the topic.

6. Arrange to discuss the topic with someone who is more knowledgeable than you.

Control Strategies for Person Variables

1. Analyze person variables such as beliefs, attitudes, motivation, characteristics for school success, etc.

a) Brainstorm beliefs about the value of the task.

b) Evaluate key factors for success. For example: Am I motivated to do well on this task? Do I have a good attitude about the task? Do I feel excited, curious, or somewhat interested in the task? What personal style variables might hamper success?

    c) Consider whether or not compensatory strategies are needed to control negative beliefs, attitudes, motivation, characteristics for success, etc.

2. Select appropriate personal strategies.

    a) Determine how doing this task will be helpful to learning something else later on.

    b) Use compensatory strategies for taking control of negative beliefs, attitudes, motivation, characteristics for success, etc.

       1. Talk with a teacher, parent, or friend about the long-term value of the task.

       2. Find something good about the task to make it more palatable to complete.

       3. Plan a reward for yourself when the task (or each subtask) is completed.

       4. Hypothesize, pose questions, and make predictions to focus interest.

       5. Select at least one personal characteristic over which you will take charge.

       6. Make a goal card and keep track of how often you demonstrate the characteristic.

       7. Talk to yourself as a coach would instruct you in using the characteristic.

       8. Reward yourself for using the characteristic.

Control Strategy Variables

1. Evaluate possible strategies for achieving meaning and remembering.

    a) Brainstorm strategies that will facilitate completion of the task.

    b) Assess understanding of how to do the strategies to determine whether or not a compensatory strategy is necessary.

2. Select appropriate achieving-meaning-and-remembering strategies and make a commitment to take control.

    a) List, or discuss with someone, meaning-and-remembering strategies needed to achieve success with the task.

    b) Ask a classmate, teacher, or parent to explain how to do any of the needed strategies for which you lack procedural knowledge.

    c) Find an alternative way to do the task.

    d) Do the task with a classmate.

Control Strategies for Environmental Variables

1. Analyze environmental factors.
    a) Determine whether you have all the necessary materials and if a compensatory strategy is needed.
    b) Determine whether the task can be completed in the school or homework period usually allowed and whether or not a compensatory strategy is needed.
    c) Evaluate the physical environment for completing the task to determine the need for compensatory strategies.
2. Select appropriate environment-related strategies.
    a) Construct and use a checklist of materials needed to work on the task at home; also construct and use a checklist of materials that must be returned to school.
    b) Use alternative materials on the same topic.
    c) Call a classmate to get an explanation of the material.
    d) Borrow materials.
    e) Arrive at school early and use materials before school.
    f) Make a schedule and monitor progress.
    g) Use time before and after school, as well as recess, for the task.
    h) Set aside time on a weekend.
    i) Ask the teacher if you can move to a quieter place to work.
    j) Talk with your parents about providing a table or desk for you.
    k) Find a quiet place to work in your house.

Presented with a formidable array of cognitive and metacognitive strategies, a teacher might well ask, "Where do I start?" "Is there a scope and sequence chart?" "What strategies are appropriate for the students in my class?" We have no clear-cut answers, no neat delineations between strategies for the primary grades and strategies for the intermediate grades. In many cases, the question is not so much at what grade or age level it is appropriate to introduce a strategy, but rather in what context and at what level of complexity a strategy is appropriate for a given group of students. Often, young children are informally exposed to a strategy several years before that strategy is formally introduced or taught.

   In general, as you will see in the following section, students in the youngest classes at Benchmark are introduced to basic reading-for-meaning and composing strategies, as well as strategies that help them to take control of the variables that will affect their learning. Our students do not outgrow strategies or move on to completely new ones, they simply learn new facets of basic strategies, learn to perform basic strategies at a more advanced level in order to deal with the demands of more complex tasks and situations, and grow more adept at orchestrating a variety of strategies at one time in the performance of a task.

Each teacher reviews, reinforces, and refines the strategies his/her students bring to class. When a new strategy is taught, it is carefully "hooked-on" to strategies that the students have learned and used before. Teacher and students discuss how it is similar to previously learned strategies and how it has been or might be useful in other contexts. Thus, ideal strategy instruction can best be described as ongoing, without discrete steps and stages. We hope that the following description of the progression in strategy instruction at Benchmark will provide teachers with some basic guidelines for the embedding of strategy instruction into a school curriculum.

PROGRESSION OF STRATEGY INSTRUCTION

Strategies for the Early Grades (Ages 6-8)

In the early grades, particularly with our students on beginning reader levels, strategies are primarily taught during reading instruction and reinforced in the content areas. The beginning-reader-level knowledge-acquisition strategies, as described by Benchmark resource teacher Penny Moldofsky, are listed below and illustrated in a lesson in the next chapter.

1. Stop and think—does the idea make sense?
2. Use a fix-up strategy when an idea does not make sense.
   a) Reread.
   b) Use one of your decoding strategies to pronounce the new words.
   c) Read on to gather more information, then return to the part that did not make sense.
3. Decode words you cannot pronounce by using the initial consonant and the sense of the sentence or by using known words with the same spelling pattern.
4. Find clues in the story that help answer your questions or the teacher's questions.
5. Connect clues in the story to what you already know.
6. Look for clues that tell about the characters, setting, story problem, and solution and identify these as story elements.
7. Use clues in the story and ideas from your head to predict.
   a) Use clues to check your predictions.
   b) Use clues to change your predictions.

Strategies that put students in charge of task, person, strategy, and environmental variables have also become part of instructional discussions during a student's first year(s) at Benchmark. These include:

1. Analyze the task. What about this selection or assignment makes it difficult? What strategy can I use to take control and make it less difficult? How do you do that?

2. Analyze person variables. What things do I sometimes do that interfere with progress? What strategies will put me in charge of these characteristics? How will I do that? What can I do to stay motivated?

3. Analyze environmental variables. What things around me keep me from successfully doing what needs to be done? What strategy can I use to take control? How will I do that?

4. Consider and select strategies that are needed for the task. What strategy is being emphasized? Why is it important? How do you do it? How will I monitor my progress?

Most of these task, person, and environmental strategies are not formally introduced to our younger students, rather the questions are asked in group discussions about how to be successful and in individual goal-setting conferences. By asking these questions the teacher attempts to mediate or be the link between a situation and the thinking processes we want students to employ. (See Chapter 8 for examples.)

Strategies for the Intermediate Grades (Ages 9-11)

As you can note in reviewing various excerpts from Benchmark lessons presented in Chapter 8, we place considerable emphasis at the intermediate level on strategies for controlling task, person, and environmental variables, as well as on processing strategies for both knowledge acquisition and knowledge production. In this way, by the time students reach the middle school (sixth, seventh, and eighth grades) they will have been introduced, at least on a rudimentary level, to most of the information-processing strategies listed earlier in this chapter. Those new strategies receiving the greatest attention at the intermediate level tend to be: creating mental images, making inferences, asking for clarification, selecting and organizing important ideas in nonfiction, and implementing basic study strategies. Composing strategies are heavily stressed at this level with application to numerous styles of writing, including writing books for publication in the library and writing research reports.

Active-reader strategies introduced in previous years are continually reviewed including: surveying; hypothesizing/predicting; accessing background; comparing new to known; generating questions; elaborating; selecting and summarizing important ideas in fiction; and monitoring/remediating. The goal is that at least the latter group of strategies will be employed independently by the students as appropriate occasions arise.

At the intermediate level teachers begin to introduce adaptations of Psych 101, the course discussed in Chapter 7. Thus, the metacognitive/motivational aspects of strategy instruction are discussed both as part of reading/writing and subject matter instruction and as separate mini-lessons.

In addition to fostering independence in strategy use, teachers encourage students to tailor strategies they have learned to fit specific task demands. An illustration of this can be seen in the transcript of Debra Wile's lesson in Chapter 8.

Strategies for the Middle School (Ages 11-14)

At the middle-school level all the strategies listed in this chapter are re-introduced, or introduced for the first time, at a level of complexity appropriate to the content with which the students are dealing. For example, identifying the central story problem or conflict requires the use of more sophisticated strategies when reading a sixth-level novel than does a five-page story in a second-level basal reader, just as identifying the author's purpose in a sixth-grade novel when the purpose is to state a point of view is a more complex task than identifying the author's purpose in a primary-grade basal story.

New strategies emphasized at this level tend to build on strategies that were taught earlier. This is particularly apparent when reading about the development of strategies in Chapter 10. Instruction in the middle school includes: paraphrasing or putting ideas from a text or lecture into one's own words; evaluating ideas critically, including an analysis of the author's intent, bias, and accuracy of presentation; categorizing, restructuring, and integrating concepts and ideas, such as recognizing literary themes and constructing conceptual maps; and transferring strategies to other subject areas and applying concepts to novel situations.

Students are regularly reminded that their goal is to become goal-driven, planful, strategic, self-assessing students. Regular discussions ensue regarding *why* they think this goal is important and *how* it can be accomplished. In most of their classes students are guided through an analysis of task, person, and environmental variables, and strategies are discussed for taking control of these variables. Because students in the middle school change classes and have different teachers for each subject, there are more opportunities for independence and across-the-curriculum practice and transfer. All middle-school students gain further impetus for achieving the goal of becoming goal-driven, planful, strategic, self-assessing students by taking part in Psych 101, a course discussed in Chapter 7.

SUMMARY

This chapter attempted to answer the question: What strategies should teachers teach while teaching their regular subject matter that would facilitate students' thinking processes for knowledge acquisition and knowledge production. We suggested strategies for processing at both the cognitive and metacognitive levels.

Strategies were suggested for two basic stages in completing a task, the *reflect-goals-plan* stage and the *implement-strategies* stage. During the first stage students: 1) analyze the task and select appropriate task-related strategies, 2) analyze person variables and select appropriate personal strategies, 3) evaluate possible strategies for achieving meaning and remembering or knowledge production and select appropriate strategies, and 4) analyze environmental factors and select appropriate environment-related strategies. During the second stage, in addition to controlling task, person, and environmental factors, students implement information-processing strategies for either knowledge acquisition or knowledge production.

Achieving-meaning-and-remembering strategies include: survey, access background knowledge, predict/hypothesize/set purposes, compare, create mental images, make inferences, generate questions, ask for clarification, select important ideas, elaborate, evaluate ideas, paraphrase, monitor and remediate, classify, identify relationships and patterns, organize, transfer and apply, and rehearse and study. Knowledge production strategies include: solve problems, make decisions, research questions, and compose. The composing strategies were further expanded to include: access knowledge, plan, draft, and review.

CHAPTER 5

Implementing Strategy Instruction

Both stand-alone and embedded instruction in cognitive and metacognitive strategies occur at Benchmark. The stand-alone course is described in Chapter 7. Embedded instruction is described in this chapter. According to Resnick (1987), embedding strategy instruction in individual subject areas has several advantages. First, it provides a natural knowledge base in which to practice and develop the use of strategies. Second, embedding strategy instruction within school disciplines provides a model for what constitutes good thinking within each subject area. Finally, teaching strategies within the content areas ensures that information about the thinking process has been presented as it applies to one subject area, even if wide transfer were to prove unattainable.

OVERVIEW

Embedded-strategy instruction at Benchmark consists of three parts. Each strategy lesson, whether prepared for beginning readers or for graduating students at an eighth reader level, is composed of the process objective (referred to in this book as the strategy), a metacognitive/motivational component, and the content objective (the vehicle for the strategy instruction). This is not to suggest that there is always an equal balance of the three parts. The amount of time devoted to each part of the lesson will depend on a number of variables, such as the familiarity or competency of the students with the relevant strategy, the nature of the content to be learned, the age and ability of the students, and the level of the students' metacognitive awareness. It is rare when there is not a great deal of overlap between these components, and at times a distinction between processing at the cognitive level and metacognition cannot be made.

Process Objective

The process (thinking skills) objective, or strategy, component of the typical Benchmark lesson is selected with the goal of helping construct a framework for thinking about or processing the content to be learned. This information-processing framework can then be used by students on future occasions for information processing. In Chapter 4 we listed the "core" strategies taught at Benchmark School.

Metacognitive/Motivational Component

The goals of the metacognitive/motivational component of the lesson are to develop *awareness* of factors which affect thinking and to teach students to *control* the thinking process. The teacher needs to enlist the *will* of the students to take control of task, person, and environmental variables and to employ strategies to process the content (ideas and concepts). Without this motivation, it is unlikely the students will put forth the effort necessary to acquire the new knowledge.

Several effective ways of fostering motivation are sharing with students the *rationale* for the strategy, telling a personal experience that illustrates the value of the strategy, and conducting an informal experiment in which students complete an assignment with and without the use of the strategy being taught so they can see for themselves that better results can be obtained when the strategy is employed. Our long-range objective is to create goal-driven, planful, strategic, and self-assessing students. To accomplish this goal it is not only important that the students understand the *rationale* for a strategy in order to enhance motivation, but also that students be induced to *self-monitor* their use of the strategy.

Content Objective

The content objective is the knowledge we would like the students to acquire as they read, listen, or observe. Content may be as simple as concepts central to understanding or appreciating a primer-level story or something more complex, such as recognizing the characteristics of the genre folk tale or understanding the concept "republic," or even as complex as understanding the events that led to World War I. Content knowledge, such as what is learned in math, literature, social studies, and science, is a necessary foundation for learning more knowledge. In the school setting, it is equally important as the vehicle for learning and using thinking strategies. Thinking cannot be carried out in a vacuum. The effective teacher uses the content of the basal reader or content-area text for teaching the thinking strategies necessary to effectively process the information.

Time Frame for Instruction

The first time a strategy is introduced to a class or group of students, it is very likely that only a few minutes will be spent introducing the content objective and a few minutes more establishing the importance of a knowledge base. The rest of the time allocated for the lesson would be spent introducing and teaching the new cognitive and/or metacognitive strategy for processing the content. On the other hand, if the strategies to be incorporated into the lesson are ones that have been taught and practiced for some time and are simply being reviewed, content might take precedence over strategies so far as proportion of lesson time devoted to instruction is concerned. Generally, as instruction regarding a strategy continues from day to day, there is a decrease in the amount of time spent discussing the strategy while the emphasis on content and motivation increases. Content receives the bulk of attention as students become more competent and motivated in implementing the strategy on their own.

Goals for the Remainder of the Chapter

In this chapter we present a picture of strategy instruction at Benchmark. We present guidelines and a basic format for planning lessons and teaching strategies. The last part of the chapter contains axioms for strategy instruction.

GUIDELINES FOR STRATEGY LESSONS

Teachers who decide to embed thinking instruction in content areas have a wide variety of teaching methods from which to choose. The Benchmark staff is continuously trying out and evaluating various approaches. As a general rule, Benchmark teachers use an explicit-instruction approach for the introduction of a new strategy. The instructional approach becomes increasingly interactive with each passing day of emphasis on the same strategy. The goal of interactive teaching is for the students to assume more and more of the responsibility for discussing and applying strategies.

Knowledge

Establish the importance of a knowledge base. We have discovered that frequent discussions of the various kinds of knowledge (i.e., knowledge of content, knowledge about how the mind works, and knowledge of "how to") and the impact of each on learning can be powerful student motivators. Such discussions remind students that they are in charge of whether or not learning takes place. We share with students that intelligent behavior results from knowledge, control, and motivation. Our goal is that students discover that success is based on what they are motivated to do to process knowledge and the knowledge of processing skills they can orchestrate, not on something that is preordained by their gray matter.

Teachers point out to students that there are different kinds of knowledge which are important to success in school. Two of these are declarative (knowledge of *what* or content) and procedural (knowledge of *how* or process).

Students are led to the awareness that content knowledge—the what—such as the knowledge learned in math, literature, social studies, and science, is the foundation for learning more knowledge. For example, understanding one principle in science, such as the principle of mechanical advantage, allows students to understand other scientific information based on that principle, such as how levers and pulleys work. Also, learning the metric system in mathematics class enables them to understand the notations in their science book in which weights are often given in grams and liquids in liters. Students are reminded that the need for knowledge to understand new knowledge is the reason teachers ask students to call to mind what they know about a topic prior to studying that topic. Incoming information can then be related to or integrated with the known or background information to construct new knowledge.

Procedural knowledge is the strategy component or the *how* of processing information. For example, when a teacher assigns a section of text to be summarized, students need to apply their procedural knowledge to know how to write a summary. Additional knowledge that affects intelligent behavior is knowledge of tasks, environments, and ourselves. Strategies for processing information, and for managing task, person, and environmental factors, put students in control of the learning process. Control of person variables such as beliefs, attitudes, and dispositions also determines motivation.

Explicit Teaching

Use an explicit-teaching model to introduce content and process objectives. Teachers begin by explaining the content and process *objectives* for the unit. For example, the *content objective* might be to discover three properties of water and the *process objective* to organize information using a chart.

The next step is crucial to student motivation, thus the success of the instruction. In this step the teacher explains *why* the objectives are important and *when* students would find them useful. Research suggests that if students believe an objective will be of value to them, they will be more motivated to learn what is being taught. We have found that including a personal anecdote regarding the value of the strategy captures the students' interest and often convinces them of the value of using the strategy.

In a lesson where students are learning to organize information using a chart, the teacher might explain the why (or the rationale) in this manner:

"Psychologists, or people who study how our minds work, have learned that it is hard to remember and use information that is stored in our heads as a lot of separate facts. However, when a person studies information, or a large number of facts, to discover big ideas and smaller ideas related to those ideas, the facts can be arranged in groups—or categories. When information is organized into categories, it is easier to remember the information. Making a chart that organizes information into categories makes it even easier to remember the information because we can form a mental picture of the chart that includes a lot of information. When you move information around, reorganize it, and can make pictures of it in your mind, it is easier to remember important information."

To increase the impact of this rationale, the teacher might share a personal experience.

"My social studies students last year felt overwhelmed by the expectation that they be able to describe the clothing, food, shelter, and travel of three Indian tribes living in different geographic areas. They thought they would have to memorize four sets of information for three tribes or 12 sets of information—much more than their short-term memories could manage. However, once we organized all of this information into categories and the students realized how location determined the clothing, food, shelter, and travel of each tribe of Indians, they found remembering it no problem at all."

Once the students have become fairly proficient at a strategy, we conduct an experiment where the strategy is used and is not used, and the results of each condition are measured and compared. The experiment helps to convince the students of the value of a strategy. Also, in a lighter vein, teachers will sometimes tell their students— especially the older students—"disaster stories" about times when they should have used the (desired) strategy and decided to take a short-cut instead.

After the *why* and *when* have been established, the teacher explains *how* to do the *process objective*.

"Charting is done by organizing information according to categories or ideas that are related. In the Indian example, we listed where the Indians lived across the page at the top of three columns, and down the side of the page we listed the information we wanted to find out: clothing, food, shelter, and travel. As we studied the material, we wrote the information related to a specific category in one of the 12 rectangles on the chart."

After explaining how to implement the strategy, the teacher uses *mental modeling* to share the reasoning used in implementing the strategy. For example, in sharing her reasoning for making a chart, the teacher might say,

"The objective for this unit is to relate where Indians lived to what they used for clothing, food, shelter, and travel. Hmmmm. Let's see. In my survey of the material, I discovered that we would be studying the Indians of the Northeast, the Southwest, and the Plains. I could outline each section with clothing, food, shelter, and travel as the subheadings; but that seems like a lot of extra writing to write those categories three times, plus the information would be spread out and hard to compare. I know I'm going to want to compare the three tribes in order to be able to see how *where* they lived affected how they dressed, ate, etc. Maybe I could just write the categories once and have a column for each tribe. That way I could compare the three tribes' clothing, food, shelter, and travel by looking across the three columns. I think I'll try that. Let's see. I'll use a whole sheet of paper for the chart and divide it into three sections for tribes and four sections for clothing, food, shelter, and travel. First, I'll make a small column down the side in which to write the categories; then I'll divide the rest of the sheet into three equal parts, one for each tribe. Next, I'll write the tribes' locations at the top of each column, then divide the rest of the length of the paper into four equal parts for clothes, food, shelter, and travel. Now, as I read about the three tribes I can write the facts I find about clothes, food, shelter, and travel in one of the 12 boxes. I think I'll read the first paragraph and see how it works....." (See Figure 1.)

Following *mental modeling*, students are given the opportunity to *practice* using the strategy as the teacher provides *feedback*. Initially the teacher usually "walks" the students step by step through the material to which the strategy is to be applied, providing as much scaffolding (support for employing the strategy) as each student needs to meet with success. In the case of charting, the teacher initially might provide the students with a chart, such as the one in Figure 1, composed of the appropriate number of boxes which the

Figure 5-1
Indian Tribes

	Northeast	Southwest	Plains
Clothing			
Food			
Shelter			
Travel			

students fill in as they read. If students have difficulty applying the strategy, the teacher *re-explains or elaborates* further about the reasoning one should use in applying the strategy. Once students have filled in a few teacher-made charts for organizing information, they should in later lessons be expected to both construct their own charts and fill in information.

The teacher explicitly explains the content objective telling *what* big idea(s) students should know at the conclusion of the unit of study and what the teacher's expectations are for assignments; *why* the big idea(s) is important; *when* the big idea(s) might prove useful; and *where* the information for study can be found. The teacher, then leads a discussion to *activate background information* and to discuss key concepts as presented in *vocabulary* that may be unfamiliar to the students.

The outline for an explicit-teaching lesson plan might look something like the one in Figure 2. (For further information about explicit teaching, see Pearson, 1985.)

Interactive Teaching

Use an interactive teaching approach for follow-up lessons on strategies that have been introduced. The same basic lesson outline is used for subsequent lessons on these process and content objectives; however, with each passing day, students are asked to supply more of the information the teacher supplied on the day the objectives were introduced. For example, the teacher asks:

> "What is our content objective? Is there anything about the material or the concepts that makes achieving this objective difficult? What? What strategies can you implement to take control? Explain how you do that. What person variables will you need to employ to accomplish this objective? What strategies can you use? Explain how you do that. What environmental factors will you take charge of? What strategies will you use? Explain how you do that. What strategy are we currently working on to process information? Why is it important? When would you use it? Describe how you use it. Questions that a teacher might use to review content and process objectives are found in Figure 3.

Cuing

Cue students to use specific strategies. Research suggests that children who have learning difficulties are the least likely to realize occasions when it is appropriate to use or transfer a strategy they have learned. Thus, it is especially important when working with

Figure 5-2
Explicit-Teaching Outline

Process Objective
Write on a chalkboard and read to students.

Content Objective
Write on chalkboard and read to students.

Process Object Explained
WHAT: "Today we are going to learn. . ."
          "What this means is. . ."
WHY: "This is an important strategy because. . ."
WHEN: "You can use this strategy when. . ."
HOW: Tell students how to do the strategy.
          Illustrate the strategy with a personal experience.
          Set up a mini-experiment.

MODEL: Model process objective using real text.
          Model any new lesson procedure such
          as working in collaborative/cooperative groups.

GRADUAL RELEASE OF RESPONSIBILITY: Walk students
through the process of implementing the strategy taught,
scaffolding (providing support as necessary.
          Re-explain/elaborate where students
          exhibit difficulty.

Content Objective Explained
WHAT: Tell content objective and expectations.
WHY: Tell why the content objective is important.
WHEN: Tell when the content objective might prove useful.
WHERE: Tell where the information for study can be found.

BACKGROUND: Help students access relevant background
knowledge.

VOCABULARY: Introduce pronunciation and meaning of
new vocabulary.

(At this point the students read the content)

Tie up the lesson
Involve Students in summarizing what, why, when, and how
of the content and process objectives.

Figure 5-3
Interactive Teaching Questions for
Reviewing Content and Process Objectives

A. *Content Objective*: What is our content objective?

1. *Analyze the task*

Is there anything about the material or the concepts that makes achieving this objective difficult?

What?

What strategies can you implement to take control?

Explain how you do that.

2. *Assess person variables* (optional)

What person variables will you need to employ to accomplish this objective?

What strategies can you use to take control of these person variables?

Explain how you do that.

3. *Assess environmental factors* (optional)

What environmental factors will you need to consider in order to accomplish the content objective?

What strategies will you use?

Explain how you do that.

B. *Process Objective*: What strategy are we currently working on to process information?

Why is it important?

When would you use it?

How do you do it?

poor achievers to *cue* them regarding occasions for strategy use or transfer. *Cuing appears to be important for all students when across-the-curriculum transfer is desired.*

Every-Pupil Response

Provide opportunities for every-pupil response. Students are more likely to be on task and actively involved in responding to instruction if teachers plan activities that require all students to react or do something. Such activities might require students to complete a response sheet while reading a text or as teacher-directed instruction is in process.

For example, in a teacher-guided activity for outlining a section of text a response sheet could be used. Students would select and write the topic of a paragraph and write a paraphrased version of what was learned in that paragraph about the topic. They would write this information on the every-pupil-response sheet *before* each paragraph was discussed by the group. This procedure requires that each student work through the process on his/her own, rather than merely copying what a teacher or classmate has worked out as the topic and phrase or sentence for the outline.

To facilitate group discussion which requires every-pupil use of the process objective, the teacher can give each student a note card with a question that can be answered only by employing the strategy. Each student must be prepared to answer his or her question during group discussion. Taking notes in one's own words or writing periodic summaries are other possible expectations that require each student to be involved.

During instruction the teacher should enforce respect for the right of each student to be recognized and heard. This is best accomplished by not responding to students who call out answers and by systematically calling on every student for a response during each class period.

Model

Model explicitly what students are expected to do before expecting them to do it. This axiom refers both to strategies that have been introduced and to the performance of activities, such as working in cooperative groups. It is good practice, during each lesson regarding a particular strategy, for the teacher or a capable student to model, or talk out loud about, the mental process or reasoning one uses in carrying out the featured strategy. In addition, modeling a review strategy seems to allow a second, third, etc. chance for the student who did not understand the strategy when it was previously explained or modeled.

Scaffold, Elaborate, Re-Explain

Scaffold, elaborate, or re-explain when students run into difficulty in discussion, seatwork, or on homework. Once a strategy has been taught, teachers scaffold instruction to help the students use the new strategy. This means that each student does as much as he or she can without assistance. Assistance is provided only when the student cannot proceed entirely alone. Thus, *to scaffold instruction means to provide each student with precisely the support he or she needs to implement the strategy, not too much, not too little.*

Students are never told an answer and rarely, as a first means of assistance, is a strategy re-explained. Initially the teacher proceeds diagnostically, asking the students questions in an attempt to have students explain their understanding of the strategy, filling in gaps or clearing up misconceptions if necessary, then guiding them to employ the strategy. If this tack is not successful, the teacher further elaborates, gives additional information about implementing the strategy, or as a last resort, explicitly re-explains how to use the strategy. The goal is to meet each student at exactly the point where he or she cannot proceed without scaffolding, and to provide the least amount of scaffolding necessary for the student to use the strategy successfully.

Throughout the lesson on paraphrasing the teacher has provided a framework or scaffold by asking questions which guide the student through the reasoning process needed to paraphrase the paragraph.

For example, after paraphrasing has been taught, a teacher might ask a specific student to state the gist of a paragraph in his or her own words. When the student states a detail, rather than the major idea, the teacher might say, "Yes, that was one thing that was talked about in that paragraph. What else did you learn?" The student might give several other details. The teacher would then say, "What word(s) could you use to express what those details are mostly about?" If the student supplied an appropriate word, the teacher might ask the student, "Can you tell me what major point the author was making about that topic?" If the student has trouble supplying the word for the topic, the teacher might supply the word and ask the student for the major point and provide additional guidance, if necessary.

Reinforce/Reward

Reinforce/reward students for improvement as compared to themselves. Some students immediately catch on to strategies when they are introduced, while others seem to struggle. It is important in order to sustain motivation and self-confidence that students not be put in competition with one another. A good practice is to make a conscientious effort to recognize each student for the improvement each makes in comparison to his or her own past performance. This is particularly important for those who are struggling.

Pace and Variety

Maintain pace and plan variety. Our experience is that a crisp, lively lesson with a great deal of teacher/student interaction maintains the interest and attention of students. When there is too much teacher talk and the pace drags, students tend to find opportunities for inattentiveness, despite the teacher's well-meaning intent that everyone should understand the strategy during the initial presentation. To ease student anxiety, we find it is a good idea to assure students that we will be working on the objective for some time and that using it will become clearer with each day we work on it together. Not all will understand the strategy on its first presentation; thus it seems better to keep the pace brisk and discussions interesting, while individually providing scaffolding for those who seem confused. Varying activities also seems to maintain student attention.

Summary of Lesson Guidelines

Nine axioms were presented for teaching strategy lessons. These included:

1. Establish the importance of a knowledge base.
2. Use an explicit teaching model to introduce content and strategy objectives.
3. Use an interactive teaching approach for follow-up lessons on strategies that have been introduced.
4. Cue students regarding opportunities to use specific strategies.
5. Provide opportunities for every-pupil response.
6. Model explicitly what students are expected to do before expecting them to do it.
7. Scaffold, elaborate, or re-explain when students run into difficulty in discussion, seatwork, or on homework.
8. Reinforce/reward students for improvement as compared to themselves.
9. Maintain a brisk pace and plan a variety of activities.

In subsequent chapters, we will present sample lesson plans as well as transcripts representing excerpts of lessons as taught in classes with a running commentary or explanation by the authors. We will conclude with a series of excerpts from one teacher's lessons to teach uses of categorizing over a school year from October to May and the authors' comments on those lessons.

It is our goal that by the end of this book the reader will have a reasonably clear picture of how strategy instruction is implemented at Benchmark as well as sufficient information to plan and teach an effective strategy lesson of his or her own.

Section 3:

Teaching Thinking Strategies in the Schools

CHAPTER 6

How Content and Process Are Joined: The Tales of Two Social Studies Teachers

Irene W. Gaskins, James Benedict, and Thorne Elliot[1]

This chapter briefly presents two stories, one told from Irene's point of view as an administrator/teacher and the other from Jim's point of view as an historian. Together they taught two middle-school social studies classes. Irene tells of teaching strategies. Jim tells of teaching history. What resulted by spring, when Jim became the sole teacher, was a social studies program which featured the best of both worlds—process and content joined into one.

A PRELUDE OF THINGS TO COME

An Administrator Searches for a Way to Become a Teacher

It didn't take long for me to discover that an administrative position is not nearly as fulfilling as interacting with students on a day-to-day basis. To satisfy my need to interact with students and at the same time experiment with the application of ideas from cognitive science, I developed a plan to become a social studies teacher. For my plan to succeed, I needed a co-teacher who would fill in for me during those times when other duties required my being away from the classroom, someone who liked young adolescents, knew something about social studies, and was willing to accept a partial-day position.

During the summer, I discovered that Jim, one of the school's summer school teachers, had decided to take a year off from his Ph.D. program in history, so I approached him about being my co-teacher for several social studies classes, and he agreed. Thus in August, I sent Jim off on vacation with our American history textbook and

---

[1] We are most appreciative of the helpful suggestions of Taffy Raphael and Richard C. Anderson on earlier drafts of this chapter.

several articles about the process approach and metacognition. We decided that he would focus on content, with his expertise in American history, and I would focus on process, responsible for teaching the students the strategies they needed to be successful with their assignments. When I was unable to be present, he would be responsible for both content and process.

Summer Musings of an Historian About to Become a Teacher

Jim's story begins the August before school began. We find him on a small lake, drifting with the current. Let us tune in on Jim's thoughts....

As I drifted on my inflatable raft, I found myself caught up in a sense of contentment. I had lined up a job for fall, and the world smiled with me. I allowed myself the singular pleasure of a carefree daydream.

I perceived with some excitement that I was now in a classroom. I took a seat in back, deciding to ride this dream out and settled down as if to watch a movie. Suddenly, the students' whispers ceased, and a teacher strode up to the front of the room, winking at me slyly as he brushed past. Ah, but this was no mere teacher. The man carried himself with professorial dignity. Was that a pipe in his hand? Yes, what a distinguished fellow! And with a gasp I realized that was me up there.

I don't remember much of that lecture now, but I know it was brilliantly conceived and delivered. I could tell from their rapt expressions and furiously racing pencils that the students were equally fascinated. At each of his questions a sea of hands rose, each battling to stretch the highest. At the conclusion of the lecture, I was not the first to stand and applaud. As the students filed out of the class, I heard the faint strains of their cherubic praises.

This, and similar musings, occupied my thoughts as that August passed. Although it is a bit embarrassing to relate, this dream embodies some truths of my actual hopes and expectations as I looked forward to my new teaching job. The realization that the school's social studies program had something to do with teaching students how to learn by using strategies was a sobering one because I didn't know how to teach students *how to learn* history. But I readily dismissed it, assuming that my co-teacher would handle that. When it came to teaching about how to learn, she knew how, I just knew.

So, I threw myself into the role of content teacher. I read books about our first topic, the Constitution, in order to gather insights not found in our text. I hoped that the wonders of history would speak for themselves, with the occasional help of an entertaining anecdote. The students would love it, and boy, would they learn! Looking back, I feel a bit silly. Because I had always loved history, I assumed all my students would too, if I could only make the people come to life:

Gouverneur Morris had a wooden leg, but he loved to dance—that's sure to capture some interest. The story of my year as a social studies teacher was to be the development from a knowledge-spouting, story teller, to a real *teacher*. This development took place gradually, but I will try to insert some of the decisive realizations and break-throughs along the way as our stories unfold.

SCHOOL BEGINS AND PROCESS LADY LEADS THE WAY

Day One

On the first day of school two very overprepared teachers entered their social studies classes. Both had spent August reading books about the Constitution and I, the Process Lady, had researched a long list of strategies that I was prepared to teach during the year. That first day I shared with the students my objectives for our forty minutes together:

- To understand the rationale for a process approach.

- To brainstorm means of coping with a text (or topic) that seems too difficult.

- To survey the chapter.

Explaining process. An overview of what processing entails followed. I told the students that I was conducting an experiment to discover whether letting students in on what psychologists know about how the mind works would make it easier for them to learn. I added that they would be learning facts about how the brain works usually reserved for psychology majors in college. Reminding the students that what they read or heard was processed by the brain, I described my role as being the one to teach them about how that process works and the control they have over it. I emphasized that knowledge is not meant to be memorized and regurgitated back as a knowledge dump at the time of an exam; rather it is meant to be *processed*. Processing means thinking of what one already knows about the topic, deciding what information in the text or discussion is important, relating the new information to background knowledge, organizing, imagining, elaborating, monitoring, and evaluating, to name only a few things a person might do when processing information.

By way of establishing a schema for the year, I asked the students what they hoped to learn in social studies. I had expected their answers to be a timeline of American history. Much to my delight, and Jim's obvious surprise, these middle-school students answered that they hoped to learn how to study so that they would be able to do well in future years.

To continue on that high note, I asked the students what past teachers had taught them that they felt had been helpful to their being successful students. Their answers sounded like a listing from any good study skills course—to survey, to predict, to turn headings into questions, to be actively involved, etc. The students' frequent use of the term "to be actively involved" intrigued me because, when asked to explain what it meant, not one student could give a meaningful explanation of the concept. My work was cut out for me!

Brainstorming ideas. Moving along to the second objective, I stated that the Constitution was a difficult topic, but that I had some tips for making the study of any topic easy and tolerable. Could the students guess what I had in mind? The students brainstormed and we settled on a list that was a combination of their thinking and mine.

1. Read an easy library book on the topic.

2. Survey the text for main topics.

3. Discuss the topic with someone who knows more about the topic than you do.

4. Read a piece of historical fiction set in the time period.

5. Enlist the support of your parents to:

    Take you on day trips.

    Read to you a book on the topic or read the book into a tape to which you can listen.

    Rent a video movie set in the time period being studied.

Surveying. The students then opened the textbook and shared with each other how they had been taught to survey a chapter. I asked the students *why* teachers teach students to survey and shared with them my rationale regarding their need for an outline prior to reading. The students seemed unconvinced. One seemed to express the group's attitude when he said, "I survey in class because the teacher makes me do it, but I never survey something before I read it when I am reading on my own." I made a mental note that I was going to have to come up with some convincing evidence that supported the *why* of the strategies that I taught.

The students *did* survey the text and they associated topics related to the Constitution with their background information. Our country was that very month celebrating the bicentennial for the Constitution, and we were in the city where that document was written, so there was a wealth of information, and misinformation, among the students. The class began to hypothesize and ask questions based on their survey of the chapter (strategies learned in previous classes), and thus began to generate interest in and curiosity about the Constitution.

Day Two

The process objective for the second day of class was "to learn to survey using the chapter introduction and bold-face type." After sharing the objective, I launched into the rationale for *why* this objective was important.

Explaining why. I shared with the class my fascination at learning in a psychology class many years ago that humans have seven memory slots, plus or minus two, in short-term memory. Anyone who chose to just start off reading and trying to grasp all the new ideas was bound to run into trouble after encountering six or seven new ideas. However, psychologists had discovered that one's memory could be increased by using those slots for "chunks" which could be composed of the big ideas and the details associated with the big ideas all in the same chunk. I suggested that the bold-face type in a book was often a clue regarding what the author thought was the major idea of a section. The bold-face type or major idea was a magnet, and if you remembered the major idea, the details would cling to that idea like pins to a magnet. The magnet and attached pins would make a chunk. Remembering isolated details didn't work, because there was no central magnet to hold the chunk together. I could tell by the looks on the students' faces and the questions they were asking that I had captured their interest. I pursued this advantage with a personal experience.

I had once prepared for a test in a college course by reading the chapter five times and was very disgruntled when I received a "C" on the test. What had I done wrong? Some of the students agreed with my study method, but others related the story to the seven memory slots. That psychology was powerful stuff! The students loved it.

Modeling. At this ripe moment, I modeled how I would survey a chapter and then guided the students through the process, discussing the surveying process for each section as we came to it. Bold-face topics were written on the chalkboard and students shared the questions they thought each section would answer. That process led into a discussion of inconsiderate text (in this case, that authors do not always put the most important ideas in bold-face type) and the need for the reader to be flexible.

Discussing homework. Jim reviewed the homework with the students and gave the group feedback regarding how their answers could have been improved. I made a note to myself that we needed to talk to the students about the benefit of finding an interest in the topic of homework rather than having their goal be to put anything down on paper. Jim gave them an option for this night's homework. The students could either watch one of the TV specials that evening about the Constitution or they could read an easy-reading book about the Constitution. The purpose was to establish a background of information about the Constitution that would make it easier to understand the textbook chapter. The assignment was to write a page telling about what they learned about the Constitution from the TV special or from the easy-reading book.

Day Three

The third day Jim began the class with a discussion of the homework. Most of the students had watched the TV special; few had chosen to read a book. The students' comments suggested a superficial grasp of what they had seen, a fact that did not go unnoticed by Jim. He had obviously enjoyed the programs and had a rich background of information about the Constitution which he used to elaborate on the remarks made by the students. I found his detailed comments enriching with respect to my own understanding of that period of history, but could not help but wonder (being the Process Lady) whether it would not have served the students better to have them analyze their understanding of events in the special TV programs about the Constitution and ask for specific clarification about concepts that seemed hazy to them. Jim was so gifted in the way he handled each student's remarks that each one probably thought he or she had made a perfectly acceptable contribution to the discussion. Great for their egos, but I have often wondered, when I am accepting of a poor quality answer, whether I am doing more harm than good.

As each student made a contribution, Jim wrote a key word or name on the chalkboard and suggested that these were important words/names that would help the students access their background knowledge. I noted that the students didn't seem to listen to one another's remarks, some repeating what had already been said, and many of them frantically copying the list on the board. At one point, when Jim was explaining the details of an event, a student interrupted him to ask him to move so he could see the list on the board. Another student used this break to ask, "When are we going to get to read the chapter?" Jim suggested that now would be a good time for me to take over and get the students into the reading. His parting comment was that the students might want to use the list on the board as a clue to important ideas to look for in the text. One student popped up with, "I don't get it. What do you want us to do with the list?"

Relating unknown to known. With that I turned the question over to the class. The students shared what they had learned in reading lessons about background information and how it enhances comprehension of new material because one has something with which to associate the new information. Next, I introduced the process objective, which had been taught to these students in previous years at Benchmark. The objective was: using maps, graphs, and other pictorial devices, as well as the text's chapter summary and review questions, to construct an outline in one's mind regarding what the author thinks is important and what information one should try to access from his or her background knowledge. I reminded the students of *why* this process is important and, using the previous chapter, modeled for them how I surveyed the pictorial devices, summary, and questions and related the survey to my background knowledge. Next, the students surveyed the chapter on the Constitution and shared what they had learned from the survey and what background information came to mind. The students seemed to like sharing their background information, but there was little evidence that they were focusing on the goal of organizing or remembering the new information by intentionally attaching what they had learned from surveying to what they already knew.

Day Four

On Day Four, Jim opened the class with a discussion of the homework. The students had each picked four terms about the Constitution or about people mentioned in the TV specials, the easy-reading book, or the survey which they wanted to know more about, and they were to have researched a bit of information about each of the four. When Jim asked them to share what they had learned, the students seemed reluctant.

Elaborating to clarify. I sensed that the students were unclear as to what was expected and probably had not understood the purpose for this assignment. Jim seemed to sense this, too, so he modeled the thought process he might have gone through in preparing the assignment. He chose the Magna Carta as a term in their text which might have caught his interest and showed them how he might use **what-when-why-how** as starters in his information search. What was the Magna Charta? When was it important? Why is it important? How does it relate to the Constitution? To illustrate information about people, he told some interesting facts he had learned about Gouverneur Morris and Patrick Henry which answered what, when, why, and how questions. Jim guided a discussion of *why* he was emphasizing the terms and people, calling the list the class had made an "identification" list or ID list. I was delighted to see the students suggest that these terms and people could be the magnets to which they attached other information as they read and listened to discussions about the Constitution.

Explaining and modeling homework. The homework assignment for the following day was to make a timeline of events surrounding the need for, writing of, and ratification of, the Constitution. Jim explained that one of the best ways to organize historical facts in one's mind is to form a picture of when key events in history happened and then associate other facts with happenings before or after those key dates. To illustrate this point Jim modeled how he would organize such events as the writing of the Declaration of Independence or Articles of Confederation as taking place before or after the Revolutionary War.

Modeling note taking. Next I began to prepare the students for reading the chapter in their text on the Constitution. My objective was to teach the students to take notes as they read text. I explained that it is easier for me to remember the things I read when I put them in my own words. Then I shared with the group a hot-off-the-press technique I had just learned from Carol Santa, a reading coordinator in Kalispell, Montana, for transposing what one reads into one's own words. It seemed to be the easiest way I had encountered to take notes. That caught their interest! Each student took a piece of paper and folded it into six equal parts, smoothed it out again, and numbered the resulting rectangles to coincide with the paragraphs in their texts. A model was drawn on the board with the heading "Confederation Limits the National Government," the title of that section of the text.

One student read aloud the first sentence in the first paragraph. As he read, I pondered out loud what I was thinking about this sentence as I tried to relate it to the section topic and delete as many words as possible to determine the heart of the idea.

> "This sentence seems to say that the reason the Articles of Confederation was written the way it was was because the newly independent citizens feared strong central power. That makes sense—they had just declared themselves independent because they didn't like living under the power of a king. I'll write 'feared strong central power' in my first rectangle."

I asked the students if any of them had thought of another way to express the major idea in that first sentence, and the class discussed the merits of each of their contributions.

This process was repeated until all sentences in the first paragraph had been summarized into phrases that were then written in the first rectangle. The class next worked on summarizing what they had learned in this paragraph, using the phrases written in the first box. The students concluded that the paragraph told why the Articles of Confederation limited the power of the national government. The reasons were fear of strong central government, fear of states losing their power, and fear that citizens might lose their liberties, so a republican form of government was proposed.

Transferring control. The students were instructed to read the first sentence in the second paragraph to themselves and share phrases that they might write in the second rectangle. The group critiqued one another's ideas and each student wrote a phrase on his or her paper in the second rectangle. This same process was used for the entire second paragraph, then a summary sentence was agreed upon by the group.

Building independence. The next three paragraphs were read and discussed in dyads. One student read a sentence and the other gave a phrase that summed up the main point. The two students discussed it, then wrote a phrase in a rectangle. Roles were reversed and the same procedure followed. The reading and paraphrasing were alternated in this manner until all the paragraphs in the section were completed. As the students worked Jim and I circulated, answering questions and giving feedback. At the conclusion of the period several students expressed enjoyment of this new way of taking notes. They also liked working in dyads and seemed to use their time constructively.

Day Five

The process objective was to introduce outlining. I explained that an outline was just one of many ways that people might use to record their notes about what they had read.

Explaining why. The important thing to remember is that the reason we write in response to reading is that writing is a way to monitor understanding, as well as to aid recall. When we try to put the ideas in our own words it is a check on whether we really understand what we read. I was anxious to convince the students that I wasn't going to overwhelm them with a new strategy a day and to show them how the present lesson was a natural follow-up to the Santa note-taking technique they had practiced the previous day. They had already done all the work for an outline when they filled in the rectangles and summarized the phrases in them.

Modeling and release of responsibility. I handed out a skeleton outline for the first section of the chapter called "The Government of the Confederation is Weak." This was on their outlines as point A. I asked the students to fill in the first five lines of the outline using their notes in rectangles from the previous day's lesson and I modeled the process for them, paraphrasing the first paragraph using the phrases from the first rectangle on the chalkboard. The students worked in dyads to complete section A of the outline and then moved on to outlining section B by again folding a sheet of paper in six parts and taking notes in the rectangles. About five minutes before the end of class, we discussed section B. The students were amazed at how thoroughly they knew the information in that section. They were proving to themselves that putting the text into their own words was a way to develop meaning and to aid the recall of information.

And so our routine was established. Jim would go over the homework first, answering questions, clarifying and clearing up any misconceptions the students might have. He would explain his content objective for the day, introduce the new concepts and vocabulary, and guide the students to access the background information they had that was relevant to the new information being presented. When he felt that the students were ready to process the new information, he turned the class over to me, the Process Lady. I would introduce or review a process objective, explain *why* it would be beneficial to the students, as well as when and where to use it, and how to do it. Mental modeling became a natural part of each lesson, as did walking the student through the new process. These steps were followed by a gradual release of responsibility to the students as they applied the process to the assigned material in the text and the two of us circulated among them providing assistance, encouragement, and feedback.

MR. CONTENT REFLECTS ON HIS FIRST WEEK AND SETS GOALS

One of my major breakthroughs in becoming a strategy teacher myself came at the end of the first week. I had been marking homework papers using a grading scale of 1 to 5. The students were obviously trying to apply the paraphrasing skill they had been working on in class and were struggling to write passable summaries of the material read for homework. But my expectations, I now realized, had not been clear. I kept hearing the shocked and disappointed, "Why is this only a 3, I worked so hard?" or the pleasantly surprised, "I keep getting 5's, boy am I lucky." The students would then compare their summaries with others' and insist that theirs were every bit as good as their neighbors'. I pondered the problem and realized that I needed to come up with some criteria that would make sense to the students for what a good summary entailed.

Make Expectations Clear

By putting summaries from the students' homework papers on overhead transparencies, I was able to interest and involve the students in discovering the characteristics of a good summary. These lessons opened my eyes to the possibilities of strategy teaching. The students soaked up these lessons. Months later I would hear students saying, "This summary is too long and fuzzy" or "This is not only too brief, but incorrect." If all of the students did not immediately improve their summary writing, they at least did have a good idea about what constitutes an effective one. How far I now was from my early dream of the history teacher! Most exciting to me was that I was putting process and content together. The students were not only evaluating summaries, but discussing and arguing over historical facts included in the summaries.

Structure Lessons for Every-pupil Involvement

In reflecting on this breakthrough, several other points hit me about the same time. First, it became obvious that, despite my fascinating talks, I was losing some of the students. My enthusiasm often led me down the path of lengthy digressions. It was difficult for me not to answer interesting but off-topic questions by some of the more curious students. At times, however, I felt I was chatting with two or three students while the rest were quietly nodding their heads or gazing into space. I knew I needed more structure in my lessons. I had to be able to run the class like clockwork, with maximum involvement for everyone.

Guide Students to Find Information on Their Own

Second, I began to realize that when students asked questions I was giving them too much information and not enough guidance. I was shamefully enjoying the repeated demonstrations of my own expertise. These students just couldn't stump me! But showing off my expertise was certainly not what I was hired to do. As a teacher, rather than a teller, I should have been coaching the students on ways to find answers on their own. I needed to phase myself out as the answer man and leave the responsibility for finding and integrating information more and more to the students.

Teach Students How to Learn

My third realization was that the chances were very good that my teaching of social studies would not be a major landmark in the lives of these students. Once I had dreamed that I could reach a few and turn them into future historians, students who one day would sit back and remember me and much of the history I had taught them. Then I realized that I could barely remember my middle-school classes, beyond a few odd bits of trivia. I wanted to leave something more lasting, of more value, with these students. The light was slowly dawning—I would use my love of history as the vehicle to teach them strategies that would help them in all their future classes, in all subjects.

These realizations and concerns provided much fuel for thought and self talk, as well as the topics for many meetings and planning sessions with the Process Lady. As a result, I became more conscious of the need to make my expectations clear and to structure each lesson in a way that kept every student actively involved. I concentrated on sticking to main points and not digressing to elaborate on extraneous topics that were of interest to only a few; and, instead, was successful in shifting the responsibility for researching answers to their questions back onto the students, encouraging them to be problem solvers. I began to devise well-organized strategy lessons and found great satisfaction in knowing that I was giving these students skills that would unlock other areas of knowledge. Although some frustration inevitably ensued, and I lost temporarily my status as a nice guy, many students seemed to appreciate this new approach. With some surprise, I began to hear the students grudgingly admit that it was a good experience for them to have to dig out the information on their own by using strategies they had been taught. It gave these poor readers a sense of security as they looked ahead to the days when they would be left more to fend for themselves in other school settings.

CHALLENGES

The Process Lady is Challenged and Conducts an Informal Experiment

On September 24, less than one month into the school year, Jim and I witnessed signs of student rebellion. As Jim and I entered the classroom a hand shot up and one of the students asked, "When are we going to stop doing all this writing and get to study the way it works best for each of us?" The thought flashed through my mind that maybe we had gone too far in convincing the students that each has a unique learning style and that they should be conscious of which study strategies work best for each of them. It was inevitable that sooner or later middle-school students would see this as an invitation to declare themselves ready to be emancipated—ready to process the information from the text and class discussion in their own most comfortable ways. Knowing my students, I was not surprised.

I asked the class to compromise. For one section of the text I would do some mental modeling. Then, for the remaining two sections covered that day, they could use the study strategies of their own choosing. We would conduct an informal experiment to discover which study strategies did work best for each of them. The students accepted the implied challenge with enthusiasm.

The objective for the lesson was to delete details or redundant information and, where possible, to combine information into superordinate categories. The result was to be a concise sentence stating the main point of each paragraph. I explained that the reason we were going through this exercise was that psychologists have discovered that manipulating information in order to put it into one's own words enhances memory for what is read. I then began mental modeling about what I was thinking as I processed the information in the first paragraph, writing notes on the chalkboard in the fashion we had used in Santa's folded-paper procedure. After manipulating the information several ways, I concluded by writing a concise sentence summary of the paragraph on the chalkboard. I walked the students through the next paragraph sentence by sentence, asking them to jot down a phrase for each sentence. For the third and last paragraph in the section, the students read the paragraph to themselves and wrote a summary sentence. When all had finished this process, we briefly discussed the section.

Then came time when each could study the section his or her own way. Asked what they thought worked best for them in studying a section of text, several said that their parents either read the text to them while they "just listened" or their parents recorded the text on a tape cassette for them to listen to and study. So it was decided that they would all close their books, sit back, and listen as I read the next section of text to them. At the conclusion of the reading, I asked what they thought were some of the main points of the section. With the exception of one student, who had grasped a lot of information from listening, few had any ideas to offer.

Another method of study many of the students felt worked well for them was "just reading, without writing." Therefore, the students read the third section silently, at their own pace. When everyone had finished, the class discussed what they had learned from this section. This discussion flowed better than the previous one, and many of the students concluded that reading on their own and *not* taking notes was what worked best for them. With that, class for the day was over.

The following day I began class by giving the students a three-question quiz: a short-essay question for each section of text covered the previous day. Each student could choose to answer any one of the questions or put down a little something about each one. The students were told that each question was worth 10 points, that only a few minutes would be allowed for the quiz, and that earning 10 points would give them an "A." Not surprisingly, every student chose to answer question one, the question dealing with the section for which they had written notes. After the quiz, all of the students said they felt good about how they had done, most claiming to have earned enough points to qualify for an "A" or "B."

A debriefing followed. I asked the students to analyze what they had learned from the informal experiment. All agreed that writing in response to what they read appeared to help them recall more of what they had read. The mini-experiment had served its purpose.

Jim Is Challenged and Guides Students to Meet Realistic Expectations

The following day Jim began the class by returning the quizzes, on which he had written extensive notes to guide the students in writing future short-essay answers. It appeared that few, if any, students read the notes. Hands went up immediately upon receiving their quizzes. "What's wrong with this? You only gave me seven points." "What was I supposed to write? I put down everything we talked about in class."

Gives explicit feedback. Jim patiently explained what a teacher looks for in a student's answer to a short-essay question and suggested that the students read the notes on their quizzes before they asked any more questions. Then they began to react to the notes he had written, some claiming that Jim had missed something in their answer, that they had actually done what his notes requested. Jim sensed that the motivation behind the discussion was wrong and that, unless he turned it around fast, all his hard work in writing comments was going to be for naught. It was obvious that the students were overly concerned about this their first grade for the year.

Provides motivation for learning from their mistakes. In this school for children with reading problems, where teachers strive to make students feel good about themselves, students had become accustomed to teachers preparing them for quizzes and tests in such a way that anyone who put forth effort and used appropriate strategies was guaranteed an "A" or "B." Being graded in a fashion similar to a regular middle school must have brought back all the old feelings of failure and insecurity. To pull us all out of this nose dive, Jim announced that it was his policy to throw out each student's lowest quiz grade every trimester. Thus, if the students felt they scored poorly on this quiz, they should learn from the experience and not worry about it.

Discovers that much cuing is necessary. Jim began to model how he would have answered each question. By the time Jim had completed discussing the first question and was in the middle of question two, it struck me that not one student had written down anything about what he was saying! It was hard to believe that there was no transfer from their "discovering" the previous day that writing helps them remember. It was at this moment that our teaching truly became *co-teaching*. I interrupted to ask, "Why do you think Mr. Benedict is spending so much time discussing the answers to each of these questions? What will you do if you are asked for some of this information on a major test or need to know it in order to understand other information in the text?" Amazingly, the students hadn't made the connection that the teacher felt this was important information, thus they would probably need to recall it for some later task. I didn't have to say more. Notebooks were opened and pencils began to fly. They seemed really excited to think they could get down on paper what the teacher thought was the perfect answer for a question they might have on a test. The question still remains in my mind, though: Why didn't at least some of the students realize on their own that it would have been a good idea to take notes?

MR. CONTENT BECOMES A DUALIST

Though I continued to be primarily in charge of content, I realized as the year progressed that I was becoming more aware of my own reading-study style and how my approach changed when I read different types of books or even different sections in the text. I was constantly on the lookout for effective strategies that I could share with the students. Prior to teaching these social studies classes I had never given reading a thought—I just did it. Now, I began to think "What would I do to handle this section effectively? What would I do to study it?"

One idea that occurred to me was to have the students reorganize the information in the text by making a chart. I tried it myself and it spiced up the reading for me; maybe the students would find it an interesting and helpful diversion. By this time I had learned enough about processing information to understand that fiddling around with information, in any way, as long as it runs through the brain, helps one to understand and remember it. So I knew that making charts was a valuable study tool. Most of all, though, making charts is fun, and proved to be a much-needed break from summarizing and outlining.

I introduced the chart lesson with some lofty title like "Reorganizing Information" which was received by some groaning, as were most of these strategy lessons. But the groans were good-natured groans, and I noticed the class straighten up and lean forward, eager to have another strategy option at their disposal. It was gratifying to see that some of the more creative students, who were not usually social studies stars, were becoming quite involved and excited with the charts. Through a variety of strategies I was discovering that I could reach all the students, not just a few history buffs.

Most of my lessons developed as a response to students' difficulties with different types of learning or thinking situations. For instance, it was becoming obvious that our forty-minute class was not long enough to finish my typical objective-plus-essay test. This was especially a problem for the students who knew the material best and had the most to say. I felt the injustice of giving the best students low grades because they hadn't paced themselves appropriately to be able to write the last essay. Yet I also felt that it was not unreasonable to expect them to finish within the time allotted. Many of the students appeared helpless in thinking of solutions to their difficulty, resorting to frustrated hostility or the constant request for more time. I convinced myself that the real world is full of such pressures for timed tests and that the students needed to learn some strategies for handling the situation while in our supportive environment.

It was fairly easy to sell the students on a week-long lesson on the time-limit problem. It was a problem for many of them, so they were all ears. Together, we brainstormed several strategies to cope with the problem: predicting essay questions, taking brief organized notes, and practicing writing the essay with a time limit—both to help in memorizing the information and to become more sure of how much information could be included in the time they had to write an essay answer.

Of all the lessons, I think this one was the biggest hit with the students, perhaps because it showed immediate results. The students had their timing down so well that, when on the next test I said it was time to move on to the next section of the test, they seemed amazed at how much they had finished, and how much ahead of schedule they were. They worked more calmly than usual and there was none of the familiar last-five-minute panic and pleading for more time. Two of the notoriously long essay writers both handed me their tests with time to spare. One of the boys could not suppress his grin as he told me, "That's the first time this year I've gotten to hand you my test without your having to take it away from me." I floated out of the classroom with a satisfied feeling.

THE CONTINUING SAGA: A SUMMARY

Process Is Never Mastered

Little did we realize when we began with our process objectives the first day of school that the strategies that we introduced in those first weeks would be the major strategies that we would emphasize, reteach, elaborate, illustrate, re-model, etc. for the entire year. Informal experiments became the most convincing way to change the students' beliefs about what they needed to do to succeed in school, and they never seemed to tire of what would eventually come to be known as "Psych 101," the process part of the lesson in which we shared cognitive secrets that only psychologists know. A few of the 14 year olds who would be graduating to a "regular" school setting at the end of the school year even approached Irene and asked why they couldn't just have psychology instead of social studies. There were others, of course, who approached Jim and asked why they couldn't have history for the entire period. And, when Irene worked her way out of the class by early spring, they thought they were having history for the entire period. There were even those in the class who, because of Jim's influence, were definitely considering careers as historians. Process and content had been successfully joined.

There's More to Learning Content Than Content

Irene learned from this experiment that process and content cannot be separated. She also learned that having an excellent background in the content one teaches, as Jim did, seems to free the teacher of content worries and to allow him or her to concentrate on teaching the process of how to learn the content.

Jim learned that it is not enough for a content teacher to know his subject well and to impart knowledge with enthusiasm and colorful anecdotes, no matter how interesting. He also learned that it is unlikely that a student will develop a deep interest in any subject in which he or she does not feel comfortable and confident, and that helping students to achieve a very basic understanding of how the brain processes information and teaching them a few strategies for executing learning tasks will make a big difference in their approach to and control over learning, and thus in their motivation. Jim still hopes that some of his students will come to share his love of history, but his greatest feeling of success now comes when he sees a student pick up a history book with a look of confidence and purpose.

Irene and Jim learned that how the mind works holds a fascination and intrigue for both young and old, students and teachers. Many of their most unmotivated students became more involved when they discussed, along with their process objectives, how the mind processes information. As in the case of all experiments at Benchmark, stories about the successes and failures of this dual teaching arrangement had soon circulated among the teachers and often became the topic of team meetings. The other teachers, especially middle-school teachers, became interested in how the Process Lady divulged her cognitive concepts and the students' reaction. Teachers frequently observed in the class and commented that they appreciated the review of educational psychology. It was not long before the teachers were asking that this information be shared with *their* students. Perhaps teaching a mini-course in cognitive psychology would be in order?

CHAPTER 7

Psych 101: A Course for Learning About Learning

The positive reaction of the previous year's students to the process lessons that included a simplified course in cognitive psychology embedded in a history course (see Chapter 6,) provided the impetus for an across-the-curriculum program in learning, thinking, and problem solving. The source of the information that teachers would infuse into their teaching at every opportunity was to be a mini-course taught to the four middle-school classes, entitled Psych 101, complete with its own manual. These classes started in the fall of 1988.

A copy of the Psych 101 manual was given to every teacher in the school and teachers were encouraged to integrate the processing concepts into their regular lessons. For the lower school, it was suggested that teachers adapt the Psych 101 material to the appropriate developmental levels of their students.

GOALS OF PSYCH 101

We decided that teaching a mini-course about how the mind works would accomplish a number of goals:

1. It would give the staff and students a common language for discussing the processing of information.

2. It would initiate the same processing objectives into the school across the curriculum. The staff, in their interactions with one another, might discuss the objectives and feel more committed to reteaching, elaborating, cuing, and reinforcing these process objectives in their own classes.

3. With circulation of the manual, special-subject teachers (e.g., science, math, health, art) could easily find out what was being emphasized in all the classes, without the difficult communication process of keeping track of the objectives the various language arts teachers had introduced.

4. Teaching a mini-course in how the mind works would provide one model for talking with students about the processing of information.

5. Teaching the mini-course would assure that the process objectives were introduced.

The staff agreed with the wisdom of adding the mini-course to the middle-school program. The director of the school was to be the teacher. It was decided that each unit of lessons would include a section devoted to background reading for the teacher. This would provide the regular teacher, in whose room the director was to be a guest teacher, with the information needed to continue the lessons on days when the director could not be present. The background reading would provide the depth of information that a teacher would need to be able to elaborate on a topic beyond the content of a brief lesson plan.

Psych 101 was not intended to be merely a stand-alone course. The intent was to introduce concepts in Psych 101 that would be infused into the teaching of all classes across the curriculum. Teachers who observed the teaching of Psych 101 in their classrooms were given the responsibility of reteaching, elaborating, cuing, and reinforcing throughout the day the concepts they heard discussed.

THE STUDENTS

On the first day of school thirteen bright-eyed middle-school students entered the classroom to begin the much discussed, anxiously anticipated "college" course that was on their rosters. They all seemed to be standing taller and looking more mature than they had appeared in the hall just minutes before. The objective for the day was to introduce the learning, thinking, problem-solving program. The presentation was largely lecture, but as the trimester progressed there would be less and less lecturing. Once the students became comfortable with the concepts, they wanted to interact.

They seemed hungry for information that would help them understand themselves. Many students seemed to see this course as a chance to find out what was really wrong with their brains so they had to attend a school for children with reading problems. Despite the fact that most of them have above-average intelligence, our students seemed reluctant to believe that they were smart. Throughout the year, no matter what the topic was in Psych 101, the students would bring the conversation around to the nature/nurture issue. Did nature, the way they were born, predetermine their thinking ability or could nurture, their environment and what they did, affect their ability to think and learn? It was as if taking control was such an effort for them that they wanted to be assured over and over again that their brains were not indelibly imprinted in a defective manner and that they could control whether or not they would be successful, not only in school, but more importantly, in life.

The remainder of this chapter takes you inside the classroom to be part of the daily Psych 101 lessons. In many cases you will be reading the actual transcripts of the lessons.

THE COURSE: DAY ONE

And, so we began...

> Today we begin a course of study that could be the most important course you will ever take with respect to shaping what you do with the rest of your life. The course we plan to teach is about how the human mind works and how you can get the best payoff when you make good use of your mind. These are facts that most psychologists and teachers know, but have rarely thought to share with students below the college level. I have asked your teachers and teaching assistants to expect you to apply these cognitive concepts when they teach you this year. They have agreed to guide you and cue you until applying them becomes a regular part of the way you function.
>
> As I talk to you during the next few weeks while we are studying Unit 1, I am going to share with you six or seven of those concepts about how the mind works. I'd like you to listen for these concepts that most teachers keep secret from you and jot them down in your notes whenever you think you hear one. We'll compare lists of secrets when I conclude this section.

Concepts From Cognitive Psychologists

> Cognitive psychologists have recently conducted studies in which elementary and middle-school students improved in reading because they were taught facts about how the brain works such as: 1) thinking about what you know makes it easier to remember what you read, and 2) making images as you read makes it more likely you will notice when you misread.

(At this point, hands were raised and students wanted to share their experiences regarding these two facts. Those who shared seemed convinced of the validity of these two facts about how the brain works.) The lecture continued...

> During the last few years, Benchmark teachers have been reading about the research of cognitive psychologists and

have been applying the ideas about thinking to your reading instruction. As a result, visitors to Benchmark and teachers of Benchmark graduates are amazed at the mature thinking of Benchmark students in response to their reading.

So far, researchers have tended to work with students in isolated subjects such as reading, math, and writing. They have not been successful in implementing a program to teach thinking across the curriculum—that is, to emphasize the secrets of how the mind works in every aspect of the school day. Benchmark was chosen by the James S. McDonnell Foundation as the school to develop just that —a program to teach students how to think and learn in all their classes.

You must be wondering, "So what's in it for me?" and "Does it mean that I will have more work?" Let me answer both of those questions.

What's In It For Me?

For one thing, this program is going to dispel some of your incorrect beliefs about intelligence and brilliant thinking. For example, many of you probably think that you were born with an IQ score and that's that. You may even have decided that you eternally are going to be either barely smart, sort of smart, not smart enough, etc., and that you have no control over your smartness. That's dead wrong! Intelligence is the result of two factors: 1) how much information you know and 2) the strategies you employ to take charge of your learning, thinking, or problem solving.

(Hands went up again to take issue with the concept of a fluid IQ. We debated a bit, then moved on.)

When you do poorly in a subject, such as math or social studies, it isn't because the math or social studies part of your brain is defective, rather it is because you either don't have enough information or you weren't able to employ the strategies you needed to take charge so you could use what you know.

Intelligence is the power to learn and understand. The power comes from knowledge—the facts you know, the skills and strategies you know, and the understanding you have of yourself. Secondly, the power comes from your effort to take charge and use the knowledge you have in a planful way.

(Pencils were flying. The students seemed invested in getting this information in their notes.)

So what's in it for you? For one thing, we will be teaching you how to be more intelligent. Is there anyone here who doesn't want to be more intelligent? There's the bell. Will everyone who wants to be more intelligent leave the room.

Everyone quickly left and that was the end of the first day of Psych 101 in Mrs. Elliot's class. During the following period the same lesson was taught next door in Ms. Scottoline's room with another group of middle-school students.

DAY TWO

Review of Two Cognitive Concepts

We began with a review. "Does anyone remember what cognitive psychologists have taught the Benchmark teachers about how the mind works?" There was a rustle of papers as students looked in their notes. Chris answered, "If you know something about what you're reading, then it's easier to read that." The teacher asked for an example, and Chris explained that reading about Dungeons and Dragons is easier for him than for some people because he already knows a lot about the topic.

He had picked a perfect example for the teacher to make the point about fluid IQ. She asked, "Does that mean, Chris, if I read something about Dungeons and Dragons and don't understand it as well as you do that you are smarter than I?" Sounding like a Benchmark teacher, Chris responded, "No, but you should pick something easier to read, something below your reading level, and just go over that first so you have a little bit of background."

Chris had obviously remembered the teacher sharing how she read easy books from the Benchmark library to acquire background information about China. She had commented that she prefers easy books for background information because these books often tell just the big ideas which give the reader "pegs in your head" onto which new information can be attached.

The teacher asked for another cognitive secret that was talked about the previous day. Frank answered, "Well...make pictures in your head." The teacher elaborated, "Good. Cognitive psychologists have discovered that, while we read, we should try to picture in our heads about what we are reading. There will be more likelihood, then, that you're going to be able to realize when you don't understand something. You're going to get that feeling of 'I just can't picture it, so I don't understand it.' It happens to me a whole lot when I'm reading technical material."

Jon said, "That happens to me when I'm reading, but I just change the picture." The teacher decided she had better pursue this and shared a story about typing her son's paper on the chemistry of nutrition, a paper on which he received a B because there were so many proofreading errors. The teacher confided that she had no picture in her mind even when she tried to proofread the paper for errors, because she didn't have the background of knowledge to attach to any of the ideas. She had no picture in her head and that confirmed that she didn't understand it.

What is Intelligence?

To move the review to the next topic the teacher asked, "I'd like your opinions and reasons about whether you think intelligence is inherited." No one put up a hand. The teacher restated the request. "Do you think you were born smart, or sort of smart, not smart, real smart?"

Jon answered, "I don't think you are born any way." The teacher agreed and elaborated....

When most of you came to Benchmark you weren't feeling very smart because you had experienced difficulty in learning to read. But, like Jon, you have worked hard and you know that you have become smarter. You have responded to the strategy knowledge and subject-matter knowledge that you have received at Benchmark and you now perform well. That is what intelligence is all about.

Intelligence is knowledge—having a lot of knowledge. Some students go into some subjects with a bad attitude— you think "that's stupid—I'm not interested in it." Well, that's like committing intellectual suicide because you're not going to have the background information you need the next day when the teacher teaches you something new based on what you were supposed to have learned the day before. You're still young and you have many school years ahead of you. If you decide to tune out the knowledge that the teachers are teaching you, you won't have the knowledge foundation to build on when you decide you want to learn something at a later time.

Doesn't it make sense to you that you are continually using what you know to help understand something new? Would you be able to understand what Mr. Young is doing this year in science if you walked in having lived on a deserted island for the last 12 years? Do you think you would understand what he's talking about?

It's the knowledge that you gain little by little by attending school, going places, interacting with people, watching television, and reading books that you use to construct meaning for the next learning experience.

The teacher shared this experience.

> I've chosen in some cases to turn off knowledge and I've been penalized for the rest of my life. I'll give you an example. When I was in high school, I took a course called Physics. From what I remember about Physics it had to do with things like pulleys and forces and power and energy. I did well the first marking period and also the next marking period.
>
> Nevertheless, I went to the teacher, one of my favorites, and told him that, because I had more than enough credits to graduate and was never going to need to know about inclines and forces and such things, I wanted to drop the course. I was allowed to, but now I regret dropping the course. There is so much about levers, fulcrums, pulleys, and mechanical advantage that I wished I had understood when my boys were growing up. But I didn't have the background to discuss with them the concepts they were learning and wanted to discuss.

Throughout the year when the teacher would share personal experiences about herself or her family, the students seemed to find it particularly meaningful in helping them understand a concept. During discussions they would often make a comment such as, "Well, it is sort of like what happened to you when you didn't have enough knowledge about physics to discuss it with your boys."

Different Kinds of Intelligence

Moving along to the next topic, the teacher continued...

> Intelligent people have different kinds of knowledge. One kind of knowledge is knowledge about the strategies you employ to take charge of your learning, thinking, and problem solving. Thus, you need not only knowledge of facts to be intelligent, but you also need knowledge of strategies to be able to do something with the facts.
>
> If you do poorly in science this year, would it be correct to say that you probably have poor potential for doing well in science, that there is something wrong with the science part of your brain? (The students shook their heads.) Do some of you do better in math than you do in some of your other subjects? (A few students grinned and nodded.) And you also know that doesn't mean that certain parts of your brain are malfunctioning or that you received defective brain parts. It might mean that in some areas you don't have

the facts that you need to work with or you don't have the knowledge of strategies or even that you have the knowledge, but don't use it. That's the way I would like you to look at any difficulties you have in learning. It is not that you're dumb. You already know that you are smart in many areas, and that you could be smart in many more.

How much you know about a topic and what strategies you choose to learn has a lot to do with what you value, what is important to you. Topics you already know a lot about are those about which you have been motivated to learn. When someone is an expert in something, does that mean that person is smarter than people who are not experts in that area? No, not necessarily. It only means that the expert has acquired more information and strategies in that area and is motivated to use those and to acquire more. What you're going to do best at is going to be related to: whether you have the knowledge about the topic, whether you have the knowledge about strategies, and whether you have the motivation to take control. That's intelligence.

A man named Howard Gardner at Harvard, who is one of the leaders in the field of intelligence, says we have multiple intelligences. Robert Sternberg of Yale, another top authority on intelligence, speaks of practical intelligence. Both are saying that a person is not just smart or just dumb or just average. Some people may be really intelligent socially. Such individuals have a lot of knowledge about people skills. There are other people who are geniuses at playing chess, but may not be too intelligent when it comes to people skills or U.S. history. The chess player had control over his becoming a chess expert. Had he spent as much time learning about people or U.S. history, he might also have looked very intelligent in those areas.

As you can see, there are different kinds of intelligence. Some people are very intelligent in music. Look at the new Miss America. She's more intelligent than I am in violin, but I'm more intelligent than she is when it comes to teaching reading.

The point I'm trying to make is that you all have relative intelligences. You all have the potential to do really well in a number of areas. Only you are in control of what you choose to learn about your area of interest, what strategies you use to learn, and how motivated you will be. It is up to you to get the background knowledge that you need, to absorb the strategies you need, and to understand yourself.

Understanding yourself is really important. A lot of people lie to themselves. I'll bet that sometimes you lie to yourself. Did you ever lie to yourself and say, "I really would have gotten a better grade on the test if the teacher had taught it better?" But, on the same occasion, did you ever look around the class and wonder why everyone else in the class earned a higher grade than you did, and they were taught by the same teacher? That poor grade wasn't due to lack of intelligence. It was due to lack of intelligent behavior. Today we have been talking about the fact that intelligent behavior results from possessing different kinds of knowledge, deciding to use strategies, and being motivated.

DAY THREE

Range of Intelligence

"Let's do a quick review. What do you have in your notes about intelligence?" Adam tells the class that he has concluded that intelligence is not inherited. Someone else says that it is inherited. The teacher mediates by telling both boys they are correct....

Psychologists believe that we each inherit a range of intelligence. (The teacher draws a graph on the chalkboard and illustrates the range with a shaded band and marks an X at the lower end.) Researchers feel that most humans don't begin to approach the limits of their potential. They perform at the lower end of the range they inherit; thus, in the end it is not inheritance that determines intelligence—it is you. It is a matter of what you do with what you have. Why do I say that?

Frank answers that intelligence comes from knowledge. The teacher agrees and tells the students several stories about children who have been read to since infancy and how intelligent they look when they enter school compared to the children who were never read to.

Intellectual Power Is the Result of Knowledge and Effort

The teacher tells the students that intelligence is the power to learn and understand. And that power comes from knowledge and effort. One of the students says, "How about strategies?" The discussion that followed was about there being a number of different categories of knowledge....

There is knowledge about school subjects, the things you learn in school, such as math facts and historical events. We'll call that category "facts." A second category is knowledge about strategies and knowing when and where to use them. A third category is knowledge about yourself.

The students asked a number of questions about the personal styles people have, such as being nervous during a test and forgetting everything or knowing you have a hard time learning something, so having to spend twice as much time studying it as something else. They also talked about people who aren't aware of how their styles can be a hindrance to their getting along socially. The group responded to the idea of having knowledge about self and taking charge to present a good image. There was a discussion of people who seem very intelligent, yet in a crisis are terrible problem solvers. "Does that mean they are or aren't intelligent?" The students were enjoying the discussion about knowing yourself, and would have liked to continue, but the teacher summarized...

> It sounds as if you have concluded that power to demonstrate intelligent behavior comes from two sources. One is the possession of knowledge—knowledge of facts, strategies, and of him or herself. We have determined that some people seem retarded socially, even though they may have a high IQ on a test that measures facts. There are other people who are strategically retarded. If they memorize information and only need to regurgitate it back in response to a test question, they may do fine. However, if they are asked to use that information at a later time to think about something new, they may not do well. The reason might be that they initially lacked knowledge about the strategies they needed to manipulate information, so they memorized it, and forgot it.
>
> As an example, some of you have caught on to why Benchmark teachers insist that you put what you've read into your own words rather than copy phrases out of the book. Jamie did a very nice job of just that today in social studies. She gave a summary of a paragraph in her own words as a means of checking whether she understood the paragraph. That's what intelligent people do; they self-assess and use strategies. Jamie assessed her understanding by putting what she read in her own words. That's being strategic. That way of functioning is going to move you more and more toward being intelligent.
>
> Second, intellectual power comes from your own effort. Your effort to take charge and use the knowledge you have. You can have all the knowledge in the world. You can know all the facts about many topics. You can listen to your teachers teach strategies. You can even understand yourself. But if you don't make the effort to put the facts, strategies,

and knowledge of yourself to work for you, then you won't look intelligent. You make the decision. You can say: "I don't care," or "I'm never going to need this stuff," or "Who cares about being in charge?" Those are all decisions over which you have control and which determine whether you will demonstrate intelligent behavior. Using knowledge in a goal-driven, planful, self-assessing, strategic way is what intelligence is all about. That's what's going to furnish the power to learn; but you're in control of that.

What's In It For Me?

I told you that I would explain what's in it for you to take part in this course. I think I have answered that question. If you put into practice all the things we will talk about in this course, you will perform in a more intelligent way, thus be more intelligent. That's a promise. We see it happen often at Benchmark. Many students, who according to someone's IQ test are not supposed to be as smart as others, put a great deal of effort into learning, using facts, strategies, and knowledge about themselves. The result is that they are successful, both academically and personally.

Now you know the secret that people have been trying to find out about Benchmark when they ask, what is the secret of your success? Benchmark is successful because students put into use the things we teach them. They learn the facts, they learn the strategies, and they take all the cues that we give them to help them understand themselves and, to those three, they add the magic ingredient, effort.

Executive Control

Now I want to talk about strategies and I'm going to read you a quote. I'd like you to see if you can interpret it. If you have trouble with it, I'll help you figure out what it means. The quote is from Ann Brown, a highly respected cognitive psychologist. She says, "Conscious executive control of the routines available to the system is the essence of intelligent activity (Brown, 1977, cited in Garner, 1987, p. 22). Sounds as if it were written in Greek, doesn't it? Let me translate for you.

Ann Brown is explaining intelligent activity. She says it is a conscious activity. In other words, you are aware of doing something; it doesn't happen automatically. She says conscious executive control—**control** means "I'm going to take charge, be in control." **Executive** means act like in your mind you are the executive or boss. I'm the executive at Benchmark School. Well, imagine that Benchmark School is you, your body and brain. You're in charge of it, you're the executive. You're saying to yourself, "I'm going to take control; I'm not going to sit here like a blob. I'm going to be in control of how this person functions."

Remember, Joanna, how I used to tease you last year that you weren't in control? You were letting social studies go in your eyes and out your hand? What do you think I meant by that? A student says, "When you copy social studies, then you forget it." That was true of you, because the social studies never passed through your head. It's a common happening. We write down notes and never let them pass through our heads, or when we see something on the board we just copy it down, but don't think about what we are copying. It went in through our eyes and out our hand. Sometimes it goes in our ears and out our hands. I did a lot of that in college. I took great notes. I always thought I would think about the information later, but often I didn't have time later. Ann Brown is saying that the person who has executive control takes charge of his/her routines. Routines include skills and strategies. That's all there is to it. She's saying that control over what you learn and what strategies you use is what intelligent behavior is.

In summary, to behave intelligently you need knowledge of facts, strategies, and yourself and you must take charge to use what you know.

DAY FOUR

Review

The teacher began by asking the students what they had learned during the first three days of class about what's in their heads. Their answers included:

- Intelligence.
- I have knowledge.
- It's part of intelligence.
- Power is knowledge.
- Understanding yourself.
- Range of intelligence you inherit, but you decide what to do with it at school.
- If you don't have effort, then you're just wasting intelligence.
- It is under your control.

Each student's contribution to the discussion was elaborated upon before moving on to the question, "What's in it for you? Why pay close attention in this class?" Students suggested:

- It will help you study.
- If you take advantage, you should know what you're supposed to do.
- You can let your intelligence grow.

Does Taking This Course Mean More Work?

The teacher began this discussion by noting that the answer to the question would depend on their definition of work.

Do you think the effort to be goal-driven, planful, self-assessing and strategic works? If so, this course will be work. You need a goal and a plan to learn. To solve a problem you need to figure out what the problem or goal is, then plan a solution. Learning and problem solving don't happen by accident.

You need to assess how you're progressing with your plan and be strategic—that means use strategies. That takes effort, so maybe that's work. I love skiing, and it takes effort, but I don't consider it work.

The students anticipated where the teacher was going with this discussion. They gave further examples of effortful activities that they did not consider work and concluded that their attitudes about learning, thinking, and problem solving would determine whether they felt this course was work.

The teacher elaborated...

So what you need to know is that if you have a bad attitude about school, a bad attitude about science, a bad attitude about math, you're sabotaging yourself. Some of the teachers use the expression, "Shooting yourself in the foot." You're hurting yourself, just as if you shot yourself in the foot, when you have a bad attitude. You're not hurting the teacher. You're not going to hurt Mr. Young if you have a bad attitude in science. He likes all of you and he would like it very much if you all liked science. But that is your choice.

The things that you like and have a good attitude about are the things in which you do well because you're willing to put out the effort. If you have a bad attitude about something, then you're not going to give the effort and you're not going to do as well.

If you like the idea of becoming a better learner, thinker, and problem solver, then you have to decide whether the result is worth the effort. If you think the result is worth the effort, this program is really going to benefit you and you're going to demonstrate more intelligent behavior as a result. But I have to be honest with you. Learning, thinking, and problem solving all take effort.

Motivation

Let me set the stage. When I was your age, I didn't use my effort to learn, I used effort to get good grades. Is there anything wrong with that?

One of the students answered, "You would know the information for a short time and get good grades on the tests and then forget it." Other students supplied similar ideas.

My effort was to earn good grades to please my parents, It never occurred to me that I could use that same effort to learn or that I could be involved in what I was learning. I memorized for tests and promptly forgot what I learned. I didn't process the information. I didn't hook it to pegs in my brain. I didn't associate the information with something I already knew, so it didn't stick.

Two kinds of effort.

Based on what I've told you it sounds as if there are at least two kinds of effort: effort to learn and effort to get good grades. Unfortunately, most humans look for the path of least resistance, the easy way. If you really want to take advantage of the knowledge we are going to present this year, and you want to become a good learner, thinker, and problem solver, you can't always be looking for the easiest way and you must stick with something until you understand it, then you have learned.

The teacher shared with the students the frequently heard statement when a teacher is assisting a student: "Just tell me what you want me to write down!"

That statement gives teachers the message that you don't care about learning, you just want to get an answer on the paper. To be a learner, thinker, or problem solver you have to be willing to grapple with frustration. Although it may sound strange, frustration is a good sign because it's your red alert saying to you, "I've come across something that I don't quite understand. I'm going to have to stick with this until I work it out or ask someone for clarification."

Do you know what many people do when they're frustrated with a written assignment? They write down something they know probably isn't correct or they give up and skip the item. A better way of coping with the problem would be to use frustration as a red alert notifying you that there is something you don't understand and, in most cases, shouldn't be put off. Rather, you should deal with it when it occurs. If you don't have time to do it right now, what makes you think you'll have time later? If you are really unable to solve the problem, make a note of it, so that later you can ask for clarification.

Effort to learn

The effort to learn is called motivation. The desire to learn comes from within you. It depends on what your goals are. If your goal is to learn enough math this year and next year so that when you leave Benchmark you will be placed in a good math section, that goal is going to motivate you to stay tuned in and work hard in math classes. On the other hand, if your goal is to get a C in social studies, when it is possible for you to earn an A, there probably isn't much a teacher can do to get you to perform better. Motivation comes from within. Few people achieve higher than their goals. If your goal is to complete assignments the fastest, simplest way, then that goal will motivate you to do the bare minimum. If your goal is to give the right answer on a test, but not to understand the material, then that is what you will be motivated to do. Sooner or later you will have to pay for that lack of understanding. However, if your goal is to understand what causes pollution because you are personally interested in protecting the environment, then there is a good likelihood that you will stick with the topic until you understand it. You will achieve your goal, which was not just to acquire information, but rather to understand it. We have already concluded that what you understand is the basis for gaining more understanding. Real learning doesn't take place without understanding. Intelligent people ask for clarification when they don't understand.

In summary, I challenge you to think about your goals. Do your goals motivate you in a positive way to be a learner, thinker, and problem solver or do your goals motivate you to get by with as little effort as possible? You now have the third component of intelligent behavior—**motivation. Intel-**

ligent behavior is composed of knowledge, control, and motivation.

FIFTH DAY

Formula for Intelligent Behavior

When the students entered there was a poster on the chalkboard that read:

INTELLIGENT BEHAVIOR = KNOWLEDGE* + CONTROL + MOTIVATION

*(KNOWLEDGE = knowledge of facts + knowledge of strategies + knowledge of self)

Students were asked to explain and give examples of the components. The discussion that followed was punctuated with questions related to each of the components. For example, a lengthy discussion took place about how background knowledge aids memory. Hypothetical cases of students missing one or more of the components were given by the teacher and suggestions were made by the students about how to remedy the problem.

SUMMARY OF THE REMAINING NINE WEEKS

The course was launched. By Back-to-School Night, the second week of school, parents were commenting that Psych 101 was the first class their children had discussed at the dinner table in years. There was much enthusiasm for the course among both parents and students!

Review of Seven Cognitive Secrets

During the second week of classes the students worked together in dyads combing their notes for **cognitive secrets**. Each dyad was to see how close they could come to matching the teacher's list of the seven cognitive secrets that had been discussed thus far in the course. Once most of the dyads had decided on five to seven cognitive secrets, the dyads shared and explained their lists of cognitive secrets. In one form or another, all the dyads expressed the following concepts:

1. Intelligence equals knowledge, plus control, plus motivation.

2. Intelligent behavior is the result of knowledge plus goal-driven, planful, self-assessing, strategic behaviors plus motivation.

3. Thinking about what you know makes it easier to remember what you are reading or hearing.

4. Making images as you read or listen makes it more likely you will notice when understanding is not taking place.

5. Knowing a lot of information is a foundation for intelligent behavior.

6. Putting forth effort is necessary to learning, thinking, and problem solving.

7. Effort toward the goal of learning produces increased knowledge; effort placed on earning good grades often produces good grades, but little learning.

In addition to those secrets listed above, some students included:

8. There are different kinds of knowledge, such as knowledge of facts, knowledge of strategies, and knowledge of yourself.

9. What people think is important affects their decision about what will receive their motivation and best effort.

Several debriefing sessions were held to tie together the concepts presented in Unit 1 before moving on to the next unit. For example, students were asked to explain and give examples of the four aspects of control: goals, plans, self-assessment, and strategies. The teacher as well as the students told anecdotes that illustrated the four concepts.

Factors Affecting Success

The next unit dealt with factors that affect success in learning, thinking, and problem solving. The teacher set the stage by giving some case studies and asking the students what factors affected success or lack of success. Then the students brainstormed examples of factors affecting success. Once a number of items had been listed the students worked in dyads. Their task was to group the factors affecting success into four categories. With guidance from the teacher, the students grouped the factors into person, task, environmental, and strategy variables. Once the categories were established, the students added more factors to each category. The finished chart was similar to the one below.

Person Variables

reflectivity	persistence	flexibility
intent	attentiveness	expectations
attribution	attitude	organization

independence	curiosity	beliefs
affect	motivation	interest
pace	bias	background knowledge

Task Variables
| topic | word difficulty | considerate text |
| complexity | subtasks | concept levels |

Environmental Variables
| desk | classroom | noise level |
| family schedule | activities | materials |

Strategy Variables
rehearsal	survey	clarification
elaboration	prediction	summarizing
spaced study	questioning	writing
organizing	imaging	self-talking/reciting
rereading	paraphrasing	relating new to old

Numerous class periods were spent talking about the meaning of each item, followed by discussing school-related situations involving each one, and how a student could take control of the variable.

At the conclusion of this unit students were again asked to add to their list of cognitive secrets. Some wrote that success is affected by person, task, environmental, and strategy variables. Others went into greater detail, listing numerous specific variables that affect success.

Control

The next unit dealt with control. Each student dyad was given six variables affecting success which they were to place in one of two columns on a sheet of paper which they had divided in half vertically. One column was for variables for which it was reasonable to expect a student to take control, and the other column was for variables they believed were beyond a student's control. For each variable in the "control" column, students were to give examples of ways to take control. For each variable in the "not control" column, students were to give a rationale as to why this variable could not be controlled by a student. After several days of discussion, the class decided on ways they could take charge of all the variables. The debates that ensued before consensus was reached were wonderful. The most hotly debated issue was whether motivation was something students could control. Many students wanted to give sole responsibility for motivation to the teacher.

At the conclusion of this unit students added to their list of cognitive secrets: knowledge about what affects learning, thinking, and problem solving is of little value unless you take control of the variables.

Task Variables

The remainder of the course delved more deeply into the meaning of task, person, environmental, and strategy variables. For example, task variables were talked about on two dimensions: the nature of the information and the demands of the task. Students were given hypothetical school tasks. For each hypothetical task they analyzed the task relative to themselves with respect to the difficulty of both the reading material and the conceptual level based on background knowledge (easy, just right, hard). They further analyzed the task by breaking the task into subtasks and assessing time, materials, and effort demands. Finally, they devised goals and plans for completing the task.

Person Variables

With respect to person variables, students were encouraged to analyze themselves with respect to their uniqueness and to devise plans to capitalize on their strengths and to take control of their characteristics that could be roadblocks to success. Students listed their person traits in three columns headed: Characteristic of me, when it helps, when it hinders. When these were shared, students brainstormed strategic plans to take charge of the traits that hinder. As a concluding activity, school tasks were suggested and the students related to the task by answering such questions as the five below, as well as setting goals and plans for taking charge of those variables:

1. What is my level of motivation? (above average, average, poor),

2. What is my attitude about the task? (good, okay, poor),

3. What are my beliefs about:

   a) the value of the task/topic? (it is necessary for other things I want to learn; it is easier to just do it than worry about it; it takes more effort than it is worth; it is something I don't need to know),

   b) the key factors to success on this task? (effort, intent to do well, a plan, powerful strategies, background knowledge, attitude, motivation, the teacher, parent, classmates, luck),

4. What feelings come to mind when I think of doing this task? (excitement, curiosity, pleasure, duty, boredom, uncertainty, frustration, nervousness, anger),

5. What characteristics of school success will be especially crucial to my success on this task? (reflectivity, persistence, interest, flexibility, independence, attention, organization, motivation, curiosity).

Environmental Variables

Factors in one's environment that could play a role in a person's success were discussed, then placed on a grid in terms of helps/hinders and possible control strategies. Typical school assignments were presented and students were asked to consider and plan for: space to work, time conflicts, noise level, appropriate materials, and support person (if necessary).

Strategy Variables

An overview of strategies was given, with students citing from experience the how, why, and when of some of the following strategies: survey, relate new to known, predict, set purposes, create images, make inferences, determine story/elements, state main ideas, summarize, analyze critically, clarify, compose and answer questions, elaborate (by thinking of examples, nonexamples, analogies, comparisons, etc.), paraphrase, outline, take notes, classify and organize, reread, assess progress, take remedial action, construct checklists, use self-talk/self-instruction, construct and monitor schedules, organize materials in a notebook, and organize materials to take home or to school.

SECOND SESSION OF PSYCH 101

By December 1st when it was time to begin the second round of Psych 101 for the remaining two middle-school classes, we were aware that language arts and social studies teachers were doing such a commendable job of integrating the Psych 101 concepts into their teaching that all middle-school students had been exposed in some form or another to most of the concepts discussed above. If a classroom teacher did not bring up one of the Psych 101 topics, then a student often would. Because middle-school students are regrouped for all subjects, and therefore are with different students, even the 26 students who had not yet been in Psych 101 were hearing about it. Also, two of the McDonnell participant-observers who observed the Psych 101 classes were also social studies teachers who carried the concepts they heard discussed in Psych 101 into their social studies instruction. Infusion was occurring!

Thus, a new course was designed using a text, *It's All in Your Head* (Barrett, 1985). In the minds of the students, having a psychology textbook definitely made Psych 101 seem like a college course. For many of the students, the reading level of the text was above their instructional levels. Letters were sent to parents requesting that parents either read the material to their children or tape record it for them. As it turned out, more students than we expected could read the material on their own. (A result of background knowledge learned in Psych 101!) A few who had their parents read the text to them seemed to gain increased understanding as a result of an opportunity to discuss the information with a parent.

The discussion topics followed the sequence in the text. In amplifying the text, most of the material for the original course described above was reviewed or introduced. The topics covered were: brain vs. mind/brain, why babies have big heads, how the brain evolved and what the different parts do, a look inside your brain, defining intelligence, measuring intelligence, the trouble with tests, nature vs. nurture, multiple intelligences, two brains are better than one, sex and the brain, what makes a person a genius, problem solving, thoughts about thinking, and memory and learning. The early topics were covered quite superficially, while beginning with the topic of intelligence, the topics were covered in more depth.

PSYCH 102

During the third trimester a 16-session course was taught to the two original Psych 101 classes. Topics covered were: knowledge vs. skills, inert knowledge, kinds of knowledge, interdependency of knowledge and thinking, problem solving, thinking, theories of how the mind works, strategies, studying vs. studying smart, learning, and remembering and forgetting.

SUMMARY

Psych 101 was a popular course with the middle-school students. It seemed to provide the rationale the students needed to take seriously the process lessons that were part of reading, writing, and the content subjects. In fact, it was not unusual for students to elaborate on a teacher's explanation of why a particular objective was being taught. Students appeared convinced of the value of understanding how the mind works. And this conviction seemed to have a positive impact on their motivation.

At the beginning of the school year eleven-year-old Mike was one of our most cynical students. However, by the end of the year he had become a good example of the difference the course could make. Though a third-year Benchmark student, Mike had not grown to accept attending a special school and continued to be convinced that we had nothing to offer him. He was passive and rigid, but claimed he could do well in school if he felt like it. In May 1989, when interviewed by one of the McDonnell researchers and asked what he had learned during the year that helped him be a better learner, thinker, and problem solver, Mike answered, "The thing I learned that was new for me was Psych 101 and that helped by showing me how my brain works. Psych 101 showed what works for most people. Maybe you are learning something, you think it is getting in, but if you think about how your head works, it really doesn't work too well. So Psych 101 helps you think of ways of remembering and learning. I learned about pegs and how to add things on. I learned categorizing. I learned a lot of things from different places. I take the idea a teacher says and I maybe think it doesn't work too well, but when I go into like reading group or social studies, I put it to use and I see that it is effective."

When Mike was asked what advice he would give a new student to Benchmark in order for him to be successful, Mike answered, "I would give him my '101' notes and tell him to study them. If he tries all those ideas, he'll be very successful."

CHAPTER 8

Strategy Teaching in the Lower School: Primary and Intermediate Grades

This chapter includes guidelines for, and samples of, strategy teaching drawn from the lower school of Benchmark School. As is true of most teaching, each lesson has its strengths and weaknesses. These lessons are not presented as ideal. Rather they are meant to represent typical lessons in which students were made aware of strategies for knowledge acquisition or production or were taught ways to be in control of task, person, strategy, or environmental variables.

What was striking to us as we read the transcripts was how quickly teachers turned over responsibility for providing the why, when, and how of the strategies to the students. This interactive procedure allowed teachers to discover gaps in students' understanding of the strategies, thus to know when it was necessary to elaborate or re-explain. The usual pattern of instruction was for teachers to give very explicit explanations on the first day a strategy was introduced; then, on the following days, to lead students in guided discussions and applications of the same strategy. One strategy tended to be the primary focus of instruction for three to six weeks.

IMPLEMENTING INSTRUCTION FOR BEGINNERS

As a prototype for a primary-level strategy lesson, Mrs. Moldofsky shared ideas for designing and teaching a lesson for the first objective we teach at Benchmark—stop and think about the sense of the story. The materials she used were written at the preprimer level.

Planning the Lesson

As a teacher reads the selection and plans, he or she thinks about questions and stopping places for applying the strategy, how to tie the story together, and how to have students reflect on the strategy. The teacher reads through the story and thinks about how much material the students should read before stopping to discuss what was read. This initially may be one page with beginners, but the amount should be extended to several pages at a time as students progress, and may be the entire selection when the students are ready. The teacher jots down questions that will encourage students to use the strategy being taught:

- Where did you stop to think as you read this?

- What things did you think about?

- How did this help you understand what Sandy was doing?

- How could you tell that Sandy was afraid of the bug? What words helped you figure this out?

- When I read that sentence, I thought it said: Sandy saw a dig bug. What should I have done?

Next the teacher thinks of a question or two that will help students pull the story together.

- What were you reading to find out? What did you find out?

- What was Sandy's problem in this story? How was it like Bing's problem in the last story? How does this story give you more ideas about how Sandy acts?

Students might be asked to reflect on the strategy by such questions as:

- How did you help yourself understand this story?

- Why did we talk about stopping to think during reading?

- Find a place where you stopped to think. Tell us how it helped you.

- Impatient people might think you should read very quickly and that that makes you a better reader. Can you tell them a better way to be a good reader?

Teaching the Lesson

There are six parts to Mrs. Moldofsky's beginning reading lesson: introducing the vocabulary; introducing the comprehension strategy; guiding students in surveying, activating background, and setting purposes; guiding silent reading; tying the lesson together; and reflecting on the strategy.

Introducing the vocabulary. Conduct a discussion of the strategies the students know for decoding words. At Benchmark these would be:

1. using context clues (thinking about what makes sense and using the words in the rest of the sentence and the initial consonant to decide what the new word could be and

2. using words they know to decode unknown words (e.g., using known words "cat" and "her" to decode unknown word "batter").

Hold up the first sentence strip. If the words are all new, read the sentence and say "blank" for the covered new word. If the words are not new, except for the covered word, tell students to read the sentence and think of what word would make sense in the blank. Have a student volunteer to read the sentence and say "blank" for the covered word. Have students offer possible words that make sense that fit in the blank. Print these words on the chalkboard and briefly discuss the relevance of each. Show the first letter(s). Have students decide if they want to "keep or change" their words. Keep or change is a concept that helps students be flexible. If you talk about "right" and "wrong," students are less likely to take chances.

Show the entire word. If a key word has been taught for the spelling pattern in the new word, ask the students if they know a key word with the same spelling pattern as they see in the new word. For example, if the new word is "met," you would print the key word "let" beneath it. Have students say, "If l-e-t is let, then m-e-t is met." The teacher explains, "This is using what you know to figure out what is new and unknown."

Have a student read the entire sentence with the new word. Ask whether or not the word makes sense. The same process is used for introducing approximately three to five words per lesson.

Introducing the comprehension strategy. Tell the students what the strategy is for the lesson, why good readers use it, when it can be used, and how it is used. *Model* the process. Use a previous story, if this is not the first story taught, for modeling the strategy.

The discussion might go something like this:

> Good readers want to understand what they read. Reading is more than just saying words. Someone wrote the story we are going to read. That author had ideas for us. One way we can help ourselves understand the ideas is by stopping and thinking as we read. For example, I read "The man was up."

(Think aloud: This could mean that the man was up in a tree or that he was awake or even up on a hill. I had better read to find out.) "The man met a bug." (The man would have to be awake to meet a bug. I don't think he was climbing a tree or on a hill because in the picture I see him in the grass.) "The dug ran away." (Wait a minute, that doesn't make sense. I never heard of a dug running away. I need to think about what I read in the sentence before this. "The man met a bug." It must be that the bug ran away. Maybe the bug was afraid of the man.) I could have zoomed through this story, but instead I stopped to think what it would mean. When something didn't make sense, I thought about how to fix it. This helped me understand what I was reading. This could help you to be a good reader, too.

Guiding students in surveying, activating background, and setting purposes. Ask the students to look at the pictures on the first pages of the selection. (In fiction it is often better not to have students look at the end pictures because those pictures often express so much of the text that students cannot have fun with predictions.) Have students read the title. Tell them that when they look at the pictures and title before they read, they are surveying. We survey to gather clues as to what the story will be about.

Have the students use the clues from surveying to think about what they know.

You said this story is called "The Big Bug" and that Sandy was in the picture. What do you know about Sandy and what he likes to do? What do you know about dogs and bugs? How could this help you when you read?

Have the students use these ideas to set purposes. Try to avoid details such as "What color is the cat?" and global questions such as "What will happen?" Write several of their purpose questions on the chalkboard or on paper for later reference.

It is important that the purpose questions are initiated by the students and not by the teacher. The teacher can model how he or she thought of a useful question, but always follow up modeling by asking students to think of their own purpose questions. You might encourage students to begin their purpose questions with "how" or "why." Be sure to discuss their purpose questions as soon as students complete reading the assigned section of the material.

Guiding the silent reading. Silent reading at this level is often noisy. Beginning readers often need to hear themselves as they read, thus they whisper-read. The point of this prereading is to allow students to use sense and clues to help themselves process what the author is saying. After students have preread for purposes (their purposes), then they are encouraged to use oral rereading to support their answers to discussion questions.

After students have read a section "silently," ask:

- What did you think you would find out?

- What clues helped you keep or change your ideas?

Using these questions repeatedly teaches students self-questioning techniques that can be used when the teacher-coach is not around.

Encourage use of the strategy by asking questions like:

- How did you make sense of what Sandy did on page 12? I thought the dog ran after the bug. Why should I change this idea? What did you read that helped you understand this?

- How did you use ideas from the last story to help you figure out what Sandy was going to do?

- Why do you think Sandy ran away? What clues helped you? What did you think Sandy would do? How did your ideas change when you read this page?

Avoid asking questions that can be answered with "yes" or "no." When asking students to express an idea, wait for several seconds after their initial response. You will find that, given think time, students learn to elaborate and other students will add on. If, on the other hand, you respond immediately to a student's answer, quickly give the answer for the question, or call on another child, students will learn to depend on others to get them off the hook. Ask a few meaningful questions rather than trying to cover every detail. Often, by focusing questions on characters, problems, and solutions in beginning level stories, you can build a pattern from story to story that aids understanding and self-monitoring.

If students give answers that fit their experience but do not fit the clues in the story, accept their ideas but ask them to find clues in the selection that led them to that conclusion. For example:

> Teacher: Why did Sandy run away?
> Student: I run away when I am mad at my brother.
>
> Teacher: Yes, that's a good idea from your head, but look in the book. There is a clue about the bug that can help you understand how Sandy was feeling.
>
> Student: The bug was big. Maybe he was afraid.

Tying the lesson together. After reading, students need to develop the habit of saying or doing something to connect the ideas of the story. This will lead to summarizing. Some suggestions for pulling the story together include: having students return to the purpose questions and discuss how they were answered; having students tell who the main characters were, where they were, how they acted, what they wanted, and how they got, or did not get, what they wanted. This is summarizing using the story elements of characters, setting, problem, and solution. Mrs. Moldofsky uses a chart to cue students. It includes:

> Who was it about? Where and when was it?
> > What did _____ want?
> > How did _____ get it?
> > Why didn't _____ get it?

Another way to tie a story together is by comparing what happened in one story with the events in a previous story.

Reflecting on the lesson strategy. While students are reading stories about childhood experiences and tales of make believe, they are mainly learning about ways to process information. By beginning and ending a lesson with reflections on strategies, students become more aware of the task, person, environmental, and strategy variables that affect success in processing information. To initiate this time of reflection a teacher might ask:

- What strategy were we using to help us understand this story?

- How did you stop and think and make sense?

- Give an example so we can see how you did it.

- Why should readers do this?

- Be the teacher. Pretend we are about to begin tomorrow's story. Tell us how we can help ourselves be better readers.

Reviewing Beginning Reader Strategies

Usually at this level, the strategy is explicitly taught by the teacher on several occasions before the daily review of the strategy becomes an interactive process led by such questions as:

- What strategy have we been using to help us understand what we read?

- Why do good readers use this strategy?

- Open your books to the last story we read. How did you stop to think and make sense? Give an example.

- How can we use this strategy today?

At Benchmark we do not dilute our discussions with students about strategies by substituting simple words for concepts such as "strategy," "make sense," and "predict." Our experience suggests that students very quickly adopt and understand this "grown-up" vocabulary and actually enjoy using the terms. Being consistent across the school in the use of these terms seems to make it easier for students to respond to the numerous teachers they encounter for various subjects and to move to new teachers each year.

Learning About Control: Mrs. Audley's Class

During the first week of school Mrs. Audley placed a huge banner across the back of her classroom. It read: INTELLIGENCE = KNOWL-EDGE + CONTROL + MOTIVATION. She told her students that this was a formula the middle-school students were learning. That formula became the springboard for many discussions during the year with her third graders who were reading on first and second reader levels. Originally the concepts on the banner were discussed as stand-alone lessons and throughout the day transferred to the teaching of reading, writing, social studies, and science. Soon, however, the students were comfortable with a basic meaning for each concept — a comfort derived from presentations and experiences that made students aware of factors affecting the processing of information and how to take control and maintain motivation. These control strategies were integrated into regular lessons.

Taking Control. "Take Control" became a phrase the students heard often throughout the year. These students needed to become independent workers. Providing them ways to take control enabled them to gain confidence and independence as learners. On September 26, for example, Mrs. Audley gave directions for students to work with partners to complete a science assignment. She concluded her directions with, "Who's in control of the intelligent worker?" "How will you show me that you are in control?" "Why is it important to be in control?"

On October 10 the students were given a science homework assignment as a follow-up to material they had been reading. The topic was atoms. Mrs. Audley reminded the students that the assignment was due in two days. The assignment called for children to summarize in their own words what they had learned about atoms:

> T: If you're not sure you understand the information well enough to summarize it, you can find the page number on the assignment sheet where you could reread. Put the ideas in your own words, that is the important step. What should you do if you can't put the information in your own words? That means you don't understand it, so what do you need to do?
>
> S: You could ask your mother to help.
>
> S: I would read in the book again and try to figure out maybe if I didn't get all the words.
>
> T: Those are good ideas. Yes, Jim, you could ask a parent to help you. Maybe you could read the article to your mother or father. I like Mary's idea, too. Rereading is a good fix-up strategy when you don't understand. I can tell you guys are

good readers! What could you do if you know your parents are going to be away this weekend and you think you might not understand? Can you think of any steps you could take ahead of time to avoid that problem?

S: Well, like, maybe you could do it tonight and ask the teacher tomorrow if you didn't get it. The teacher could help you.

Mrs. Audley's students were taking control. It is quite apparent they have learned strategies for ensuring that they will be able to get a difficult assignment done.

Predicting and Using Background About Genre: Mrs. Downer's Class

Mrs. Downer's class, composed of eight- and nine-year-old third graders, began the year reading on first grade level. In fact, several of her students were virtually nonreaders. What follows are excerpts from two reading lessons which both took place in January.

Making predictions.

T: Today we're going to continue to practice predicting. That's going to be a review objective, because we've been making predictions to help us get involved in our stories all year. We're going to read a story about Penelope. That's kind of an old fashioned name. A lot of people say Penny for short. "Penelope Gets Wheels." Now in your head when you hear that title, it could mean what?

S: It could mean like he got roller skates.

T: Penelope is a she.

S: She got a bike. Or, maybe something like maybe a new, something with wheels.

T: Okay. It probably is something new with wheels or she wants something with wheels on it. Today we also are going to work on accessing background knowledge. That means we are going to use something we already know to help us understand something new. We've also worked on this objective before. Why is background knowledge important in reading?

The students could not explain clearly why background knowledge was important. Finally, one student gave an example the teacher had used previously. Mrs. Downer was not convinced the example was meaningful for the student, thus she made the example personal.

T: Until you rode on an airplane, you would not have understood a story about riding on an airplane as well as you would now. Your background knowledge and experience are very important in determining how well you understand.

Four new words for the story were introduced. Based on those words and the title of the story, the students made predictions using their background knowledge, then read to see if their predictions were correct.

Using genre to understand the story. On another day Mrs. Downer had the children use genre, another kind of background knowledge, to help them make predictions and understand the story. This, too, was a review objective for her students.

T: What I want you to know today is more about the fantasy genre and how it helps you understand the story. Today's story is a fantasy, and we're going to talk just for a couple of minutes about what we mean by the fantasy genre. Then we are going to discuss why and when we use this knowledge and how to use this knowledge to understand what we read. Who would like to start and give me one characteristic of the fantasy genre?

S: Animals talk.

T: Yes, Sue, animals often talk and take on human characteristics.

S: Sometimes they're magic?

T: Sometimes there's a little bit of magic.

S: Sometimes there's a universal lesson.

T: And what do you mean by the universal lesson?

S: What the author is telling you.

T: And often something important for life. Universal lessons tend to be things that are always true, like if you're kind to people, they'll be kind to you. If you work hard, you'll be more successful than if you don't work hard. If you lie sometimes, after a while people may not believe you even when you are telling the truth. That thing that's kind of generally true is usually universal. Anything else about the fantasy genre?

S: Good vocabulary.

T: Very good vocabulary, which is kind of neat because it

helps you in your writing. Reading and writing are very closely connected. Fantasy reminds us to use better words to make our writing more interesting. And often the setting is elaborate. What is the setting?

S: The setting is like where it takes place.

T: Good. Some other characteristics are they usually have a happy ending and they're really written to entertain. They're written to be funny and enjoyable stories. How can we use knowledge of story genre to help us when we are reading?

S: So you can maybe tell what's going to happen.

T: So what we're going to do today as we read this story is think about which of these characteristics that we just discussed are present in the story and how knowledge of them helped you understand the story. When you're finished reading, I would like you to make a note on a piece of paper that will help you remember what the universal lesson is.

Books were passed out and the story was read and discussed.

IMPLEMENTING INSTRUCTION AT THE INTERMEDIATE LEVEL

Strategy Teaching during the First Month of School: Miss Robinowitz's Class

Miss Robinowitz taught nine- and ten-year-olds, most of whom began the year reading on second grade level. She was the students' teacher for language arts and reading, and social studies. As is the most common pattern in the lower school, science, math, art, gym, and music were taught by other teachers.

Typical of most of the Benchmark classes, learning strategies for awareness and control of information processing was a priority in this class. Concepts the middle-school students learned in Psych 101 were integrated into Miss Robinowitz's teaching across-the-curriculum, as well as occasionally taught in separate mini-lessons.

Learning about active involvement: Knowing when you do not understand. At the beginning of social studies class on September 14, the first full day of school, Miss Robinowitz told her students that her objective was for them to be actively involved in learning. One way to do this was to recognize when you understand and when you do not understand something and to seek clarification.

T: What can you do when you do not understand something?

S: Ask questions.

S: Look it up in another book.

T: Why is it important to stop and do something about it if you don't understand? Why is asking for clarification an important strategy?

S: So you can understand—if you don't know what a word means, you might get the whole question completely wrong.

Next, this teacher led a discussion of *why* this objective was important and *how* and *when* they would apply it.

The students were studying geography when they were introduced to the objective of knowing when you do and when you do not understand. They were using a packet of material the teacher had assembled. After surveying the material with the students, the teacher asked them what they wanted to learn in this unit that they did not already know. Suggestions were given and listed on the chalkboard. The teacher walked the students through the first section of the material, encouraging them to ask for clarification when they were unclear about any of the information.

The objective remained the same in social studies for some time. Every day the students would talk about what it meant to be actively involved and what specifically they should do when they did not understand something. On October 5 in social studies, Miss Robinowitz asked the students what the objective was that they had been working on for three weeks and why it was important.

S: To be actively involved so you can become a better student.

S: You know when to ask questions.

S: It will be more clear and it will be easier to learn.

S: You will notice your way of learning.

T: Okay, Joe, that is a good point. It might help you figure out how you best learn because maybe you need to ask lots of questions to learn.

Learning about active involvement: Using background knowledge to make predictions. "Today we are going to talk about another way to be actively involved in learning. We are going to think about what we know about a topic — that is our background knowledge. This background knowledge, and the predictions we can make because of background knowledge, will help us stay actively involved in what we are studying. You're going to think about what you already know about the topic. It's a broad topic today, United States geography. And based on what you know about the topic and what you learn from surveying the material, you can make some predictions about what to expect when you read this material. This will keep you actively involved.

"If you know something about a topic, it also can help you learn something new. You can attach new information to the old information. So calling up, or activating, your background knowledge can help you in two ways: it can help you make predictions as to what will be in the text and it can give you something to attach new information to." At this point Miss Robinowitz thought she had concluded her initial explanation of the process objective; however, she was in mid-sentence, in introducing the content objective, when she realized that something was amiss.

T: I'm not sure you all understand what I am saying about background knowledge and why it's important. You have used background knowledge in your reading groups. How have you used background knowledge to help you when you are reading?

S: Well, if you, like, know something about what's in the story it can help you understand better.

S: You make predictions?

S: It helps you get actively involved. Like I got lost once and I could feel how that girl in the story the other day felt when she got lost.

T: Yes. You've used background knowledge, or what you know about a topic, to make predictions and to help you understand what you're reading. You attach what you're reading to things you already know. The other day, when we were in language with Mrs. Silio, she said something like, "This is a fanciful tale. How do you think it will end?" And one of you said, "Well, I expect it's going to have a happy ending. I know in my background that fanciful stories always have happy endings." And so you used your background knowledge to make a good prediction about a story. Can you tell me how we have used background knowledge in our word identification lessons?

S: You mean like if we know key words?

T: Good! Can you tell me how we use key words?

S: Well, like, uh, if you know "made" then you can say "grade."

T: That's right. We use our background knowledge, our key words, to figure out new words that have the same spelling pattern. We are using something we know to figure out something new. Do I see those blank stares going away?

Maybe if we try putting this strategy to work for us now, it will become even clearer. I'm going to put six words on the board and we're going to share some of our background knowledge about these words.

Miss Robinowitz put a number of words related to the geography unit on the chalkboard, "desert," "river," etc., and the group talked about how the meanings of the words were alike and different and then they classified the words. Miss Robinowitz pointed out to the students that they used their background knowledge to classify the words.

On October 19, Miss Robinowitz once again told the students in social studies class that the objective was to be actively involved in learning. Students were asked to suggest how they could do this. One student readily suggested using background knowledge about the topic and this was followed by a discussion of why this strategy was important. The students then surveyed the material about explorers that they would be studying during the next week or two and quickly concluded that they did not have much background knowledge about the early explorers. She suggested that to keep themselves actively involved they might think of questions for which they wanted to find answers as they read. Questions were listed on the chalkboard.

On the same day in reading group, Miss Robinowitz asked the students before they began reading to tell her some of the things good readers do while they are reading.

S: Stop and ask themselves if they understand.

T: Why? What do good readers know in their heads about stories?

S: That stories have to make sense.

The strategy set as the objective for that reading lesson was to make predictions and change them if you find evidence that you are wrong. Miss Robinowitz then modeled her thinking as she surveyed the story, made a prediction, read a bit of the story and found her prediction was wrong, and changed her prediction based on the new evidence.

Selecting Strategies: Miss Wile's Class

Miss Wile taught a class of ten- and eleven-year-olds, most of whom were reading on a third grade level at the beginning of the school year. On October 12 Miss Wile conducted a reading lesson that integrated several strategies that students had learned previously, as well as made students aware of how to make decisions about strategy selection and why flexibility is important.

Preparation for reading. "The content objective we want to keep in mind as we read today's story is to discover what causes weather. What process objective have we been learning in social studies to help us organize and recall the information we read?" A student answered, "Outlining." Preparation for reading continued with questions such as "Why is outlining important?" "When can you use it?" "How do you do it?"

Miss Wile next introduced the process objective: "Our process objective today is two objectives combined into one. One part is to take charge of a personal characteristic called **flexibility**. We will have to be flexible because our objective is to select strategies to organize and remember information that fit the ways the author has organized the information. Today's author was not as considerate in the way he organized the selection as our social studies author was. What does it mean to be flexible?" A discussion of flexibility followed, with the teacher eliciting examples from students.

"The reason it is important to be flexible about the strategies you use is that certain strategies are more helpful than others, depending on how the material is written and your purpose for reading. The purpose of using strategies is to improve your chances of understanding and remembering information. If the strategy you use isn't the most powerful strategy for the way the selection is written, your purpose, and the way you learn, then you are not getting the best payoff for your effort. It would be just like using the wrong tool for a project, such as using a spoon to dig a ditch when using a shovel would be more efficient.

"Let's see if we can decide which strategies fit the way the author has organized the information we are going to read today. First, we will have to think of the strategies we know for organizing information. Can you tell me what some of these might be?"

S: Use background knowledge.

T: Activating background knowledge. Yes, we use what we know about a topic to help organize the new information we are reading. What do you know about weather that might help you understand this selection?

A number of students supplied information they had learned in science class about moisture, humidity, temperature, and the shape of clouds. A discussion followed about how these facts might help students organize the information in the material they would be reading.

T: When might accessing background not be useful?

S: If you don't know very much or if your knowledge is messed up.

T: Yes, when you don't have much background information about a subject or your information is incorrect. What other strategies can we use for organizing information?

S: Survey the story.

T: Why do we survey. How does that help you?

S: To find out what the story will be about and to think of what we know about it.

S: To look at the headings and turn the headings into questions.

Miss Wile asked a student to demonstrate surveying the selection by talking out loud to share his thinking as he surveyed the selection on weather. Other students volunteered their suggestions, too. Although surveying had been previously taught and used in this class, Miss Wile noticed that some of the students did not seem to know what to do. She asked different members of the group to share what they do when they survey a selection and she elaborated on each of their contributions.

T: Surveying gives us an overview of the author's organization. An overview can help you decide which strategy might be the most helpful for organizing and remembering the information in a selection. Can you think of any other strategies you have used for organizing information?

S: You could look for the main ideas.

S: Summarizing, like when you put it in your own words.

S: Make a picture—I mean chart?

Miss Wile modeled the thoughts she had had as she read the selection the previous evening. "I looked at this selection on weather and thought, 'Hmm. It's nonfiction, so I guess I should outline it since that's what we are learning to do in social studies. I'll use outlining to organize the major ideas.' I'm afraid I wasn't being very flexible. I kept trying to outline it because that was the strategy I had been practicing recently. I was trying to make an outline like we did yesterday in social studies, but that didn't work very well because the text has so much information and it isn't very well organized.

"I knew I was going to need some kind of strategy to help me keep track of the information, but this selection seemed to have too many important facts and no details. I tried setting purposes based on the heading, but that didn't always work either. This selection answered so many questions that one purpose-setting question caused me to ignore a lot of important information that didn't answer my question. There were sections where I felt the whole paragraph was the main idea, so I couldn't do a main idea and detail outline. What I finally concluded was that when I'm reading something hard which has a lot of information which I may have a difficult time understanding and remembering, I might have to be flexible and use a number of different strategies.

Using strategies to process information. "What we are going to do is read this story about weather, section by section. As we do so, we will try to figure out what strategy that we have already learned will help us understand each section." Miss Wile asked what speed they should use in reading this piece of nonfiction. One of the students answered that they needed to read it more slowly than when reading fiction, because nonfiction usually contains more information. Students then decided to read the first section to answer the question posed in the section heading, "Where Weather Comes From."

After silent reading, Miss Wile asked, "Where does weather come from?" The answers were isolated bits and pieces of information. It appeared that students were using their background information to try to answer the question, rather than information in the text. Miss Wile pointed out to them that using their background knowledge to answer a text-based question would not prove a fruitful strategy if they did not have sufficient background information.

Miss Wile then led the students through the section, analyzing it with them, paragraph by paragraph. Finally, she asked them again to state in their own words the answer to the question posed by the section heading, which also happened to be the main idea of the section. The students concluded that the best way to organize the information in this section would be to make a summary statement.

The second section was read silently. The students realized it contained a list of four things scientists have to know about weather. They concluded that an outline would work well for this section, and they had no difficulty selecting the four main points and supporting details.

The section titled, "What is Water in Air?" followed. When students finished reading, they again began offering isolated details. Miss Wile reminded them that they needed to relate what they were saying to the question posed in the heading. Separating important from unimportant details, as related to one's purpose, seemed difficult for these students. Miss Wile decided that her students would benefit from some more instruction in main idea/details before they worked on outlining again.

Miss Wile used mental modeling to illustrate one way of reasoning about the next section. "I'm thinking about the first paragraph and trying to figure out the main idea. It doesn't seem to have one main idea, it has lots of ideas. I need all those ideas to be able to get the right picture in my head. I think the best way to learn the information in this section would be to draw a picture. Stating a main idea might leave out a lot I need to know."

After reading the last section of the article on weather, the students concluded that the section did not lend itself to outlining or to drawing a picture, but it did clearly have one main idea. They agreed with Miss Wile that, when they could finally explain or summarize the section in their own words, they also understood it. Miss Wile summarized, "Thus, explaining information in your own words is an excellent way of testing your understanding."

At the conclusion of the lesson, Miss Wile asked the students why it was important to be flexible when choosing strategies. The students decided that it is important to be flexible when choosing strategies because many texts do not lend themselves to all strategies and finding a good match between text and strategy is necessary for efficient organization of information.

A Reading/Writing Lesson: Miss Ostertag's Class

Joyce Ostertag taught nine- and ten-year-olds who at the time of this lesson in January were reading on third reader level. In reading group she had been teaching them strategies for identifying and summarizing important points of a story. One strategy for summarizing stories the group had already learned was to identify the central story problem and tell how it was resolved. Her students were now using this strategy for sharing reviews of the books they read independently.

In this lesson students were practicing a second strategy for writing summaries of stories. This new strategy was to identify one or two key words per page, jot them down as they read, then expand them into a written summary. Because identifying key words was a complex strategy for the students to master, the teacher spent much time sharing and elaborating her thinking processes, encouraging the students to do the same.

Preparation for reading/writing. The teacher began by asking, "What is the strategy we have been learning?" "Yes, we are learning to summarize stories." She continued, asking, "Why is this an important strategy?" "When would you use it?" Then she asked, "How do you do it?"

> S: Sometimes we use the central story problem and how the problem is solved. Now we're learning a new way by finding key words.

S: You taught us three ways to find key words.

T: Can anyone tell me one of these ways?

S: When you look in the paragraph it's usually talking about something special.

T: Okay, so when you start reading the page you find something unique or different that sets it apart from the other pages.

S: Words are repeated.

T: Good. Words that are repeated in a paragraph are usually important as long as they're not "a" or "the." What's the last one? Sometimes a word isn't repeated very often, but what about it?

S: They're like explained.

T: Yes. For example, do you remember the story about Christina? (Takes from shelf and opens book.) Now what's the key word in this paragraph? I think it is castle. Castle is only mentioned once in this paragraph, but it connects all the other words together because all the other words describe the conditions of the castle. So a word that connects a lot of ideas together is a key word.

The students were asked to open their books to page 83, to read the title, and to make predictions about the story.

Using strategies to process information. They were then asked to read the first page and jot down any key words that seemed to sum up ideas on the page. The teacher also read and jotted down words. Students in the group shared the words or phrases they had chosen and why they had chosen them. Miss Ostertag wrote students' contributions on the chalkboard, then summed up the discussion.

T: I have to tell you I have what Kristy had. I have Mom. What makes Mom probably a better choice than the other two? You can leave these other two because they might trigger something you want to write when you are summarizing, but what makes Mom a better choice?

S: Because it's mainly about Mom.

T: Okay. The author's organization seems to be Mom as the main topic and under that we could put Mom's work and Mom's building. So those are really smaller ideas about Mom just like you can say apples and pears are both examples of fruit. Work and building both tie in with Mom, so I would push them all together under Mom. Work and building would be legitimate key words if we found out that the whole story was about Mom. Then we would want to say specific things about Mom. So you may want to revise your notes a little bit as we go along.

Students read the next two pages and compared notes. Again, there was a variety of ideas. The conclusion was that the first of the two pages was about Dad.

"Okay, that's about Dad's work. It's not repeated a lot, but each paragraph is about Dad just like on the previous page each paragraph is about Mom. Then, for the next page everyone wrote either Fanny or babysitter, which is the same thing. Kristy, Brian and I also wrote mushy eggs. We picked up on the idea that there's probably going to be more about Fanny, so what's unique about this page is they're talking about mushy eggs, whereas on other pages you're going to find out about other special things that Fanny does. I'm predicting right now. So, on this page I might want to remember that she's talking about mushy eggs."

The students continued reading pages of text and discussing the words or phrases they had selected to aid them in summarizing the story. Miss Ostertag accepted what each said, had them evaluate each other's contributions, then summed up the discussion before moving on. Another example of her summarizing follows.

"I think you could almost use one key word that will trigger what happened on both of those pages because leaving and going are really kind of the same thing, so on one page you find out that she's leaving and on the other page she's actually leaving. If you use just the one key word, leaving, it will work, which teaches us a valuable lesson about writing key words down. You can be a little flexible about that. So in this case we can just say leaving."

At a later point in the lesson she reminded the students of the criteria they were using. "Remember we said there are three things that make up a key word. One is that it's repeated a lot. A second is that it connects a lot of things together on a page or, what's the last one?"

S: It's special.

T: Right, it's special about the page. So in this case when they mention the new babysitter a little bit at the end, it is special for this page and so I think all of us had the sense, "Yes, we should probably put this down" because it's important to the end of the story. You did a good job of picking out key words. Let's put these together in summaries.

Miss Ostertag asked the class to "take five" and write a summary pulling together their key words. Students shared their summaries, and Miss Ostertag gave feedback. For example:

"You might want to say that. You're repeating a lot of 'ands'. It's good to use other words like 'at the end' or 'so' or 'also' to show connections."

At the end of the lesson, the teacher reviewed the objectives, emphasizing what they discovered about using the strategy during the day's lesson.

Using Background Information and Imaging: Miss Soja's Class

Miss Soja and Miss Robinowitz often worked together planning lessons, thus sharing the same lesson plans, materials, worksheets, etc. It is interesting to note that the same plans do not have to be delivered in the same way to be effective. For example, using the lesson plans that she and Miss Robinowitz had written together, Miss Soja taught this lesson on using background information.

Using background information. On October 5 Miss Soja said to her class of below-level readers, ages 9 to 11, "Let me tell you a little bit about what we're going to do next in social studies. It is something that some of you are learning about in reading group. We'll continue to say it is important to be actively involved and to recognize in your head when you understand and when you don't understand and to take some kind of action when you don't understand something. That will be important all year long and whenever you are learning, no matter what the subject is."

> T: The next thing I want to teach you is to be actively involved in learning by calling to mind relevant background knowledge. The first think you might say is, "What do you mean by background knowledge?" Did you ever hear about background knowledge? Those of you in Mrs. Sheridan's reading group have been talking about it for a couple of days. Christian, would you like to share what you have learned?
> S: It's what comes from the back of your head that you know about the story.
> T: Okay. It's knowledge that's in your head. Your background is what you already know about something. So the knowledge you bring to whatever you learn is called background knowledge. It's really important whenever you try to learn something new to think about what you already know about it.
>   People who study learning and memory say it's a good idea to think of something you already know about a subject and then you can attach the new information to what you know. That's why background knowledge is so important— it's why, when you are in reading group, Mrs. Sheridan will

say, "What do you already know in your head that will help you understand this story?"

It is the same thing in social studies, the same thing in science. When you're learning something in science, you can think, "What do I already know about it?" It will help you learn the new information. So, when I ask you for homework to find out what states you have already been to, there are two reasons for that. One, is for you to start to locate states you have visited. You can label them on a map and start to learn some new states. The other thing you will be able to learn, if you know what it's like in those states you have visited, is what the geographic features may be for the states around the ones you already know.

Activating your background knowledge or calling to mind what you already know helps you to get ready to read or to gain new information.

Tomorrow when we continue talking about this, we will see what you already know about these geography concepts. You will find that you have heard and learned a lot of information about the geography of the fifty states and by calling to mind what you already know, it will be easier to learn the new information. We will be continuing to study the United States and the fifty states, something most of you began studying last year.

Imaging. On October 21 Miss Soja was teaching a reading group.

T: We've been talking in reading group about creating images or making pictures in our head as we read. Does anybody remember why that's an important thing to do when you read? Carly?

S: Because sometimes the pictures that are in the book don't help you and you try to look at them and they don't give you the right idea or when you have a book and they don't have any pictures.

S: It would be like if you were reading a book with no pictures, you could get it from your head mostly.

T: I was thinking that sometimes picturing helps you to understand, which is what Carly and Jim and all of you are talking about. It could also help you remember. Maybe you don't have to remember something from reading group, because you are reading just for fun, but in another subject you may have to remember. So picturing helps you understand, it helps you remember, and third, it may help you enjoy a book more, especially when you're reading something like a chapter book. You'll also discover that picturing alerts you to when you don't understand. Is there another subject, besides reading group, in which you could use picturing? Jim?

S: I use it in science when I do a test. There was this question where he asked us if it was like a physical change. It was a question like if you chopped down the tree, is there a physical change or a chemical change? I said there was a physical change?

T: And how did picturing help you do that?

S: I pictured somebody cutting something down and thought it must be a physical change if I couldn't see that the parts of the tree looked any different after it was cut. It was just the same tree in two pieces.

S: Does anybody remember this morning when somebody asked you to picture something.

S: Like a "t" in handwriting.

T: Yes. Sometimes when you are writing you have to stop and picture a cursive letter you want to write. Yesterday in social studies we talked about picturing the Indians, picturing where some of them lived, and that picturing could help you figure out how they lived. Today I want to read you a story about a mouse called Pippa Mouse and then you're going to read a story about her. But first I want to see what pictures you can get in your head from what you hear, then use those pictures to help you when you're reading.

The teacher read the story to the children, stopping periodically to have the children explain the pictures they had in their heads. When she concluded the story Miss Soja modeled what she was picturing:

"I picture Pippa as a little mouse in a little blue dress, living with Mom in a mousehole house, that sometimes isn't very clean. The information in the story that I used to make those pictures was .... I know that the pictures I make up must be based on the facts in the story and when the story doesn't give me all the details for a picture, I fill in the picture from my background information, like when I said..., I was using... from the story and ... from my head."

"The story that we're going to read today is about Pippa Mouse in the wintertime. What pictures can you make about what Pippa Mouse might do in the winter?"

New words for the story were introduced and the students made predictions about the story. The students began reading to check their predictions and to make pictures in their heads. Miss Soja stopped them periodically to discuss what each student was picturing.

Miss Soja summarized the objective at the conclusion of the discussion by saying, "If you're really making pictures in your head as you're reading, when you get to something that's confusing, you won't be able to make a picture because you won't know what it means. That will give you a clue that you should stop and do something about it. Maybe ask a question or read ahead a little or reread. Making pictures in your head is a way to check your understanding. So, if you weren't making pictures as you went along, at least you should stop and try to picture the story before you try to talk about it. Picture when they're finished sledding, what made them go home? What about those tracks? Some of you weren't really understanding whose track they were, you couldn't picture the big tracks, so you didn't know they were fox tracks. When something doesn't make sense, you need to do something about it.

"If you're reading a story that does have pictures and you're trying in your head to check the pictures that you're getting, your picture is going to give you a clue as to whether you understand.

"It's really important because the main goal, whenever you read, is that reading has got to make sense. You have to be doing some things in your head to make sure that what you are reading makes sense. Making pictures in your head is one way of checking to see that reading makes sense."

Taking Time to Think and Explain to Yourself: Mrs. Poosti, Mathematics Teacher

Ferdows Poosti teaches four classes of math during each school day. The lesson below was presented to a class of ten- and eleven-year-olds.

Analyzing the task. On December 8 Mrs. Poosti was teaching a class how to analyze a story problem. The strategy required reflection. The students in this class had a habit of rushing through story problems, only half reading them; searching for numbers to pull from the text; and scribbling the figures on paper.

Students were supplied with a workpaper and were to answer the word problem by following the steps listed on the workpaper, also using it as scratch paper to complete the problem. Mrs. Poosti reviewed the procedure with the students, then said, "We read and think. The first step in thinking is explain to yourself. Can anybody explain the problem to me?" A student attempted to tell the answer he had written on his paper. Mrs. Poosti continued, "Explain the problem in your own language."

Mrs. Poosti modeled her thinking, "I'm going to tell myself,

'There's a girl who's trying to sew some skirts.' That's the way I explain it to myself. 'She has 38 yards of material. She wants to make some skirts.'"

T: Who will continue explaining it?

S: Um, well, how much material do you have left over?

T: You are stating the question. Your explaining is not finished yet. A girl wants to sew some skirts. She has 38 yards of material and for each skirt she's going to use how much material?

S: Four yards, so I...

T: Stop a minute, four yards. The next step, which you find by explaining to yourself, is "Find the question." Can anybody tell me what the question is?

S: How many are left over?

T: No, wait, it's asking two questions. How many skirts can she make? How much material will be left over?

Mrs. Poosti continued that she was aware that the students have no difficulty with the calculations involved in the word problem, but their errors are usually the result of not taking time to think and not using a step-by-step process as outlined on their workpapers. She continued to model, "Now we have found the questions. Now I'm going to dig into my head to see how we're going to answer these questions. Sometimes I make pictures or I draw graphs. Let's see what I can do on this problem."

She involved the students in helping her set up a picture on the chalkboard, then continued. Referring to the picture on the chalkboard, she said, "Actually, what I'm doing, I'm trying to take a group of four out of 38 for one skirt and another group of 4 out of 38 for another skirt. So what I am doing is dividing 38 yards into four parts. See how many fours you can find in 38." Mrs. Poosti continued to work through the problem with the students, concluding, "When you have a word problem, tell yourself, 'First I read, then I think.' When you're thinking, explain the problem to yourself in your own language and weed out the question. Then get back into your head and see how you can figure out the answer to the question."

SUMMARY

Excerpts from lessons taught by Benchmark teachers suggest that these teachers are aware of the need to **explicitly explain** to students how to employ strategies that will help them process information to achieve meaning and to remember. Teachers state a process objective for each lesson. They discuss with the students how to implement the process and explain why it is important and when it can be used. In addition, they (or a student) usually model their reasoning as they apply the process, then teachers guide the students through the process of applying the process, giving them feedback, and elaborating on how to do the process as needed. As students become more proficient, teachers turn over more and more of the responsibility to the students for taking control of both discussing and using the process. Once a process is taught, teachers expect students to use it across the curriculum as appropriate. When this is not done, teachers cue the students to use a specific process.

CHAPTER 9

A Team Approach to Awareness and Control: The Middle School

The forty-eight students in the Perot Middle School of Benchmark School could not have escaped instruction about awareness and control during the school year 1988-89. It was infused into every aspect of the curriculum. If these eleven- to thirteen-year-olds had not at least picked up a new vocabulary from their teachers, they would have been sure to do so from listening to the other students.

In reviewing the transcripts for the year, we realized what great strides most of our middle-school students made. What we had to overlook, though, was the slow start we got off to in implementing the new curriculum of strategy instruction about which we were so excited when school opened. Time and again, the awareness and control objectives we had planned to teach had to take a backseat to meeting the students where they were, as you will see. For most of the teachers, it was four to six weeks after the start of school before strategy instruction could be given its fair share of daily instruction time.

ORGANIZING NOTEBOOKS AND OTHER ASPECTS OF SCHOOL LIFE

At the opening-day inservice, when teachers received a list of powerful strategies which they had generated the previous year, we never dreamed that one of the most powerful strategies was not even on the list, *organization*. Our students seemed to need explicit instruction regarding all aspects of **being organized.** For example, they needed to be taught what section of the notebook to open when they entered a class, as well as to put sheets of notebook paper in each section, so they could take notes in the section of the notebook that corresponded to the class they were in. They also had to be patiently taught how to organize notes and handouts in a particular section of their notebooks. On several occasions early in the school year, entire class periods were devoted to talking students through the rationale for organizing the random accumulations of papers that were stuffed in their notebooks.

In mid-October one class needed a refresher course. The teacher had noticed that their notebooks were again in disarray.

"Our objective today is to have organized notebooks. Why is organization important? Let me give you my reasoning. Did you know that an organized person can accomplish two or three times as much in a day as a person who is disorganized?"

The teacher then told a personal story about the cost in time of being disorganized. The teacher continued, "Our goal is for you to think through being organized so that your life will be more efficient.

"They say that an organized person has an organized brain. Now if we looked at your notebooks today, we might discover some very disorganized brains. But if you keep the papers in your notebooks organized, you'll also keep things organized in your head. What is well organized, will also be more useful to you. So you're going to be more efficient.

"When do you work on organization? Well, you organize as you go along. I'm going to model for you what you have to do." The teacher showed the students her notebook and how it was organized by date, teacher, and subject. She related how her notebook was organized to show how the students should organize theirs.

Next, the teacher explained,

"You should have a place for everything and always put things in the place reserved for that subject. In other words, there should be a social studies section in your notebook. People who are efficient and organized would have the first day's notes and papers first in the notebook, followed by the next day's, and so on. Keep your papers in order so that when you're studying, everything will be in sequential order. Does that make sense?

"You should use your dividers to separate notes for each class. I watch some of you when you leave social studies. You jam everything in your notebook in any old place and run when the bell rings. You have all discovered that it takes only 15 to 30 seconds to make it to the next class, and some of you take science right in this room. There's no need to rush. Therefore, taking a few seconds to get everything in the right place and in order is much more efficient than losing or misplacing papers in a race to get out into the hall."

Students were given further suggestions.

"If your notebook is too full, take out some of the old papers and put them in a two-pocket folder and label the folder telling what is in it. Don't rip paper out of your notebook. If you do, you can't put the paper back and expect it to stay put. Use reinforcements where the holes are torn on your papers."

Students were told to use the next 15 minutes to organize their notebooks and teachers were available to coach and assist them.

Not only did students have to be taught to organize notebooks, but they were also taught how to keep track of assignments using an assignment book, how to organize their lockers, how to make sure the right materials went into their bookbags to take home, and how to organize themselves at home to get back to school with completed homework and books.

ESTABLISHING BEHAVIORAL EXPECTATIONS

In the early weeks behavior was also an issue. Social needs were definitely top priority for these middle-school students, and it was never more obvious than during the first four to six weeks of school. Any strategy instruction that students heard was perceived through an affective-social filter. While teaching was going on, it appeared that at least some of the students were thinking things like: "Is it cool to put up my hand to answer a question?" "Will they think I'm a goody-goody if I stay after class and ask the teacher what she meant?" "I wonder if Jeff is joining the newspaper club; I'm not joining if he doesn't." And, of course, there were those who did not keep those thoughts to themselves.

Students seemed happiest in classrooms where teachers had iron-clad, but reasonable, rules which they had had a part in making and which were consistently enforced by the teacher. Social issues did not take an obvious paramount position when students could blame the "strict" or "mean" teacher for their staying on task and not socializing. The students clearly did not like to be isolated from the class, so that one warning for a behavioral infraction, then dismissal from the class, seemed sufficient to keep most students looking on task most of the time. Student contentment also seemed associated with teachers reinforcing their efforts to apply strategies and teachers guiding them through activities, by asking questions that students could learn to ask themselves, when they experienced difficulties.

We were reminded again, as we are at the start of each new year, that until the behavioral expectations for the class are in place and teachers are very consistent about enforcing them, teachers will not have the opportunity to teach the lessons they have worked so hard to prepare.

CATEGORIZING

While dealing with the organization and behavioral issues during the first weeks of school, there was some teaching of process objectives. The students needed explicit instruction regarding how to think about information they discussed in class, read each evening for homework, and studied for tests. Nothing could be assumed regarding their understanding of what should be done, why or when it was beneficial, or how to do it.

In social studies, for example, students seemed to feel safer attempting to memorize dates and names rather than thinking about what they were reading and categorizing the information into some logical framework. As a result, lessons were devoted to **categorizing** — teaching students to put the details they were studying into categories. The rationale given for this strategy of grouping ideas was the by-now-familiar seven slots, plus or minus two, that the brain has for storing information. If they wanted to store all the information gleaned from class and homework in such a way that it could later be accessed or recalled, they would have to store it in connected "chunks" (e.g. superordinates and ordinates, categories and examples). The students were instructed to look for key words that represented big ideas that could be used to connect more specific names, dates, or details. The teacher made the forest-and-trees analogy. This kind of hunt became fun. A common phrase became, "You're lost in the trees again; we are looking for the forest."

In reviewing U.S. history during the first several weeks of school as background for the study of American history beginning with Reconstruction, students were asked, "How would you categorize the historical events surrounding the people you just listed: LaSalle, Coronado, Hudson, and Marquette?" Blank stares were the only response. The teacher drew trees on the chalkboard and on each tree she placed the name of an explorer. She asked the students to name the forest. After a few hints from the teacher, the students named the forest "exploration."

Another early problem: the students did not understand why homework is assigned and how to make it a beneficial experience rather than 15 minutes of wasted agony. To develop these understandings, teachers often had to put aside the lesson prepared for the day and guide students step by step through how to complete homework assignments. Asking for clarification was considered a virtue and those who asked for clarification were warmly reinforced.

On one day a middle-school teacher was reviewing homework with students. The goal was to survey the new chapter for major ideas under which students could categorize information as they read. She asked, "How much of this do you think you're going to be required to know? How important is this chapter introduction in terms of the names of the people and the dates?"

A student responded, "You want us to just know the forest and not the trees."

The teacher asked what that meant.

The student's response was, "Not the details, but the main idea."

"Okay, so tell me again, what's the point of this introduction?"

A student replied, "What leads up to the Civil War."

"Yes, but what is it that leads to the Civil War?"

"The fist fight."

The teacher teases the student, "Oh, you're giving me a tree."

"The arguments in Congress."

"You've almost got it. Can anyone add anything?"

"The arguments in Congress about slavery."

"You've got it. So the introduction is trying to give you the flavor. It's telling you one incident but it's saying that people were pretty upset about slavery. So upset, they were even having fist fights in Congress. So that was the purpose of having you read the introduction and most of your introductions will be similar—they will set the tone. Authors try to grab your interest and they know that kids love to hear stories about fist fights. So they try in an introduction to give you something that will be of interest to you, but often it's a detail, not something you have to remember. The author is just setting the scene for what is to come.

"Now we are on the third paragraph of the introduction, where it says, 'The Brooks Sumner affair was one of many violent events that took place in the 1850's.' Yes, Jamie?"

"What does violent mean?"

A short discussion of violent followed. "So there were many violent events that took place during the 1850's. When does the Civil War begin?" A student answers, "In 1861." The teacher continues, "I was thinking as I was reading this, 'The fist fight took place in 1856 and the war didn't start for five years. That's a long time to have violent events going on in the country.' Does anyone know why I do that kind of thinking when I am reading?"

A student answered, "Because you don't want us to memorize all the dates, just to attach the little dates to the ten important dates we have to memorize in American history."

There were some detours along the way, as we realized the necessity of reviewing or reteaching processes that we had wrongly assumed were in place. However, students were internalizing concepts such as "associate little ideas with major concepts" and "use words that tie together details rather than memorize details." It was encouraging to see that the students were beginning to realize practical benefits to categorizing.

USING BACKGROUND KNOWLEDGE
TO REMEMBER NEW INFORMATION

Students still needed to be reminded about how to get ready for class to begin, as this excerpt from an October 18 transcript illustrates.

"Okay, we are ready for social studies. You should have out on your desk your notebook and your social studies book. Your social studies books should be open to the place where we left off yesterday and you should have a blank piece of paper in front of you in the social studies section of your notebook."

What

"The objective of our lesson today is to access background information. What that means is that in order to understand the topic, you need to think about everything you already know about the topic. During the next 60 seconds I would like you to write a list of words that you think of when you think of Reconstruction." (Students write.)

"All right, the next thing I would like you to do is talk to a person sitting beside you. You have 60 seconds to talk to your partner and add to your list of brainstormed words about Reconstruction. Also, I'd like you to ask your partner about the meaning of anything on the list that you don't understand." (Students talk and write.)

Why

"Okay, I think we've exhausted our brains. Put your desks back where they belong and we're going to talk about what we know about Reconstruction. Now, I told you when we started class today that our goal was to talk about the importance of accessing background information. You have heard that forever from Benchmark teachers, right? Do you have any idea why we ask about background information?"

Students gave answers such as "To make it interesting" and "So we will know what we are reading about." The teacher finally clued them to think of something they had learned in Psych 101.

A student answered, "We have to organize information."

Another said, "You want us to make forests instead of have trees."

Another said, "We only have so many slots, so we save room by hooking it to stuff we know."

The teacher summarized the theory of memory that had been discussed in Psych 101. "Psychologists believe we have seven memory slots, plus or minus two, in short-term memory and that chunking information together and hooking it to what we already know are good ways to be able to remember more."

The teacher then told a personal story about trying to remember a whole chapter of information for which she had very little background information and asked the students what would be one way she could have handled the situation. They seemed to enjoy hearing about the teacher's personal experience and sharing ideas for its solution.

The teacher summarized, "So why do we access background information? We access background information so that we can attach the new information to it. We can use background information like a magnet. All the metal shavings are what you're going to read. As you read, the metal shavings are going to attach to the magnet, which is your background information."

PARAPHRASING

Once the organizational and behavioral issues were under control, the awareness and control program really took off. Students seemed comfortable with the structure we had imposed on their lives and were ready to respond to instruction. Lessons were beginning to sound more like this social studies lesson from the third week in October.

What

"What was the objective I said we would be working on today?"

A student answered, "To put things in our own words?"

"Yes, to put things in your own words. There are many different ways you can summarize or put things in your own words. I won't be fussy, if you don't summarize exactly as I do, as long as you get the big idea in your own words."

Why

"Why do teachers ask you to put what you read in your own words?"

A student replied, "So you can understand it better and if you know it in the way you understand it, not the way the book says it."

Another student said, "I think that you could use your own words to make sure that you do understand it and so those words that we get really confused on...

The teacher elaborated by telling of a recent incident when she wrote something for Benchmark's research seminar that another teacher did not understand. "Because it was in my own words, does that mean I understood it?" The students all thought that it did. The teacher continued, "If you're trying to put something in your own words and you're not clear on it, you probably know that you are mixed up, don't you think? Well, that is exactly what happened. I didn't understand that paragraph, but instead of discussing it with someone to get clarification, I just wrote something down. My not being able to write something that made sense to others proved that I hadn't understood what I read. That's one reason that it's important to put notes in your own words. Having to put something in your own words lets you test yourself to see if you really understood what you read. Sometimes it's a good idea to have someone else read what you have written to see if they think it makes sense, just like I did in research seminar. I had tried to fool myself into believing that I understood what I read. When I had someone else read my summary, that person confirmed that I was still mixed up."

When

"When do you think you should take notes or summarize?" The class made a number of suggestions and the teacher summarized. "You've got it. That's exactly right. When you read for information. When I'm reading a novel, I don't take notes on it. I'm reading that just for my own enjoyment. The only time you need to take notes is when you will be tested on the information, want to use the information for some purpose such as writing a report, or want something to refer to at some future time. Every time I read a professional book or journal—on learning and teaching, for example—I take notes on the things I want to remember. I frequently refer back to those notes. So there are two kinds of reading. One kind is for pleasure—that's like when you read a basal reader or a novel for fun. When I read *Good Housekeeping* I sure don't take notes. The second kind of reading is reading for learning and remembering. You're going to take notes because you know that you're going to remember more if you have to put the ideas in your own words."

How

"Now there is one problem with this idea of taking notes. We have discovered that some people have a very interesting disability. It's called the "Eye-Hand Disease." What the person reads goes in the eyes, down the neck, down the shoulder, out the hand, onto the paper, without passing through the brain. Have any of you ever had that disability? We trick ourselves into thinking we are being good students and doing the right thing by taking notes, but we aren't thinking. We aren't putting what we are reading or listening to in our own words. What we need to be reading or listening to find are the most important words. These are often the words that your background knowledge tells you are important to this subject or words that have been used often in the passage. We jot those down and put them together in a sentence.

"Researchers tell us that underlining and highlighting are two of the most passive ways you can interact with your reading material because you don't have to think to make lines with a pencil or highlighter. A much more active way to interact with a book is to put what you are reading in your own words. You can't put it in your own words without passing the information through your brain."

Modeling

"I'm going to model my thinking for you on the first paragraph we're going to put in our own words. As I model, you can jot down the key words and then you'll have the first paragraph about done."

The teacher then modeled her thinking as she read and wrote her notes on the chalkboard.

"'Some Republicans disagree with Lincoln's programs.' Okay, so this is going to be about people who don't agree with Lincoln. He's a Republican, but they don't all agree. All right. 'Instead of punishing the South, President Lincoln wanted to heal the nation quickly.' Let's see, what are the two or three key words there or the two or three key ideas? Oh, it's about not punishing and healing. Okay, it's about punishing (writes on board) or healing. I think I'm going to do it this way so I can remember. (Writes on the board.) About punishing or healing. Okay, the next sentence. 'Therefore in 1863 he offered to pardon...' Pardon, what does pardon mean? I'm going to have to write that down at the bottom and look that up later to make sure that I'm right on pardon because I want my words right. (Writes on board.) 'Southerners who swore they would be loyal to the Union.' Okay, the important words are what? Umm, it seems to be about pardon and loyalty. Okay (writes on board), let's see, pardon is for loyalty. Okay. 'The only people who could not take part in this plan were those who had served in the confederacy.' Okay, so I need to write here, except in confederacy. Okay, I think I'm getting it. 'As soon as 10 percent of the citizens who had been qualified to vote' — okay, 'ten percent of the citizens who could vote in their states in 1860 took the oath,' Oh gads, what is oath? (Writes oath on board.) 'They took the oath of loyalty and agreed to...' Oh, oh, 'e-man-ci-pa-tion.' Oh, emancipation. I wonder what that means (writes emancipation on the board.) Boy, I'd better be sure on that one — she's going to put that one on the test, you'd better believe that, she likes those big, fat words.

"Okay, let me start this over again. 'As soon as 10 percent of the citizens who qualified to vote in their state in 1860 took the oath of loyalty and agreed to emancipation' — this sentence is killing me, it's too long — 'that state would be accepted back into the Union.' Okay, ten percent, 1860, took oath of loyalty, emancipation, state back in union. I see all of you have been jotting down those key words as I read. Let's all try to use them to summarize in our own words what we just read."

The students seemed at a loss to tie all of the words and phrases together. One student threw up her hands and said with a wry chuckle, "I guess we need some fix-up strategies!" That remark seemed to cue another student to recall that there was a dictionary of terms in the back of the social studies book that might be consulted for the unknown words. "Figuring out" the meaning of the paragraph so they could put it into their own words became a cooperative and enjoyable learning experience. The teacher guided the paraphrasing by "asking for clarification" when their phrasing was not clear and writing and revising on the board as students dictated, but she left the students in control. They were pleased with themselves for putting this sophisticated concept into their own words.

In these middle-school classes, more and more responsibility was being shifted onto the students and they were thriving on it.

WRITING ESSAY ANSWERS IN LITERATURE: DAY ONE

What follows are excerpts from two reading lessons taught in early December to sixth and seventh graders who were just completing the fifth reader level.

"Today we are going to begin a new book called *From The Mixed-Up Files of Mrs. Basil E. Frankweiler*. This book is about a young girl approximately your age and it takes place in the Metropolitan Museum of Art in New York City. Some of you may have been there and may come upon some descriptions you recognize. I've been there, and I had lots of fun looking for familiar scenes. I loved the story, too.

"Our objective for this book, our kind of long-term objective, is going to be to write clear and complete answers to essay questions on a book. Which means at the end of the book you will get what, Chris?"

"An essay."

"An essay test. Where have you had an essay test before? I know you have had them in social studies. So you probably know that they take more planning and organization than shorter answers. Did you learn about different *kinds* of essays?"

Students discussed their experiences with essay tests.

How

"How do you write an essay answer? Well, an essay answer doesn't necessarily have to be long, but it's different from an objective test such as a multiple choice or a true/false test. Over the course of reading this book, we will be exposed to essay questions and will see that essay questions have a particular format. There are problem and solution essay questions as well as compare and contrast, and we're going to analyze them together and try to learn how to write a good essay answer for each of the different kinds of essays."

Review of Previously-Taught Strategies

Strategies for active involvement. "Before we can even get to the point where we're thinking about essay questions, we have a lot of other strategies to review in order to prepare for reading. First of all, we need to call up strategies that we've learned, to begin to get ourselves involved in this book, in particular, and in reading in general. We brainstormed with the other reading group, and we made a list of what we usually do to get ourselves actively involved in our reading. We talked about surveying. Do you all survey when you read a book? Do you think that's useful?" The students discussed their different experiences with surveying when reading a novel as compared to surveying in preparation for reading in social studies, science, or health.

"Well, one strategy that I use to decide whether I even want to pick up the book is to look on the back of it or I look on the cover and I read the information to see what it is about.

"Another strategy that we decided you could use to get actively involved was to make predictions when you read, and you can revise your predictions if and when you find they're wrong. You can set purposes, you can make pictures in your mind, you can focus on the story elements, you can summarize. Anybody else have any other ideas, anything else that you do that gets you involved in your reading?"

One student said, "Well, like usually I put myself in one of the little people's position if I'm really into the book."

The teacher responded, "So in other words you take the point of view of a character?"

The same student clarified, "No, not really, but I don't do everything, I feel like I'm watching it like in a TV set."

The teacher asked, "Do you make pictures in your head?"

"Yes, I do, but I feel like I'm really there, like I'm hiding under a rock."

"So you try to put yourself into a setting."

"When I'm reading I try to picture what it's like...."

Fix-up strategies. The teacher continued, "Those are all the kinds of things we need to do to get involved in the book. Then, in the other group, we made this list of fix-up strategies. What happens after we've done all these things and we are reading along and we don't understand what's happening, which happens frequently? In the last group somebody said they reread, another person said they ask questions, another person, who I think was me, talked about being attentive in reading group. And then we talked abut what happens when you come to a word you don't know." Students shared ideas about what they do when they don't understand what's happening or when they encounter a word they can't pronounce and what they do when they encounter a word they can pronounce, but do not know what it means.

"That's fantastic. And Chris, you usually don't get stuck over the actual decoding of the word. I think using the context, going ahead, reading the sentence, and saying "blank" is usually a very helpful strategy for figuring out the meaning of a word. I know I use that lots of times when I come across a word I can decode, but I may not know the meaning. So I have to go ahead and read the whole sentence, or maybe read the whole paragraph or the whole chapter, to see if I can make any sense of that. And I have to decide whether the word is important enough to my comprehension to worry about it.

"Am I the only teacher who has talked to you about fix-up strategies? Where in real life or in other classes have you ever had to use fix-up strategies?"

The students discussed fix-up strategies needed in math and social studies. The teacher reminded students about the time she got lost on an orienteering course during the November middle-school camping trip and had to get fix-up help from Mr. Hurster.

Predictions. The students then surveyed the book, reading the back cover and looking at chapter titles. They next began predicting what the book would be about. "Okay, this girl wanted to be appreciated and she wanted to feel different. She said she always felt the same and she wanted to feel different."

Themes. The teacher gave the students "theme sheets" on which she had listed a number of themes commonly found in children's literature. Theme had been a topic of discussion in several books they had read earlier in the school year.

"Based on the little bit of information gleaned from your survey, and looking at this theme sheet of ours, what do you think a theme of *From The Mixed-Up Files of Mrs. Basil E. Frankweiler* might be? Do you think it might have anything to do with good against evil? Probably not." Students made various suggestions as to what the theme might be and gave reasons for their choices.

"Survival. Anything else? How about growing up and searching for the truth? When you're running away and you're trying to be different, do you think that has anything to do with growing up?"

A discussion followed which led very naturally into the teacher's establishing background for the story by asking the students what they knew about art museums and whether any of them had visited the Metropolitan Museum.

Characters. "The next thing I'd like you to do is to turn to the first page, the page with the words in italics, and I would like you to read that now, carefully, to begin to get into the story." Students read silently. "What characters have been introduced in this? What is the format of what you have read so far?" The students said that it was a letter to a lawyer from a Mrs....

The period ended. The students began the next day where they left off.

WRITING ESSAY ANSWERS IN LITERATURE: DAY TWO

"I said yesterday that our long-term objective was going to be to learn how to give really clear and complete answers to essay questions by analyzing the essay question and then answering it using good specific examples."

Study guides

"There are a number of ways that you can go about doing that. One way is to make a study guide for yourself and take notes while you're reading. So we're going to make a study guide while we're reading this book. Have you ever made up a study guide before?" There was a debate among the students as to whether they had made up their own study guides before. The reason for the disagreement was their different definitions of a study guide.

Study guides had been taught and prepared by these students in earlier contexts. This failure to recognize a previously-taught strategy in a new context is an example of students' failure to *transfer* strategies taught to new situations.

"I can see that we don't all have the same idea about what a study guide is. Well, let me show you what I have here that I made for you. There are no specific questions on this. This study guide is something on which you can take notes. There is a sheet for vocabulary, a sheet for themes, a sheet for characters of realistic fiction, and a sheet to write the problems that Jamie and Claudia encounter and their solutions.

"These are the categories that we're going to focus on to gather information as we're reading the book. Does that make sense so far?"

Traditionally, the students in this class meet with the teacher at the reading group table for instruction and for discussions on the reading. Students read at their desks and then complete independent seatwork. Seatwork consists of a written response to the reading, often some questions related to the teacher's objectives for the book they are reading.

"Now, what I'll have you do for your seatwork will be traditional seatwork questions, but I've only put two of them on this sheet because I also want your seatwork to include filling out information on your study guide. I thought it was too much to expect for you to fill out information on your study guide, which we will do at the reading group table, plus answer seat work questions. So your seatwork grade will be based on the answers to two comprehension questions and the information that you've written down on your study guide pages. Now, your study guide information is notes. You don't have to write in complete sentences, the spelling doesn't have to be perfect. Do you think the notes have to be legible?" "Yes, you certainly have to be able to read them and I'm going to determine whether they are legible or not.

"I have specific things that I want on your study guide. You are to find three vocabulary words for each chapter and write down the page number of each. Your second assignment is to list characters who have been introduced so far and any notes that will help you better understand the characters."

Model of study guide

"I've filled out my own study guide sheet to show you as a model. Let me show you what I did for characters on my study guide sheet. I put one character here and skipped a whole bunch of lines because I want to be able to go back and fill in things about the character throughout the book. You should leave plenty of space under notes on theme and problem, too, for elaboration."

Why

"Why are we doing these study guide sheets?"

A student answered, "So when the essay comes, we have the information."

"Yes, so you'll have the information organized in categories. Then you're probably going to have to reorganize that information after we've analyzed questions or raised questions, and you'll have the information here and should be set to go with some specific examples to be able to answer the essay questions. Does that make sense to everybody?"

Clarification

"Just because you have only two questions to answer on the sheet doesn't mean these are the only two things that I expect you to know from the chapter. During our discussion of each chapter, I will ask you if you need any clarification on your comprehension. This book is not an easy book. But to me it's a terrific story, so you're going to have to read carefully, and if you don't understand anything, use your fix-up strategies, come to reading group, and we'll discuss it.

But you need to generate the questions, you're going to have to be responsible for saying 'I didn't get this' or 'I didn't get that' because we're going to focus a lot on the process of filling out this study guide and I'm going to expect you to come to me with questions about content. Clear?"

"Okay, you can go back to your seats and read chapter one."

MAKING INFERENCES: A LESSON PLAN

The following lesson was taught in January to students who were seventh and eighth graders reading on a seventh grade level. Most had attended Benchmark for many years. In fact, two had been at Benchmark for six years, having begun as nonreaders.

New Book Introduced

"We are going to be reading a genre of literature that is different, in form at least, from that of any other book we have read this year. This story is written as a play. It is called *Raisin in the Sun* and was very popular on Broadway some years ago. It has also been made into a movie, which we might try to get on video tape when we have finished reading the play."

Genre Described. "The genre here is really one that you are very familiar with—realistic fiction. It is only the format of this story that is new to us as readers. I know you have all seen plays. In many ways they are similar to movies. The main difference between reading or seeing a play and reading a book is that the play gives the reader or audience fewer sources of information. In a play, there are only two sources of information available to the reader or viewer: one, there is the *stage set* and two, the *dialogue and actions* of the characters. The playwright does not have the same opportunities that other writers of fiction have for providing background information, description, thoughts of the characters, etc. For the benefit of the play's director and the audience, the playwright describes just how the stage setting should look and the reader or audience must "read" a lot into this setting. For the reader of a play, all stage directions are important because he or she cannot see the expressions and gestures of the characters."

Objective Introduced

"Our objective in reading this play will be to learn to **make inferences** about the characters and things that are happening in the story, just as you do in all the stories you read. I know that **making inferences** is a strategy that you learned several years ago and that it is frequently reviewed both in my class and other classes. The big difference today will be that you will have fewer clues, less information available in the text, on which to base your inferences. All of your information will have to come from the stage set, the stage directions, and the dialogue. Naturally, you'll have just as much background information, that information in your head, available—won't you? Who will review for me how a good reader makes inferences?" The teacher and students briefly reviewed the process of making inferences, a thinking process on which they had been working all year.

Why

"Why are we working on making inferences in the context of a play? Why are we 'studying' stage directions? Why has dialogue become so important? When you are in high school, plays will become a common form of assigned reading. You'll soon be reading Shakespeare. You need to be ready to get the most out of this kind of reading. As I mentioned earlier, stage directions are always important to the understanding of a play. The reader needs to pick up the clues that help him/her understand characters' situations, motives, feelings, etc. If you don't pick up these clues, it is not likely you will fully understand the play. Stage directions will be the basis for many inferences you will have to make as you read this play and many plays in the future."

When

"When will you use playreading skills? You will read stage directions every time you read a play. However, you need to make inferences *all day, every day* — in *all* reading that you do, in your interactions with other people, observations of situations, and events around you."

How

"How will you make inferences based on stage directions and dialogue only? You will read all stage directions carefully to see what 'picture' the playwright is trying to create. Make pictures in your mind (as you should always do when you read) and ask yourself what information about the characters you can extract from those pictures. Read carefully everything the characters say. 'Listen' to what they are saying. As you always do in making inferences, combine what you see and hear with what you have in your background knowledge to make inferences about characters and action."

Active-reader strategies reviewed. "Before we open our books, let's review the active-reader strategies we always need to employ when reading. What is the first thing a good reader does when getting ready to start a new book?" For the next few minutes, the students reviewed the strategies they habitually use — or know they *should* use — when reading. These included surveying before reading, accessing background knowledge, predicting, monitoring, applying fix-up strategies when comprehension breaks down, 'picturing in your mind,' and constantly measuring what is going on in a story against your background knowledge.

Surveying/Predicting. Students read the book cover, the excerpts from reviews by the critics, and the short poem by Langston Hughes (an introduction) from which the title of the play was taken. "Tell me what you think this play is going to be about. You can use the old familiar story grammar elements of setting, characters, problem and solution to make your predictions." A lively discussion ensued in which students used the information gleaned from their survey to make predictions about characters and story plot/action and set their purposes for reading.

Following the introduction to the book and these prereading activities, the students were assigned a number of pages to read and then returned to their seats to read. When they had all completed the reading, they returned to the reading group table for discussion.

Discussion. Although teachers include numerous questions in their lesson plans as reminders to themselves of points they would like to have discussed, usually only a few questions are asked to stimulate discussion and the remaining questions are asked only when the discussion needs to be restarted or redirected. The basic questions used to direct the discussion are designed to achieve the teacher's objective.

"Would anyone like clarification? What information do we get about the Younger family from the stage directions at the very beginning—even before the curtain rises on Scene I?

What are the 'indestructible contradictions' referred to in the first sentence? You need a clear picture in your head to pick up these clues.

What further light is shed on the family's situation when they are getting up in the morning?

How is Ruth feeling—her mood—as she gets up and gets her family up? Where can you find clues to tell?

What are relationships like between family members?
- Clues to go on?
- Signs of affection between mother and son?
- Signs of affection between father and son?

Did Walter give Travis money out of affection for Travis or to bug Ruth?

Why does Ruth simply keep telling Walter to eat his breakfast, go, etc.?

What is Walter's complaint about Ruth and colored women, in general?"

Wrap-Up. "How did reading stage directions in this scene help you to understand the characters and action in this play? What active-reader strategies are you using to help you understand this book? Are they working for you? Did you come to any places where you had to stop and use a fix-up strategy? Tell us about it. Are you making pictures in your head? How is making pictures in your head when reading a play similar to what you do when you read a novel? How is it different? How does the author help you in this play?"

The following day, this teacher introduced her *second objective* for this book, to recognize the *theme*, or author's message. Throughout the reading of the book the students worked on both making inferences and recognizing theme. Study guides were used by the student to take notes on dialogue and action in the play that supported/illustrated the theme. The notes were written by students as they worked in a group at the reading-group table. This was "independent work," with the teacher in the background offering guidance and direction when the students needed this support.

SUMMARY

In the Perot Middle School, students review, practice, adapt, and refine strategies to which they were introduced in the primary and intermediate grades as well as learn new, more sophisticated strategies to meet more complex task demands. The team approach to teaching in the middle school results in many of these strategies being implemented in a number of classes in the same time frame. At any given time, students are often learning to categorize events in history, organisms in science and examples of theme or point of view in a novel, etc. In this way students learn how one broad information-processing strategy can be adapted to fit many diverse learning situations. Teachers release responsibility to the students as each is ready, providing scaffolding as needed. After a strategy is initially presented, as a new strategy or as a familiar one to be adapted, interaction takes precedence over teacher talk. The focus may remain on one strategy through a unit or a novel as the foregoing excerpts suggest. The teacher's major goal, as students approach the end of their Benchmark experience, is to create students who can independently orchestrate an array of strategies to complete a learning task.

CHAPTER 10

One Teacher's Reading Group Instruction: A Case Study

Have you ever visited a class, seen students demonstrating a high level of awareness and control with respect to learning, and wondered how the students were brought to that level? Many of us have had that experience, so we decided to analyze transcripts for one teacher, teaching one aspect of the curriculum during a six-month period. The following is based on information from four sources: transcripts of Sharon Rauch's reading group instruction from October 1988 through March 1989 jottings in journals written by observers; Mrs. Rauch's lesson plans; and interviews with Mrs. Rauch.

The purpose of this chapter is to demonstrate how a teacher plans and carries out instruction over a school year. A teacher's first consideration in planning strategy instruction is what the students already know about the strategies. Their awareness of strategies becomes the basis for discussion about each phase of the instruction. For example, the twelve students in Mrs. Rauch's reading groups were eleven- and twelve-year-olds who, with the exception of one, had attended Benchmark for a number of years. They were students who had made exceptional progress in their time at Benchmark and had received several years of strategy instruction. Thus, Mrs. Rauch was able to cover the basic active-reader strategies at a review level and devote the preponderance of her instructional time to higher-level information processing strategies.

Mrs. Rauch had two long-range objectives for her class. Both of these objectives emphasized ways for students to take control of their learning. The first was to convince her students that implementing strategies for active involvement is worth the effort. The second was to increase students' awareness of classifying as a useful strategy for organizing and remembering information as well as to teach them how to implement the strategy. You will see how, in doing this, she was constantly either encouraging students to draw on their repertoire of strategies in other subjects or to see how strategies used in reading could transfer to other areas.

Some of the axioms of strategy instruction that are consistently found in Mrs. Rauch's instruction are:

1. Application or transfer of previously-learned strategies can never be assumed and should always be reviewed and guided by the

teacher (who re-teaches, clarifies, or elaborates as needed) if the strategies are needed to perform the new task at hand.

2. Initial instruction about the strategy is very explicit, with the teacher doing most of the talking on the day a strategy is introduced. The teacher informs the students why the strategy is important, when and where it is useful, how to execute the strategy; models the strategy; and relates the strategy to some personal experience using the strategy.

3. Instruction becomes increasingly interactive as the teacher gradually shifts responsibility to the students.

4. Students are given many opportunities to practice and apply the strategy, thus maintaining the active participation of all students.

5. The teacher is always supportive of students and encourages risk-taking.

6. Review, re-teaching, and clarification are always ongoing.

THE READING GROUPS

When the school year 1988-89 began, the twelve students shared by Mrs. Rauch and her co-teacher, Mrs. Gutman, were sixth and seventh graders who were all ready for instruction at the sixth reader level. The teachers rotated the reading groups, consisting of three or four students, in such a way that both taught each of the twelve students at least once a trimester, the rotation often taking place when a novel was completed.

Generally, the students in a reading group met with the teacher each day for the introduction of the portion of the text that was to be read that day. The lessons followed a standard format. The new objective was taught on the day it was introduced, re-taught and/or reviewed on subsequent days as necessary; relevant previously-learned strategies were reviewed; and background knowledge, unfamiliar vocabulary, predictions and purposes were discussed. This discussion could take ten minutes or more than an hour, depending on students' needs and their familiarity with the process objectives being featured. After the initial introductory discussion at the reading table, the students would return to their desks and read the assigned material. When all of the students in the group had completed the reading, the group would meet for a discussion.

We enter Mrs. Rauch's reading instruction in early October, as the students are preparing to read *Prince Caspian*, the second novel of the *Chronicles of Narnia*. The reading groups had recently completed *The Lion, The Witch, and The Wardrobe*, the first novel of this series by the author C. S. Lewis. As you follow the students through *Prince Caspian* you will see that many of the strategies that are being emphasized had been introduced in the earlier novel, and some even in previous years.

Prince Caspian — Day One: Becoming Actively Involved

On the day the novel was introduced, the students brainstormed strategies that helped them become actively involved in their reading. The strategies elicited were all ones that had been taught and practiced in depth over a period of several years. Their list included: 1) surveying, 2) predicting, 3) setting a purpose, 4) identifying story elements (characters, setting, problem/conflict and solution/resolution), 5) thinking about what you already know, and 6) monitoring your understanding and applying fix-up strategies when comprehension breaks down. After a discussion of why, when, and how to use these strategies, the students returned to their seats and read silently the first chapter of *Prince Caspian*.

After reading, the group again met to discuss their reading and to share which strategies they had used and found helpful. To wrap-up the lesson, the group summarized Chapter One and discussed the strategies that had helped them understand the chapter.

Day Two: Task Defined

On the second day active-reader strategies were again reviewed. Mrs. Rauch encouraged students to think of strategies they used in other subjects that also could be used effectively in reading a novel. She stressed that most strategies can be useful across the curriculum (e.g., using the structure of a text in social studies or science to predict; in reading you can use titles, pictures, and text structure to predict).

At this point Mrs. Rauch shared with the students what their task would be as they read this book. At the end of the novel they would be given an essay test. In keeping with Benchmark's goal of producing students who take control of their learning, Mrs. Rauch did not explicitly tell the students what sort of essay questions they should expect. Rather, she guided them to ask her questions that would help them analyze the task for themselves (Will there be a question on theme? Will the questions be the sort of questions we've had on other novels?, etc.). The students elicited from Mrs. Rauch that they could expect questions regarding character, theme, and genre in their essay test.

The students expressed concern about being able to decide what would be important to remember for the test and how they would remember everything they would need to know. Mrs. Rauch suggested that they think of strategies they had used to remember information in social studies and science. The group then brainstormed possible strategies that would aid their studying for an essay test. Different methods of long-range preparation for the test were proposed. Among these strategies were: keeping lists of character and place names, since the unusual character and place names were giving students difficulty; saving seatwork papers; and discussing among themselves what sort of questions they might anticipate and what might be important to know/remember (cooperative learning).

After this, Chapter One was briefly reviewed, new vocabulary for Chapter Two was presented, and students made predictions and set purposes. Next, Mrs. Rauch challenged the students to use some of the strategies they had just brainstormed to start preparing for the test as they read. Then the students returned to their seats to read. After reading, the students met for discussion and wrap-up of the lesson.

Days Three-Six: Strategies for Active Reading Reinforced

On each of these days, the students read another chapter of *Prince Caspian*, following the usual reading lesson format. No new process objectives (strategies) were introduced, and Mrs. Rauch continually elicited from the students which active-reader strategies they were using, how they helped, and, on occasion, why they had not been helpful. She continued to ask if anyone wanted clarification (an explanation of words, concepts, etc.) and to praise students who talked about strategies they had used. It was not until Mrs. Rauch felt the students had developed sufficient involvement in this novel and in their reading in general that she introduced her overall objective for this novel, in Chapter Seven.

Chapter Seven: Classifying Information Introduced

This seemed like the opportune time to introduce her classifying objective. The students had been conscientiously collecting lists of character and place names they felt they might need for the test. Some of them were showing signs of panic as to how they would ever remember them all or keep them all straight, or whether they even needed them all.

Mrs. Rauch opened the lesson by introducing her overall process objective for *Prince Caspian*: to have students understand and develop ways to classify and organize information so that it is easier to access, or remember.

> T: Many of you have begun to talk about how you can decide what's important to remember for the essay test, and I've

also heard people here say they don't think they can remember everything they'll need to know. What do you do in social studies and science to remember?

S: (Students offered making timelines, outlines, and charts or diagrams as ways of organizing information in these areas.)

T: You've already begun to get yourselves ready for this test in several ways. You've been keeping the worksheets I gave you for seatwork on this novel, and you've been keeping lists of important characters and places. Today we'll talk more about things we can do with your names lists that will help you get ready for a test. Lists can be assigned key words that help in identifying the names in the list. When I was in school, I used to keep lists like this for English, social studies, and science. I would read the lists over and over and hope that I'd remember most of the terms. Then one day I found I was grouping the names together because they had something in common, like I'd group the South's generals together, and the North's generals. When I did that I remembered better. It was only many years later in psychology class that I understood why. Does anyone in Psych 101 know?

S: You probably didn't have enough slots in your brain to remember so many names.

S: We learned that you can remember better if the information in your brain is organized.

T: Very good! I wish I'd had Psych 101. So, if we really want to remember the names in our lists, what can we do?

S: Organize it?

T: Good! Yes. Does anyone have any suggestions as to how we could organize the names to help us remember?

S: We could leave out the names that are not important.

T: Yes, that would make it easier. Can you think of any common traits or characteristics we could group them under?

S: Well, there's good characters and bad characters.

S: There are all different kinds of characters like dwarfs, and animals and real people. We could do them like that.

Mrs. Rauch guided the students to select key words that would identify the different categories on the board and under each placed the names and places the students provided. Using the category names, and under the guidance of Mrs. Rauch, the students designed study guides (Figure 1) they could while reading use to gather important information that they might need for the essay test.

As this lesson proceeded, Mrs. Rauch discussed with the students how and when this classifying strategy might prove useful in social studies and science. The students suggested that this kind of classifying was very similar to the way they grouped rocks — as to whether they were igneous, sedimentary or metamorphic; in social studies they had grouped explorers as English, French, or Spanish explorers. As a group, the students now seemed to feel quite confident that this study guide would work to help them organize and remember. However, Mrs. Rauch assured them that they could bring their lists and study guides to reading group every day after reading and that they would share names and categories. This seemed to be just what the students wanted to hear. Mrs. Rauch realized that this activity would provide her with daily opportunities for assessment of the students' grasp of this strategy, as well as for any further teaching, elaborating, or clarifying that might be needed.

New vocabulary was presented, predictions made and purposes set, and the students returned to their seats to read Chapter Seven. After reading, they reassembled for discussion, bringing with them their lists of names and places.

> Now, what we want to do before we talk about this chapter is to look at our lists — what the categories are that we chose, and we can change categories, add to them, take names off or keep what we have.

There was much discussion and debate by the students regarding additions and changes. Throughout the discussion, Mrs. Rauch asked for the reasoning behind each statement or suggestion. Once they were ready to discuss the chapter, Mrs. Rauch began by asking if anyone needed clarification about anything. Several students asked about places about which they were not clear, and a lively discussion ensued as students tried to work out the meaning together. The teacher guided or confirmed, was always supportive as she encouraged students to take risks and praised their insights, but she did not supply answers to their questions.

Day Eight: Reinforcing Lesson on Chapter Seven

This day's lesson was used to reinforce the lesson taught for Chapter Seven and to re-teach as needed. Mrs. Rauch began with a review of the previous day's strategy.

> Who remembers what strategy we were learning yesterday to help us get ready for the essay test? How is this useful? Who has used it before in other subjects?

Figure 10-1
Study Guide

Prince Caspian

Old Narnians		New Narnians	
Name	Key Words to identify	Name	Key words to identify

Common characteristics of Old Narnians	Common characteristics of New Narnians

The discussion that ensued included talking about what makes a category, eliciting simple examples from students, and reviewing reasons for the categories generated by students the day before and which now occupied a "permanent" place on the chalkboard behind the reading group table. (This information remained there for additions and revisions until the students finished the book.)

After this, the students summarized Chapter Seven, new vocabulary was presented, purposes were set, and the students read Chapter Eight. When the group met to discuss, additions and revisions were made to the lists on the board. Students were asked to give reasons for selecting a name or place as important and to consider whether changes should be made on the basis of new information. (For example, a character might be removed from the list of dwarfs and put under a category "dangerous criminal" on the basis of new information about the character.)

At this point in their categorization, students were encouraged to start anticipating the kinds of essay questions a teacher might generate from this list. Mrs. Rauch modeled: "I might ask, 'Name two Telmarines and tell how they are alike and different.'" She elicited similar questions from the students, but did not go into this strategy in depth at this time. She had planned a lesson on predicting test questions to be taught closer to the end of the book.

Once again, the reading lesson ended with a discussion of the chapter, with Mrs. Rauch guiding and encouraging, but rarely providing answers to questions, followed by a summary of the chapter and the strategies used.

By this time the students were demonstrating a fairly high level of confidence with respect to classifying the names and characters in this novel. Mrs. Rauch decided to move on to the more complex concept of theme. Identifying themes in a story had been a main objective while reading the previous novel, *The Lion, The Witch and The Wardrobe*. Her new objective would be to have the students understand and develop ways to classify and organize information regarding the novel's themes. She wanted them to see how major ideas in each chapter fit into themes and to begin to think about the author's message.

Day Nine: Categorizing As It Relates To Theme

Mrs. Rauch began the lesson with a review of the categorizing they had been doing:

T: What kind of information have we been categorizing?

S: We've been categorizing, like the names of the characters and sometimes the places, like holy places.

T: Yes. And there are other kinds of information that we can also remember better when we categorize. This kind of information is the important ideas that the author develops. We've already talked a lot about these important ideas when we've discussed... Many of the big or important events in a story are related to theme. A theme is really a category for important ideas. Who remembers some of the themes we found in *The Lion, The Witch and The Wardrobe?*

S: Wasn't one survival?

T: Yes. Good. Any other?

S: Yeah. Good versus Evil?

As the students offered themes, Mrs. Rauch wrote them on the board.

T: Do you think any of these themes are in *Prince Caspian,* too? Do you see any other themes?

Once again, Mrs. Rauch wrote all of the themes on the board. She did not reject or confirm any suggestion, but consistently asked, "What makes you think that "survival" is a theme?

Mrs. Rauch wrote student responses on the chalkboard under the heading "survival" (Caspian runs away from home to escape death, Caspian must find food to live, Caspian is nursed back to health, etc.). Similar ideas were written under "growing up," etc. She was forever questioning, and her questions followed a familiar pattern: How is what we just did like the way we categorized our lists? How might this help you in an essay test? Is it similar to anything you do in science and social studies?

From here on, the lesson followed Mrs. Rauch's usual pre- and post-reading format. (See earlier chapter lessons.) Students now brought lists of important events and ideas related to theme, as well as lists of characters and places, when they came to reading group.

Chapter Ten: Categorizing As Related to Theme Reinforced

The objective for the first part of this lesson was to reinforce the students' understanding of classifying ideas related to theme. Questions heard during pre-reading discussion were, "Who remembers what strategy we were using yesterday to help us get ready for the essay test?", "How could it help us get ready for the test?", "Do you have any important ideas you would like us to add to the themes before we read?"

When the group met to discuss Chapter Ten and to go over their lists of characters and places, and ideas related to theme, Mrs. Rauch turned the focus on important information that adds to themes.

> We said that a theme is a group or category of important ideas and that the author usually tries to give the reader a message about the theme. Let's look at the themes we have so far to see if we can get any idea of the author's message. (Reading from the chalkboard) Let's see.... We have survival, good versus evil, real versus supernatural, growing up.

As was typical, Mrs. Rauch guided her students through that zone between what they could do entirely on their own and what was beyond their understanding without a great deal of support. She gave just enough support to help students arrive at answers on their own, but never more. She never gave them answers. The following excerpt is an excellent example of *scaffolded instruction*.

> T: Let's start with survival, because that's the theme under which you have the most ideas and events, at least so far in the book. When you think about these examples of survival — the kids having to find food on their own, Caspian having to live on his own and find food and make friends to help him, having to fight wars with his old acquaintances and friends in order to survive — what do you think the author might be saying about survival and about a person's ability to survive and what makes it possible for a person to survive? Do you have any ideas? What do you think he might be saying?
>
> S: ...hard because it's hard to get food because you can't know if you're killing the right animal or not, and it's kind of a confusing place because...
>
> T: Well, it's 'hard to survive on your own' (writes on board). Do you think the author is saying that there's anything that can help you to survive? What was helping Caspian survive after he left Merehouse — what is helping Caspian to survive the battles or the fights? What is helping the kids to survive on the island?
>
> S: The first one is talent.
>
> T: How does talent help you?
>
> S: Well, ability helps you survive.
>
> T: Okay, now we're getting closer to another idea. Who helped Caspian get a sword, get armor, be prepared to fight?
>
> S: Well, Merehouse helped him to do it.

T: Merehouse gave him his first training, but remember when he ran away? When he was in the forest, who helped him and who helped him get the equipment that he needed to survive? I don't need a particular name, — just in general?

S: (Students suggest a number of names, including Cornelius, the dwarfs, the animals, friends, etc.

T: Yes. That seems to say that people need people and you will survive best with help from your friends. (Writes on board) 'You need other people.' Now, is that a message we could live by as well as people in another time?

S: Yes, you need other people, you can't just live alone. I guess you could do that, but it gets awfully lonely, but also people help you.

T: So the message that an author would give is not just a message for characters in the story, but also for the reader. And I think he is saying you need friends to survive. How about good versus evil? What message would the author be giving us about good versus evil? Think about fairy tales, how they usually end.

S: Good wins.

T: Good wins. So I think we have a simple message here in that 'Good wins and triumphs' (writes on board). We'll see for sure if there's actually that message in this book, but if it follows the fairy tale mold, good will triumph over evil. How about real versus supernatural...

Mrs. Rauch continued to lead a discussion similar to that above; however, the students were increasingly in charge of the discussion as they became more familiar with the concept of author's message.

Day Eleven: Categorizing as Related to Genre

In this lesson, Mrs. Rauch introduced a third use of the categorizing strategy. This time her objective was to have the students use the genre of the book to help them make predictions and to categorize information (characteristics of the story that fit the genre adventure story). The concepts of genre and adventure story were not new to these students since genre is the core of the Benchmark Literature Program. Because they were now also familiar with categorization, the students quickly caught on to this new use of the strategy. Rather than give her students the rationale for use of the strategy, Mrs. Rauch was able to elicit this from them.

T: Recently we've been spending time putting information into categories. What kinds of information have we categorized?

S: Well, we did the names — like characters and places.

S: The themes.

T: Good! Why have we done this? How is it going to help you?

S: It's going to help us for the essay test, like remembering better.

T: Yes, organizing information helps you remember better. Today we are going to categorize another kind of information in a way that will help us remember. When one of my daughters was in 9th grade, she had to memorize the characteristics of different kinds of stories. She hated it because she didn't know why she had to do this. We are going to look at the characteristics of an adventure story, but we do have a good reason to study them. We can think of these characteristics as categories. Let's see what facts from our story fit into these categories....

Mrs. Rauch then elicited categories/characteristics, as well as examples from the story to back them up, and wrote them on the chalkboard. These were discussed and revised until the students as a group agreed upon them. The students then copied these lists so they could be added to other "study guides" (lists) they were keeping in preparation for the test. When the students returned to their seats to read the chapter, they were told to look for characteristics of an adventure story in the new information they would be reading.

There are several things that should be noted in Mrs. Rauch's lesson. She was constantly assessing just where her students were in the awareness and control of the strategies she wanted them to use, so she was able to draw on their strengths, and to shift more and more of the responsibility onto them (gradual release of responsibility); she always related the new information she was giving them to what they already knew and had been doing; she kept all of her students actively involved and participating in the lesson and moved at a brisk pace; she maintained interest by relating personal anecdotes or stories related to the strategy she was teaching.

Day Twelve: Categorizing by Characteristics of Genre Reinforced

Along with the other usual pre- and post-reading activities in her reading lessons, Mrs. Rauch had the students continue adding to the categories under characteristics of the genre adventure story. These were put on the board and copied onto individual study guides.

Day Thirteen: Predicting Essay Questions

By this time, the students were almost at the end of this fifteen-chapter book. Mrs. Rauch had noted, and indeed anticipated, a fairly high level of student anxiety over the upcoming essay test. She decided to make the most of the opportunity to reinforce her rationale for using categorizing as a strategy (it helps you remember better), while allaying student anxiety at the same time. In other words, she wanted to convince them that this strategy was an effective means of readily accessing (recalling) information. In order to do this, she would have to insure that the students were well prepared for her essay test. Therefore, teaching students how to anticipate essay questions was in order.

Mrs. Rauch began the lesson by asking her students whether they felt sufficiently prepared for the essay test. Receiving the expected negative response, she asked the group what they thought they could do at this point to better prepare themselves. Again, a student helpfully said, "We could figure out what kind of questions will be on the test." And there was the perfect rationale for the strategy Mrs. Rauch had planned for this lesson.

> T: Yes, we could try to figure out what kind of questions might be on that essay test. Anticipating test questions is something I know you've done with Mr. Benedict in social studies. I bet you've done it with Mr. Young in science, too. Tell me what you did to help you predict test questions in social studies.
>
> S: Well, Mr. Benedict said you could tell when he talked about something a whole lot.
>
> T: Yes. That's a good indicator. When a teacher talks a lot about something, you can infer that the teacher thinks it's pretty important. Are there any other means you've used to predict test questions...

Mrs. Rauch patiently elicited from the students that all the categories they had come up with and kept track of should be a help in predicting the essay questions. The students decided that they would use the three broad groups of categories (characters/places, themes, adventure story-genre) to predict essay questions. In the following excerpt, you will see them working on themes.

> T: Remember, we talked about how theme is really a group

of ideas the author wanted you to think about and they all come under a category that he is also giving a message about. For example, survival is a theme that we have tons and tons of examples of. We decided the author was trying to say that you need other people to help you; it's hard to survive alone.

What we need to do today is think about what essay question a teacher could ask that could draw on the general idea of theme. Can you think of a question that I might want to ask?

The students made suggestions and the teacher helped them shape what they said and asked questions to cue their thinking. The students struggled with being able to state a question that would tie together the ideas they had written under the "survival" theme and the lesson that it is hard to survive alone. Again, Mrs. Rauch scaffolded the lesson, guiding students with questions that led their thinking until it arrived at this connection. Finally, a student tied these ideas together in a question that Mrs. Rauch wrote on the board: "How was Caspian able to survive all the things that happened to him?" Next, Mrs. Rauch asked the students to brainstorm ideas to include in an essay answer to that question. This activity generated so much enthusiasm on the part of the students that they continued to work on this predicting strategy throughout most of the reading period. Being able to predict possible essay questions and find the information needed to answer them right in their study guides seemed to give their self-confidence a big boost.

One of the students pointed out that there were two parts to answering the essay question. One was getting the facts straight and the other was putting them together right in your head — the thinking part. Mrs. Rauch took this opportunity to explain that the reason for categorizing is to help you get the facts organized ahead of time so you have "lots of slots" left over for thinking.

Mrs. Rauch has a talent for catching students doing something that she would like to see more of and reinforcing that behavior. For example, one student asked if he should copy the information Mrs. Rauch had written on the board during the preceding discussion. Mrs. Rauch responded, "It was great that Bert asked if he needed to copy this information, because… What were you aware of, Bert, when you asked the question?" The student replied that he knew it would help him study for the test. With that, the other students also began to copy the information.

How much more effective any activity is when the initiative comes from the students! This is one big step in the direction of students taking control of their learning. Mrs. Rauch seldom missed such an opportunity.

Conclusion of Prince Caspian

During the next four days, the students finished reading the novel and prepared for the essay test. When students met at the reading table to discuss each of the last two chapters, there was an even greater emphasis put on the active-reader strategy of monitoring your understanding (which is a part of every reading lesson). At these times they were told to look back on the whole story (make summaries in your head) and ask for clarification if there was anything they did not understand. They were also encouraged to go back over their notes/study guides to see if they understood everything they had written down. By reminding the students to use their active-reader strategy of self-monitoring comprehension and using the fix-up strategy of asking for clarification when meaning breaks down, Mrs. Rauch put the students in charge of their learning. They were responsible for making sure they had everything they needed to be successful in this test, and she would be there to give them any support they asked for prior to the test.

Mrs. Rauch gave her students one more opportunity to take control of their learning when she gave them the choice of how they would spend the final reading period. They were to use this period to study for the test, but had a choice of how they would spend their time. The consensus was that they would each study with a partner (their version of cooperative learning).

The next day the students took this test and, to Mrs. Rauch's delight and credit, all passed the test. Some students were pleased with how they had done on the test; others were disappointed they had not done better. As is always the case in Mrs. Rauch's class, the test became a learning opportunity for both students and teacher.

Self-evaluation is another characteristic of Mrs. Rauch's teaching. She learned that if students are going to study in pairs in preparation for a test, **they need very specific guidelines about how to spend their time.** This would become an objective for her in preparing her students for similar tests in the future. She also learned that her students could benefit from some explicit lessons and practice in writing essay answers. As one of her students had so aptly commented, it is putting ideas together in an essay — "the thinking part" — that is often the hard part of writing an essay answer. Integrating notes to write an essay answer would continue to be a priority objective in the writing lessons Mrs. Rauch prepared for her students.

Taking (and passing) the essay test helped convince the students that categorizing information does in fact help them remember. The test also helped them realize that, in preparing for an essay test, predicting questions and brainstorming ideas that answer the question are not always enough. They came to the conclusion that practice putting the ideas together ahead of time can be a big help and that they should have practiced writing out the essay answers as part of their preparation for the test.

THE VOYAGE OF THE DAWN TREADER

This book, the sequel to Prince Caspian, and the third book of the *Chronicles of Narnia*, was assigned as homework reading just after the two reading groups had completed *Prince Caspian*. The purpose of the assignment was to provide these students with an opportunity to practice, semi-independently, the categorizing strategies they had been taught as they read *Prince Caspian*. Although the reading was done at home and emphasis was put on making study guides and collecting information on their own, the groups met for a few minutes at the start of the instructional reading lesson each day to discuss this book. Students were asked to share the strategies they were using and how these strategies helped. Mrs. Rauch asked whether anyone had any questions or wanted clarification regarding strategies and/or content. This provided an ongoing review of the categorizing strategies and gave Mrs. Rauch the opportunity to guide and cue the use of skills and strategies and to re-teach, clarify and elaborate, if needed, by individual students. As in the earlier books, students were guided in the gathering and categorizing of names and places, of ideas relating to theme and author's message and of characteristics of the story that fit the genre adventure story. They used the information in these categories to predict essay questions and prepare for an essay test.

SING DOWN THE MOON

Continuing her year-long objective of increasing student awareness and control of classifying as a strategy for organizing and remembering information, Mrs. Rauch chose the novel *Sing Down The Moon* as the vehicle. In this book the students would find and categorize examples of an author's point of view in order to decide whether to agree (with the author) or disagree.

On February 2 and 3, 1989, the introductory lessons were presented by Mrs. Rauch to the entire class. Since these lessons would require a high level of critical thinking, Mrs. Rauch realized she would have to review and reteach this thinking skill, taught at a more elementary level in previous years.

Mrs. Rauch introduced this unit of study by explaining that as they read *Sing Down The Moon* the students would be learning another classifying strategy. They would be finding and organizing examples of an author's point of view so that they could decide whether or not they agreed with this point of view.

When it became clear to her that few of her students had a clear understanding of the concept **point of view**, Mrs. Rauch gave examples relating to the American history they were studying — contrasting views held by North and South on slavery, etc. Once Mrs. Rauch felt the students could see what it meant to agree or disagree with a point of view, she explained that to form or take a point of view required critical thinking. She solicited the students' understanding of the various levels of thinking and asked when and where they had been expected to think at the literal, inferential, and critical levels. She shared several personal experiences to demonstrate her use of critical thinking as a child and as an adult. These personal experiences seemed to capture the students' interest and clarify for them what critical thinking "looks like." Mrs. Rauch invited the students to share experiences about when they had used critical thinking, such as thinking through whether Benchmark should build a cafeteria. At the conclusion of the students' analysis of the cafeteria situation, Mrs. Rauch said, "I just wanted to give you an example of how you do think carefully about things in deciding what you believe."

The students were then asked what they thought would be a good definition of critical thinking. As students made suggestions, the teacher wrote their suggestions on the board and helped them shape the various contributions into a definition. The end result was: "To think reasonably and carefully about something we are to decide or what we are going to do."

Mrs. Rauch asked them to relate critical thinking to reading. "Have you ever had to think carefully about your reading in order to decide what the author believes or what his message is?" Numerous suggestions were made, but none was an example of critical thinking. Mrs. Rauch said, "Where have we looked to find the author's message?" Students answered, "Themes."

"So sometimes, and especially in reading, you're not only thinking about what you believe, you are thinking about what the author believes, so you have to think that through very carefully."

To reinforce the rationale for analyzing point of view, as well as the transfer of strategies across the curriculum, Mrs. Rauch asked the student to think about when in their own lives analyzing a point of view might be important and when and where it might be important in other areas of the curriculum. Two examples given related to responding to advertising and voting in a democracy. After some discussion as to why analyzing point of view was important in both of these contexts, Mrs. Rauch asked, "By the same token, why is it important to decide what an author's point of view is and how he is getting to that point of view?" The students made several suggestions, then the teacher continued,

"So the main reason we are teaching you to analyze what an author believes is so you can decide whether you want to believe it, too, or whether you want to believe something different."

"My reading groups and Mrs. Gutman's reading groups are going to be reading *Sing Down The Moon*. This is a story about Indians who were moved by Kit Carson from their home to a reservation. We wanted to give you some background on Kit Carson before you get into the book, so I'm going to read you a short biography about him. We're going to find examples of the author's point of view, either about Kit Carson or about the Indians."

Mrs. Rauch reviewed with students the categorizing they had done in *Prince Caspian* and *Voyage of the Dawn Treader*.

"In this new book, we can again make use of this strategy to organize and remember information. As we organize this information, you will see that it will help us to analyze the author's point of view. Then we can decide whether we agree or disagree. Now, in order to categorize examples of the author's point of view, we are going to put them into three categories. The categories show three ways an author could show the point of view he is trying to get across. I will put these categories on the board and you can use them to make study guides."

"One category includes 'things a character says or does' (writes on board). Now, another way you could figure out the examples we are going to do could be through 'author's description' (writes on board). A third way would be 'through situations the characters themselves are in'" (Writes on board).

Mrs. Rauch then read several excerpts (a sort of "preview") from the book and the students discussed the excerpts and decided which category they would put them under. They seemed to have caught onto this concept.

Then Mrs. Rauch began reading Kit Carson's biography to the class. She would pause periodically to solicit the students' input about the author's point of view and write the example on the chalkboard under one of the three categories of evidence.

After about thirty minutes of reading, with many illustrations and much discussion, Mrs. Rauch caught a student doing just what she wanted, and she reinforced that behavior:

S: It's not like the Indians are being mean, because the first thing that happened is that they took the Indian's land. The author is making it look like the Indians are wrong.

T: So then, what are you doing now? You are doing something very good. What are you doing?

S: Being critical?

T: You are being critical. You are deciding — you are taking what you know in your background about this subject — and you are deciding whether you are believing in the author's point of view.

At the end of the class, Mrs. Rauch again related the taking notes in categories on the board (as she was reading Kit Carson's biography) to their categorizing as they read novels earlier in the year. She elicited from the students what objective they had been working on in class and what critical thinking means.

As Mrs. Rauch continued to read the Kit Carson biography aloud for the next several days, she consistently required the students to recall and organize major ideas they had gained from previous days' reading and to relate this analyzing of author's point of view to categorizing they had learned earlier and in other areas of the curriculum. Discussions became increasingly lively. These students seemed to be enjoying looking for the author's point of view. You sensed that they felt like detectives although the analogy was never made. Finally, Mrs. Rauch said, "What we see happening here is that you are all beginning to do some critical thinking. What are you actually doing? We said critical thinking is to think carefully about something. What are you thinking carefully about in this discussion that we are having?"

S: Well, the author doesn't like Indians.

T: You've been thinking carefully about the author's examples about the Indians. And what did you decide?"

S: What the author believes.

T: What the author believes. Fine. And then of course another step after that, which you have already begun to explore, is to decide whether you agree or not. Okay. Good job. I think you guys came exactly to the point we hoped you would. We weren't really sure whether you would be able to handle this or not, but I think we have a successful beginning.

As a preliminary to starting *Sing Down The Moon*, the main vehicle for learning how to analyze an author's point of view, Mrs. Rauch reviewed what her objective regarding point of view was, how this categorizing strategy was done, and why and when it was important. Students had difficulty explaining why it was important to be aware of the author's point of view and Mrs. Rauch related the importance to social studies and newspaper reading. Students seemed convinced of the importance of reading critically in those materials.

The students surveyed their new book, and were asked to predict (and explain their prediction) the point of view of the author. Finally, one of the careful readers pointed out that it said on the cover that the story is written from the Indian's point of view. They all had a good laugh.

After pre-reading activities, and before they read each day, Mrs. Rauch set the students up for a successful discussion by providing them with a worksheet on which there were a few open-ended questions "to use in monitoring your comprehension." They were not required to write answers to the questions, but they were asked to "rehearse" the answers in their heads. To structure their gathering of data reflecting the author's point of view, they were given study guides consisting of a page for each kind of evidence that had previously been on the board.

The first time the group met for discussion, several students began by asking for clarification on various points. In addition, Mrs. Rauch noted that the examples students had gathered to illustrate the author's point of view were very general, for the most part. The students were definitely struggling with this task. What follows is an unusual amount of teacher talk for Mrs. Rauch, as her pattern was to be much more interactive, with students usually doing as much or more telling then she. It was clear that Mrs. Rauch felt the students needed some re-explanation.

> T: Yes, we are trying to find examples. Any examples. Whether they are situations the author creates, whether they are descriptions he gives, whether they are things he has his characters say or do. Something that gives us a clue as to what his point of view may be. Now, do we know at the beginning, definitely, what his point of view is? Are we expected to know after reading the first chapter? Hmmm. (Models.) "Oh, yes, okay, this is his point of view now, I'm going to collect this information." When do you make a conclusion about his point of view?

> S: After you...after you start skimming the problem?

> T: Somewhere along the way you start to test your ideas. You say to yourself — it is like making a prediction, you know how you keep revising your predictions — somewhere along the way you may say to yourself, as we did, "This author is pro-Indian, this author is biased towards the Indians." Now you may read along and say to yourself, "Now wait a minute, this sounds to me like he is against Indians. Maybe I am going to have to change my idea about the author's point of view." Or, you may stay with it. So it is a

little like making predictions in that you might keep revising your thoughts on the matter. It's not something you would absolutely have carved in stone. Now, yesterday we began to collect examples of the author's point of view, either toward the — do you remember what the two groups are that we are considering the author's point of view about?

S: The Indians and the white man.

T: Yes. The Indians and the white man. We decided, well, I had told you that what I had done was to start to list examples of what I thought was a point of view, the author's point of view about the Indians in one place and the author's point of view about the white man in another place. We are using the same three categories — what the characters say or think, how the author describes the characters, and the situations the characters find themselves in. Now, remember that I told you that later we were going to go through the steps that you go through when you are thinking critically, but I asked you to keep in mind the very first step when you are looking for these examples. What is the very first step that we want to keep in mind when we are thinking critically about authors' points of view?

S: What we want to find out?

T: Yes.

S: Think about your goals?

T: Think about your goals, because it is easy to kind of get into a situation where you find a nice description and you write it down, but it doesn't really have anything to do with the author's point of view. So you want to make sure you are thinking, does this tell me anything about the author's point of view? If it does, I'll write it down. If it doesn't, I'm going to just pass on that one. Now, here are a couple of examples you found yesterday. This is under what characters say. "Last summer they," and that was referring to the Long Knives, "threatened to come back and burn our village." And somebody suggested that this was an example of the author's point of view about which group?

And in this manner the group reviewed the several examples discussed the previous day that seemed to suggest the author's point of view. Mrs. Rauch also shared, as she often did, her thinking as she was reading: "You know what helped me with that, I was thinking about the Kit Carson book. I kept comparing in my mind that author's point of view and how this author is developing her point of view about the Indians."

These daily discussions continued, and although the students were initially frustrated with categorizing examples of author's point of view, the teacher's re-explanations, plus her accepting and supportive attitude, seemed to have carried them through the frustration they felt, to a feeling of confidence about handling the assignment. It could only have been instances like the following that supported this change:

> S: How about, gave the impression?
>
> T: Okay, gave the impression. I like that. (Writing on the board.) Yes, you are right. She didn't actually say those words, it was the look on her face that the narrator interpreted. Well, I think you guys got pretty much of what I picked out. Let me see if I have anything else here. (The teacher flips through her study guides.) You got everything that I was looking for! Did anybody else find something in addition that we haven't gone over? You did a really fine job of picking out those examples. So now, let's kind of sum up for a minute.

By the start of the second week, the students had collected and categorized quite a few examples of the author's point of view. It seemed to Mrs. Rauch that they were ready to move on to developing tentative conclusions about this point of view. As is characteristic of Mrs. Rauch's instruction, she moved into this phase by first reviewing their definition of critical thinking and relating it to what they had been doing so far and how that would help them with the objective.

> T: We are going to be talking about Chapters 7 and 8 today. Keep in mind that our objective is to do critical thinking. When we talk about critical thinking what we're really talking about is thinking very carefully, very reasonably about the material that you've been reading in order to decide what we want to believe or sometimes to decide what the author believes. Now, in this book we're using the characters in order to figure out what?
>
> S: The author's point of view.
>
> T: And you're quite right. Often the author speaks through some of the characters. Do you get a sense of who the characters are the author may be speaking through?
>
> S: I think he's speaking through Bright Morning.
>
> T: It's likely. Remember we said that we don't want to say absolutely that we know what an author's point of view is, it could switch. But it seems that way so far.

Often during discussions of author's point of view, Mrs. Rauch would summarize. This is one example:

> T: So we have these people with their old culture and their religion and their way of life, and on the other hand we have these other people with their power gotten from guns and technology trying to force the Indians to do what they want, basically. Is there anything bad about the Indians, so far?

The students respond to this question, and again Mrs. Rauch summarizes.

> T: Well, I think it's like what you said. They're holding on to the old culture. This is what they've always done. I think you're right. They have no leader to bind them all together. So we have this positive view of the Indians and this negative view of the whites so far.
>
> Every step in Mrs. Rauch's lesson plans exhibited the care with which her lessons had been planned. Toward the end of the book the students were to discover another reason why (in addition to providing background) she had read to them the biography of Kit Carson.

> "...we have almost the opposite view of the white man in this (*Sing Down The Moon*) book. The reason I brought up the Kit Carson picture again, the other author's viewpoint of Kit Carson, is that in these next chapters we're going to be reading about Kit Carson, although they don't mention him by name here. He is the person who is leading this group of Long Knives. So I would like you to keep in mind that picture of Kit Carson from the other book and then see how you think the author of this book is painting Kit Carson and what bias he had."

The teacher's pattern continued to be to summarize at the beginning of each lesson the progress the group had made to date, as she did the day the last chapters were read:

> T: We have pretty much gone through the steps of what you need to do if you think critically. Back in the beginning, you had to keep in mind what you wanted to find out. Remember that we said if you found a great quote somebody said, but it didn't show a point of view, that wouldn't be something you wanted to write down on your sheet. You did a really great job of keeping in your mind that you were looking for examples of the author's viewpoints. And then we talked

about being open-minded, and what does that mean, to be open minded?

S: It means that you just take in any point of view and you don't...

T: You don't judge. We were getting examples of the whites being bad and the Indians being not as bad. We needed to keep an open mind about what the author believed. We had to think about both of those positions and say, "I'm not sure yet what the author believes." But now we're at the point where we are beginning to take a position and we've already generated some character traits for each group that we think seem to be, at this point, the point of view expressed by the author...

There was a bit more discussion, then Mrs. Rauch summarized again.

T: ...So, that's where we stand at this point and now we're going to solidify our position. What do we believe the author is telling us about these two groups of people? We're going to finish this book...I do want to give you one word of advice about this Postscript. It isn't neutral. It does take a point of view, and later on, when we start to talk about the essay you will write on Tuesday, I'm going to give you some material that gives you a neutral view of what the Indians' and the white people's conflict was all about."

After completing this book the students wrote essays in class on the author's point of view. Mrs. Rauch and Mrs. Gutman wrote an essay on the Kit Carson biography which they shared with the students as a model. They helped the students select examples from their notes they might use in writing their essays and these were discussed. The notes were used by the students to write the essay in class over two class periods.

At the end of February, all the students in the class were introduced to *Johnny Tremain*. During the reading of this book students did part of their reading in class and part of it at home. This book, too, was used to gather information reflecting point of view and to analyze the author's point of view.

Section 4:
Implementing A Strategy Program

Engaging, Training, and Supporting Teachers and Administrators in Developing a Content-Process Curriculum: Principles and Practices

If you have read to this point, there is a good chance we have convinced you of the value of integrating the teaching of content and process and that you are anxious to get started. You even may be thinking about attending a few workshops or trying to convince someone else to work with you in teaching thinking across the curriculum. Great! But before you stumble into any of the roadblocks we have encountered, let us share with you some of our experiences and conclusions related to engaging, training, and supporting a faculty involved in curriculum change.

In this final chapter we discuss the lessons we have learned from a history of change and seven principles for implementing curriculum change we have derived as a result. You will learn how our over-zealousness regarding an exciting idea on occasion has proved to be a roadblock. Carried away by our enthusiasm, we neglected such basic principles as selecting an innovation that meets the demonstrated needs of students or involving the staff in planning the innovation. These two principles, and others such as helping teachers acquire the knowledge they need, fostering an attitude of "becoming," and creating a safe environment, are fundamental to the success of engaging, training, and supporting a faculty in developing a content-process curriculum and are discussed in this final chapter. Two final principles we discuss are: expect change to take time and require ongoing support; and set aside time for reflection and renewal.

Principle 1: Select Innovations That Meet Demonstrated Needs of Students

A powerful source of motivation for teachers to implement change is the frustration they feel when they are not meeting the needs of their students to the degree they would like. The importance of taking into account this frustration, and selecting an innovation that addresses teacher concerns about student needs, was the first lesson we learned in our efforts to implement change at Benchmark and is our first principle for implementing change.

An Example: Twenty years ago our first attempts at innovation were to guide teachers to teach directed reading-thinking lessons and decoding skills. We assumed that teaching students to read was our teachers' primary concern. After all, poor reading ability was the reason most children were attending Benchmark. What we discovered, however, was that teachers were more concerned about classroom management and appropriate seatwork (Gaskins, 1988a). Teachers were struggling to reconcile their philosophies of ideal teacher-student interactions with the reality of chaos. Student choice of learning activities and a voice in how to use their time sounded exciting in the abstract, but these concepts were not working for us. Teachers were having trouble getting students' attention to teach *any* lesson. Before teachers could process and implement ideas about reading instruction, they wanted and needed guidance and support regarding classroom management. We quickly discovered that in-service programs about behavior modification and contingency management were much more welcome than those on how to teach phonics or a directed reading-thinking activity.

Another example: Teachers were also frustrated because the commercial seatwork materials available at the time appeared to be irrelevant to our students' needs. What our students needed was to do a whole lot of reading and there was not much reading on a workbook page.

We temporarily suspended inservice on reading instruction while we researched answers to the classroom management and seatwork dilemmas. Possible solutions were tried in the classrooms. Classroom management and seatwork became more satisfactory.

These early successes, due to making decisions about change based on student needs and teacher concerns rather than lofty ideals, buoyed our spirits for attacking other areas of concern.

The foundation for across-the-curriculum strategy teaching was laid over many years beginning with a program to teach students strategies for coping with difficult social studies texts, an issue that was of great concern to teachers (Gaskins, 1981). This was followed by projects to teach students strategies to cope with maladaptive learning styles (Gaskins & Baron, 1985) and word recognition problems (Gaskins, et al., 1988), again student-centered issues that concerned teachers. Next, was our 1987-88 pilot strategy project to join content and process (see Chapter 6); the issue again was our students' difficulties in processing the information taught in social studies classes.

Thus, when Benchmark embarked on developing a program to teach thinking strategies across the curriculum, teachers recognized the program's potential for meeting a host of needs — those growing out of information processing problems, maladaptive style problems, and learning and thinking problems in general. They were enthusiastic; however, many were initially intimidated at the prospect of volunteering for such an ambitious project. An initial step in implementing the pilot project was to enlist our first disciple by convincing at least one teacher that joining content and strategy instruction was worth trying.

We have discovered that change projects that address staff concerns about students' needs have the most potential for success. Once the student needs of greatest concern are identified by teachers, possible ways of meeting those needs should be discussed and studied by the staff. Based on these discussions and research, plans should be made by the staff for implementing an innovation to meet the identified student needs. We believe, along with others (e.g. Fullan, 1982, and Klein, 1989), that staff initiative in identifying needs, and staff involvement in planning a curriculum are critical ingredients for a successful change project.

Principle 2: Involve the Staff

If you want to increase the chances of staff follow-through on a good idea, even when the good idea meets a student need about which the staff is concerned, you must involve the staff in formulating the program. The greater the staff involvement in planning the program, the higher the likelihood the program will be implemented. We learned this principle when teachers were not sufficiently involved with a great idea.

Our First Example: Our search for a program to address our students' dysfunctional responses to instruction resulted in two projects: gathering data on the characteristics of students who had attended Benchmark over a five-year period (Gaskins, 1984) and an experiment to develop a program to help students cope with three maladaptive cognitive styles most prevalent in our population — impulsivity, rigidity and non-persistence (Gaskins & Baron, 1985). We were fortunate to enlist a well-known researcher, Jonathan Baron, to help us set up the experiment and to plan a program of cognitive-behavior modification. This program encouraged students in the experimental group to "take charge" of their individual styles and to replace their previously dysfunctional styles with reflectivity, flexibility, and persistence. The two trainers administering the program also served as mentors to the students they each taught, meeting regularly with them for training in small groups and individually to support their efforts to adapt their styles. The results of the eight-month study were not only statistically significant, but exciting. Students in the experimental group exhibited more reflectivity, flexibility, and persistence than the control group on both laboratory tests and teacher ratings (Baron, Badgio, & Gaskins, 1986).

We were surprised to find this project had relatively little impact on the school as a whole. Almost everyone thought the mentor program was outstanding, but since most of the staff had only been observers on the periphery of the project, they were not able to carry any of the techniques into their own practice. We learned the importance of staff involvement in an innovation if it is to take root and grow. When the time came to embark on our next project, we knew where we must start.

Another Example: This book is written near the completion of a three-year research and development project to develop learning and thinking strategies across the curriculum. From the time this project was initiated, we have held staff meetings for the purpose of explaining the project, gathering reactions, and updating the staff on the status of the project. Volunteer participants were solicited. At these meetings staff members who had observed the pilot class for combining content and process (see Chapter 6) also shared what they had observed. Some even shared how they had begun to experiment with strategy teaching. They also shared their successes and the frustrations they had experienced. The staff seemed to enjoy particularly hearing the authors tell of their mishaps as they attempted strategy instruction. These tales appeared to make teachers more willing to experiment with new ideas for strategy instruction. As they became involved, they soon realized that none of us held the success formula for strategy teaching and that any strategy program we developed was going to be a joint effort.

The more opportunities there were for staff involvement, and the more frequent the communications about what was happening regarding the project, the more comfortable the teachers felt about the idea of teaching strategies across the curriculum. Teachers became involved in numerous ways. Several traced a teacher's strategy instruction over a period of months (see Chapter 10). Others wrote plans for strategy lessons and shared them with other teachers for feedback. Some participated in Psych 101 (see Chapter 7). Some also volunteered to react to manuscripts that were being written to codify our thinking about applying cognitive science to the classroom. As the strategies-across-the-curriculum project progressed, sharing continued, both formally and informally, as teachers discussed their attempts at strategy instruction and solicited ideas and assistance.

As with many new projects, and despite the fact that there had been numerous and frequent opportunities for staff involvement, this project has had varying degrees of support from the faculty. Although the need for our students to know and apply strategies is acknowledged by all, not all faculty members are stressing strategy instruction to the same degree, nor with the same level of commitment, comfort, or expertise. Naturally, we feel that it would be in the best interests of our students if all our teachers would implement the program fully. However, at this point in developing the program, participation in the project is voluntary. It is our firm belief that the only teachers who will be successful in implementing the program are those who are enthusiastic about the merits of the program and are willing to acquire the knowledge to implement it. Fortunately, with the increasing success of our students, more and more teachers are willing to become involved.

Principle 3: Help Teachers Acquire Knowledge

A knowledge base is crucial to the success of any innovation. When knowledge is lacking on the part of either teachers or innovators, it can be the stumbling block to implementing a desired change. To illustrate this point, we will relate the initial failure and subsequent success of a program at Benchmark.

An Example: In the early eighties Ann Brown and her colleagues lectured and wrote about helping students become aware of and take control of factors affecting success in learning. Those of us who attended these lectures and/or read the articles and chapters returned to the school full of enthusiasm about developing students' awareness and control. We told other staff members that they should be teaching students about awareness and control, that they should teach students how to set goals, plan, monitor, and self-assess. Although we were able to convince the majority of the staff that this was an important goal, those who were taking a lead in advocating this innovation were imprecise and tentative about how to accomplish the goal. There was little, if any, published material at the time about how to guide students to develop awareness and control. As a result, only a few teachers were willing to experiment with implementing such a program in their classrooms.

Staff leaders soon recognized the need to help teachers acquire more knowledge about the factors affecting success in learning as well as the confidence to experiment with metacognitive instruction. They began sharing with other staff members tales about the lessons a few teachers were piloting and analyzed together what seemed to work and not work. The director and supervisors taught lessons to model metacognitive instruction for teachers, and arranged inservice and sharing meetings about teaching awareness and control. We read and discussed the professional literature searching for guidance. Once the staff had the knowledge they needed to implement a metacognitive program, a great deal of enthusiasm resulted. Teachers began to take initiative in implementing such a program in their classrooms.

Our initial failure to enlist teachers in implementing a program to promote awareness and control taught us the importance of teachers having the knowledge required to implement change. When we were ready to undertake our next big project, helping teachers acquire the relevant knowledge became a top priority. The faculty's knowledge base for developing the learning and thinking strategies program has been accumulating gradually since the program's inception. Those who attend the research seminar have been discussing the theories and research underlying across-the-curriculum strategy instruction for a number of years. The faculty has attended inservice meetings, observed pilot teachers, experimented with methods of fostering thinking, attended workshops and conferences, and discussed ideas with colleagues — all in support of gaining a knowledge base. Our resource teacher taught model strategy lessons in classes where new teachers and teaching assistants were being trained, and supervisors and the director have also taught model lessons.

How does a school administration achieve productive staff involvement in an innovation project? How does it help teachers acquire the knowledge they need to understand the possible causes of the problems students are experiencing, as well as what possible solutions have been tried or recommended to ameliorate the problem? What are the essential components of a program to help teachers acquire the knowledge necessary for innovation? Benchmark's experience suggests that such a program requires:

1. **Leadership**: someone taking a leadership role in professional development.

2. **Sharing**: a social system which fosters active collaboration.

3. **Observing**: the development of images of what the innovation should look like.

4. **Training**: the provision of ongoing inservice and of professional literature for reading and discussions.

Leading. The drive to support the faculty in acquiring the knowledge base needs to be spearheaded by a decisive, visible, and knowledgeable lead teacher, supervisor, or administrator. These leaders must think of themselves as "adult developers" who ensure that both *adequate funds* and *release time* are allotted for *ongoing* professional development. To fulfill this role, school leaders must value and work toward professional growth and change *in themselves* before they can expect growth and change in others. They must also respond to adults as the unique individuals they are and provide individual-ized, professional development opportunities, i.e., opportunities beyond those aimed at "group growth."

School leaders at Benchmark foster professional growth in a number of ways. Supervisors meet weekly with their supervisees, participate in classroom instruction either by conducting demonstra-tion lessons or by observing and giving feedback, and serve as a sounding board for or co-developer of units of instruction. A teacher's communication with his or her supervisor often is further enhanced by use of an interactive journal. Using the interactive journal, the teacher is encouraged to write questions, objectives, plans, and areas of focus for the supervisor who then observes and writes notes about the lessons, as well as asks and answers questions in the journal. The teacher then reflects on the notes and responds in the journal to questions and suggestions. This is especially effective when times to meet individually are at a premium.

Sharing. Regardless of the combination of staff development options one selects, the key to having the staff learn complex academic content and new teaching strategies seems to be an active state of interchange, a **productive collaborative atmosphere**. Within such social systems collegiality is valued and encouraged, and sharing among staff members is common. Active peer interchange is fostered by leaders who encourage and/or orchestrate frequent opportuni-ties for discussions. For example, a leader might say, "I think Dawn just tried that. You might want to ask her about it."

Sharing also takes place when a Benchmark teacher meets weekly with his or her supervisor, as well as during the weekly meetings with the director. The agenda for these meetings usually is set by the teacher, who may choose to discuss an administrator's observation, a lesson taught to his or her students, problems with a student, difficulties in implementing a strategy lesson, or the appli-cation of an idea from a journal article or book.

Faculty members share with one another, in formal sharing meetings (e.g., weekly team meetings, teacher-led inservice) and informally on a small group or individual basis. The very act of talking about an idea among colleagues helps a concept become explicit. With this new understanding, change is possible and ideas take shape. In such an environment, those in the most active state of growth inspire others to get involved.

Observing. Change is facilitated by teachers observing others teach. An image of what an innovation looks like is truly worth a thousand words. Observation is particularly influential in advancing the cause of change when teachers are observing an innovation for which they see a need and about which they have some choice regarding whether or not to adopt, adapt, or merely observe and learn. Observations can be arranged between teachers with an agreement to share notes or critique one another or as just a visit to learn what another teacher is doing. At Benchmark, teachers not only observe other teachers teach, but they frequently invite their supervisor or the director to present a series of demonstration lessons in their classrooms.

As a result of observations, the teachers who are to implement the change acquire not only images, but an intellectual understanding of why the innovation is beneficial and how it is to be implemented. Understanding the why and how and accepting the rationale into one's belief system are the starting points on a road that leads to commitment and mastery. Images incorporate one's beliefs and, according to Au (1988), are the organizers of knowledge. And, it is the images of what one believes teaching should look like that guide classroom practice.

Training. Workshops, faculty meetings, conferences, courses, and discussion of professional literature are an integral part of the professional's life at Benchmark. For example, a ten-day August inservice is provided each summer for new teachers and teaching assistants, monthly inservice meetings are presented by national experts or our own faculty members, and a research seminar meets weekly. In addition, teachers regularly attend national, state, and local conferences. However, the effectiveness of any one of these practices in bringing about change in the classroom depends on several factors.

Foremost is that **training must be ongoing** rather than consist of a few one-shot workshops. One or two inservice exposures to a skill or an idea, without follow-up support, are ineffective in bringing about change. For a new skill or idea to be owned by a teacher, the teacher must go through the process of transforming it to fit the students, subject matter, goals, and the way the classroom is managed. All these need to be considered if the skill or idea is to be applied appropriately and forcefully.

Another essential factor is that the plan for professional development must have an impact not only on what teachers *do*, but on what teachers *think*, their belief system. Doing, which involves use of materials, new skills, and new behavior, too often receives the bulk of attention, yet it is the teachers' belief systems — their philosophy, theories, knowledge, and attitudes — that will determine both the amount of effort the teacher expends in implementing the change and the quality of the moment-by-moment decisions made while a teacher is providing instruction. Knowledge about the rationale underlying an innovation is crucial to bringing about changes in beliefs and attitudes.

In addition, an ample supply of professional journals and books needs to be provided in the school's professional library. At Bench-mark, teachers sign up for the professional journals they are inter-ested in reading. These are routed to them when they are received. Numerous books are added to the professional collection each year. Both the books and journals are discussed in weekly research semi-nars.

Our hunches about the importance of training, as well as other aspects of knowledge acquisition, were confirmed in a recent study (Pressley, Gaskins, Cunicelli, Burdick, Schaub-Matt, Lee, and Pow-ell, in press). In this study of teachers' opinions about strategy teaching, the factors that influenced the strategy teaching (and the percentages) are: interacting with other teachers (97%), reading and reacting to Benchmark manuscripts (87%), reading professional articles (87%), attending monthly inservice with outside experts (81%), interacting with supervising teacher (81%), interacting with school director (81%), observing other teachers (74%), attending team meetings and other sharing meetings (68%), attending research seminar (65%), reading professional books (42%), observing the director teach (35%), and observing the supervising teacher teach (26%). (See also Au, 1988; Fullan, 1982; Hall & Hord, 1987; Joyce & Weil, 1986; and Levine, 1989 for further ideas on supporting teachers in the process of acquiring knowledge.)

Principle 4: Foster an Attitude of Becoming

It is our contention that a school composed of teachers who feel they have not yet "arrived" is the very school that has a high probability of successfully implementing curriculum change. Those of us in leadership positions began creating this atmosphere in the seventies by modeling for the staff the attitude that we still had a lot of learning to do, and by valuing and reinforcing any interest the staff had in professional growth and change. The attitude that "I can always get better" seems to lead naturally to an interest in professional growth and change.

Our experiences in implementing curriculum change and the conclusions of those who study change in schools suggest that this attitude of "there is still a lot to learn" is a key factor in bringing about change. Researchers consistently note that schools which stand out because of the quality of their programs are those schools with a faculty which is constantly in the state of *becoming* (Klein, 1989; Lieberman & Rosenholtz, 1987).

An attitude of *becoming* does not just happen. It needs to be nurtured by an administration that places top priority on providing students with the best possible education. One of the things we do to accomplish this goal is to engage in ongoing formal and informal research and development to identify and revamp areas of the school's program in need of improvement. Each teacher's daily interaction with our students, and our placement counselor's follow-up of each graduate, provide the faculty with input regarding the strengths and weaknesses of our programs.

An Example: An occasion for putting into practice our belief that we still have a lot to learn about meeting the needs of students with reading problems became vividly obvious during the early eighties. Teachers were dissatisfied with their success in alleviating the tremendous difficulty most of the students who enter Benchmark have in decoding unknown words. Despite the best decoding instruction the teachers knew how to impart, a high percentage of our students seemed to have no independent strategy they could use to unlock an unknown word except to guess based on context. The faculty's desire to become better teachers of decoding led to what has been at this writing an eight-year (and still ongoing) research and development project regarding word identification (Gaskins, et al., 1988).

The attitude that they still had a lot to learn about how students break the code led the faculty to spend the 1982-83 school year reviewing the educational and linguistic research looking for clues as to what decoding strategies we should be teaching students. Chomsky (1972) and Cunningham (1975-76) seemed to hold the insights for which we were searching. We invited Patricia Cunningham to present an inservice to the staff regarding the approach to decoding that she was recommending, an analogy approach. The staff became enthused. Using a chapter Cunningham had written (Cunningham, Moore, Cunningham, & Moore, 1983) as their guidebook, many of the 14 head teachers began inventing their own programs. Ideas were pooled and a program was written. Richard Anderson of the Center for the Study of Reading heard of the project and initiated a research project to collect data and, along with Cunningham, helped formalize the process of researching and developing a word identification program. The staff was excited about what they learned from that experience, as well as the product that resulted — manuals with daily student lessons and explicit instructions for the teacher.

The word identification project was a great success for many reasons. The most important reason, undoubtedly, was that the program met a very visible student need. Furthermore, the word identification program was faculty-initiated, and was driven by the faculty's desire to become better teachers of decoding. Through this project we learned once again that an innovation has the best chance of succeeding if it meets a student need that is of concern to the faculty. We also learned that when a faculty has the attitude of *becoming*, the process of change can be an exciting adventure.

Principle 5: Create a Safe Environment for Expressing Concerns

The attitude of *becoming* is often found where there also is a safe environment for expressing concerns. Teachers and administrators who value professional growth and curriculum improvement learn to regard concerns as valuable input and come to realize the importance of creating an environment where all concerns receive a fair hearing.

An Example: When we shared with the faculty the vision of creating self-regulated learners — learners who knew how to set goals, plan, and self-assess — by implementing a program of strategy instruction across the curriculum, the announcement was accompanied by a wave of anxiety and a bevy of concerns: How can we squeeze one more thing into our already crowded school day? How will we know how to teach strategies if the program is just now being developed? Where are we going to find the time to learn how to teach this way? Why can't someone teach a few strategy courses to the students rather than having the whole faculty change their programs?

Opportunities had to be provided for these and other concerns to be expressed and addressed. We discovered that, when we looked at each concern from the point of view of the one expressing it, we could see the legitimacy of most concerns. There also were misperceptions. By providing a safe environment for expressing concerns, we had the opportunity to clarify them individually rather than allowing them to go underground and undermine the success of the program. Many open forums for discussions about our vision have been held and continue to be held. We have found that often a teacher expressing a concern also offers a nugget of genius which we can use to improve the program.

We are the first to admit that there are days when genuine concerns sound more like complaints and we feel weary from making adjustments to the program. In hindsight, though, we always can see the value in having provided the safe environment where all concerns are heard and considered.

Environment. Our theory of change suggests that any idea for change, no matter how fitting, how well researched and well planned, will play a viable role in the life of a school only if a school culture exists that is supportive of change. Orchestrating a change in the way teachers teach is a delicate process. To be successful, the innovator must be well grounded in an understanding of the change process and help create a satisfying and safe school climate which also has a sense of excitement, where concerns can be expressed, and which comes to be an energizing professional ambience.

Visitors to Benchmark School tell us that the faculty's openness, both to express concerns and to change, seems to be part of a more general ambience which pervades the school. This ambience is no accident. We work hard to create an environment that is not only "energizing" (Joyce & Weil, 1986), but safe for one to express concerns, inadequacies, or a need for help. Staff morale is a priority. From the moment people walk through the door of the school we want all that they see and hear to mirror the professionalism and dedication of the staff and faculty.

How does an administration create an environment in which teachers feel safe to express concerns? It begins by basing administrative decisions primarily on two factors: first, the best interests of students and, second, the support the faculty must have to accomplish the task without its being overwhelming. We strive to keep morale high by listening to the concerns of the staff and by finding ways to make the school an exciting and satisfying place to work and learn. Trust and camaraderie are fostered by applauding those who are willing to ask for help, yet are also good problem solvers. Teacher ownership of ideas is developed by encouraging and supporting teachers as they try ideas and adapt them to the needs of their students. Because we are careful to recognize their efforts and reinforce their victories, the faculty exudes pride in the school and in what each of them is contributing to making this a convivial setting in which children prosper personally and academically. Without striving for this kind of school culture, it is doubtful that teachers will express their concerns. Once expressed, a teacher concern must, of course, be addressed.

Concerns. A lesson we learned, often the hard way, was that we must listen to staff members' concerns as they wrestle with the pain and confusion often associated with change. We find that teachers and supervisors need to be aware that, with each new change, faculty members experience a temporary sense of disequilibrium. We each seem to pass through the "zones of uncertainty" that Schon (1971) speaks of, "the situation of being at sea, of being lost, of confronting more information than you can handle" (p. 12, quoted in Fullan, 1982, p. 25). (See also Schon, 1983.)

Change can bring with it frustration, anxiety, pain, and other uncomfortable feelings. Means of coping with these uncomfortable feelings should be set in place to avoid teachers giving up a great idea due to despair. For example, opportunities for peer coaching, which are particularly helpful when one is beginning to implement a skill, should be orchestrated by the administration. Time for discussions with supervisory and administrative personnel should also be scheduled. Teachers need to be encouraged to be their own advocates in seeking out the support which is so crucial to their working through the replacement of a comfortable routine with an unfamiliar one.

During our history we have found ways to minimize the discomforts inherent in change by having the innovators be the ones who first implement the program in classrooms, by initially making involvement voluntary, by allowing for the gradual implementation of a program over a period of three to five years, and by providing time for reflection and the exchange of ideas. However, we were not always so wise, and change has not always come easily. The eventual success of previous change projects is testimony, however, to a staff that has become knowledgeable about how to implement each change, and to innovators who are understanding and have guided the implementation of an innovation with concern for the adopters, and with patience.

The innovators' openness to hearing and addressing individual concerns is a crucial means of support. Our experience suggests, as does that of others (e.g., Hord, Rutherford, Huling-Austin, & Hall, 1987), that concerns must be addressed before staff members can look at a proposed innovation objectively. The person charged with implementing the change should actively ask questions of individual staff members, questions that stimulate them to express concerns. In addition, they should be prepared to respond to those concerns in a non-defensive and supportive manner.

Some common concerns with which we have had to deal include: how is this different from what I am already doing; if I am already a good teacher, why do I have to change; how can I make my program creative, fun, exciting, etc. if I have to learn and follow the new program guidelines; how much preparation time will it take; will I have to write another set of lesson plans; and how will I be evaluated. The keys to resolving the concerns staff members have about a change include being understanding, seeing the problem from the staff member's point of view, and individualizing support to the developmental level of the individual (Gaskins, 1988a).

Principle 6: Expect Change to Take Time and to Require Ongoing Support

Curriculum change is a complex process that happens over time. For us, the time is measured in years. We have learned that it is not possible, nor desirable, for a school to have a program in place one year and by dictum declare another program in place the next. At least, it certainly has not worked that way for us.

Time is necessary for a number of reasons. One is that real change (that is, basic change in one's thinking about an innovation) cannot be imposed, but must evolve in response to teachers' recognizing the needs of students and understanding how the proposed change meets those needs. Sometimes, when we have tried to implement a new idea, the results have been disappointing because we have not allowed time for assessing needs and gaining understanding. A second reason that time is needed is that change requires a period of incubation and preparation. Several times, in our enthusiasm about a good idea, we had not analyzed carefully the impact of the change on teachers, including their need for support in making adjustments in knowledge and know-how. In such instances, we had neglected a basic premise — **individual teachers do the changing, not schools.**

Change that involves both long-held traditions and abstract concepts is the most difficult to establish and maintain, while change that involves a familiar text supplemented with innovative materials prepared by the change agent is easier to establish and maintain. We learned this truth by experience.

One of our early curriculum change projects was the school-wide implementation of a process approach to writing (Gaskins, 1982). Another was to develop a way for our students to handle difficult content-area texts (Gaskins, 1981). The two innovations met with very different responses.

An Example: The first of these changes was slow in being established and sometimes traumatic. It was the late 1970's. Donald Graves (1975) was pioneering a new idea in writing and we were eager to learn from someone who might teach us how to guide our students to improved written expression. We invited Graves to Benchmark. As a result of our work with Graves, we asked teachers to pack away their English textbooks and throw out their story-starter worksheets — the very materials teachers had relied on for years. And we were replacing these, not with more materials, but with an idea. The idea was that students should be allowed to write about the events and things about which they had the most information (e.g., dinosaurs, sports teams, my pet gerbil). Further, this writing would go through many drafts. The students' concept of "first draft, last draft" was to be substituted with a teacher first responding only to content, then to organization, later to clarity, and lastly (and only if the piece merited being revised for an audience), to spelling, punctuation, grammar, etc. Initially only one Benchmark teacher was willing to try the process approach to writing. Her successes, as well as her openness in sharing what went on in her classroom, were instrumental in giving the innovation the boost it needed. As other teachers followed her example, process writing was established at Benchmark.

Nevertheless, ten years later, with normal staff turnover, we still struggle to keep that innovation in place and the story starters and red pens in the closet. We have discovered that an innovation is not put in place once and for all, but rather that it needs constant support to keep it from falling into a routine that little resembles the original intent of the program. We attempt to provide this constant support by appointing one teacher as the coordinator of the school's writing program and by supervisors' routinely working with teachers in the classrooms.

There was much less resistance to the content-area innovation. We attribute the greater ease in implementation to the fact that this change was more concrete and not a radical change from tradition — as was the writing program. The innovators piloted this program in classrooms over long periods of time while the classroom teachers observed and assisted. Once the innovators were no longer modeling in the classroom, they provided the teachers with sample lessons and materials.

In summary, not only does a new innovation need ample time to take shape and become established, but it needs continual maintenance to remain in place and healthy. Providing knowledge or theory without also providing follow-up support, such as demonstrations, practice, feedback, and application with coaching, has a high probability of having little impact on classroom practices.

Principle 7: Set Aside Time to Reflect and Renew

One final lesson that extensive curriculum development and change have taught us is that it is very important to set aside time to reflect and renew. The staff needs time to step back and assess its progress and its goals.

An Example: One of our most unusual staff-development projects resulted in a book. In this project volunteer teachers selected an area of the Benchmark curriculum to research and update. Each researcher wrote a report sharing his/her finding with the staff. Staff members read and reacted to these reports and the final products became chapters in the book, *Teaching for Success: Administrative and Classroom Practices at Benchmark School* (Gaskins & Elliot, 1983). We were all surprised to find that the reports brought to our attention many good practices we had unconsciously altered or let slip from our usual routines. Two of the rewarding results of writing the book were better teaching and a better sense of how all aspects of the program fit together.

The book-writing project was repeated in 1986-87, with the chapters written by teachers presented to the research seminar for editing suggestions. The finished chapters now serve as the handbook used for new-teacher training, and revisions and additions are ongoing.

Another means of allowing time for reflection and renewal has been to have retreats. Some have been held during weekends, while others are held on a school day with substitutes being hired for the teachers involved. During the retreats teachers are given the opportunity to write lesson plans and to discuss their plans with an administrator or another teacher.

SUMMARY OF THE WHY AND HOW
OF IMPLEMENTING STRATEGY TEACHING

Why

To be successful in the 21st century men and women will need to know how to think about and access information. Self-regulated learners, thinkers, and problem solvers will have the edge on rote learners when applying for colleges and jobs. Employers will increasingly seek out lifelong learners rather than those who simply earned good grades in school. Knowledge accumulated from one's school days will provide merely a base for thinking. Being able to generate new ideas will be what is in demand. For these reasons it is crucial not only to our students, but to the stability of our economy, that teachers value and know how to guide students to become goal-driven, planful, self-assessing, and strategic learners.

How

There are those who will read this book and say, "Sure you can teach strategies across the curriculum in a unique school like Benchmark, but implementing a strategy program in a school like mine would be impossible." Such a statement is contradicted by the research. There is ample evidence that strategy programs with goals similar to those of the program described in this book are being implemented in both public and private, urban and suburban schools throughout the country. (See the citations in the References for descriptions of some of these programs.)

You are undoubtedly wondering what the authors of this book would do if they were given the challenge of implementing a strategy program in an urban school in a large city. Interestingly, we have been given that challenge, so we have given the idea considerable thought. We think our seven principles will be crucial to our success, so considerable thought and planning, not to mention years, will go into putting each in place.

Gathering Information. We plan to begin by scheduling a series of meetings with the faculty to discuss teacher concerns about the academic needs of their students. If the teachers desire and agree that it would be helpful, we will observe in classrooms and read student records, as well as chat informally with teachers and volunteer to teach demonstration lessons. We will share our impressions with the faculty regarding their concerns and invite their participation in a dialogue about the possibilities a strategy program holds for dealing with their concerns. In the process of these interactions we will strive to foster in each faculty member an attitude of *becoming*.

Sharing Knowledge. Teachers and administrators in the target school will be invited to visit Benchmark or another school where a strategy program is being implemented. These faculty members will be encouraged to spend extended amounts of time in classrooms where exemplary strategy teaching takes place and to meet individually with teachers and administrators to learn first hand about the difficulties and joys of undertaking such a project. In the best of all worlds, one or more teachers and/or administrators from the target school would spend a semester, or even better, a year working as a co-teacher in a classroom where strategy teaching is being successfully implemented. This apprenticeship model would allow these faculty members to return to their school with both knowledge about and enthusiasm for the innovation. If visitations are not possible, videotapes of exemplary strategy teaching will be presented and discussed with the faculty.

In addition, we will share with the faculty of the target school articles and chapters in professional journals and books that suggest remedies for the concerns addressed by the teachers, as well as provide knowledge about the theory and methods of strategy teaching. We will encourage a nucleus of the faculty who are interested in piloting a strategy program to meet as a group to grapple with the ideas they encounter in their reading. After this group has met several times on their own, and if they would like to share their conclusions with us, we will meet with them again. We will be particularly conscious of creating an environment where faculty members will feel safe to express concerns about this program change.

Planning and Implementing Pilot Classes. Based on the concerns of the faculty about student needs and on knowledge about the theory and methods of strategy teaching, the faculty of the target school will be encouraged to take part in planning a strategy program for a few pilot classes. We will share with the group transcripts and lesson plans for units of content/process instruction that have been taught at Benchmark. These transcripts and lesson plans can serve as prototypes as teachers design lessons appropriate for their students. We will encourage the teachers to tape their lessons as they implement their program and to critique not only their own lessons, but one another's. Meetings will be held where troublesome aspects of strategy teaching will be pondered and tapes illustrating these points shared and discussed.

When invited, we will present demonstration lessons in classrooms, preferably over a period of days so that the continuity of lessons can be shown. The faculty will be asked to write notes regarding the demonstration lesson to facilitate discussion following the lesson and to help us evaluate the progress the group is making in understanding strategy teaching. Administrators and teachers or pairs of teachers will be encouraged to support the development of a strategy program through the use of interactive journals.

Establishing, Maintaining, Reflecting, and Renewing. Though only a few members of the faculty may volunteer initially to participate in the innovation, we will continue to have periodic meetings with the full staff to answer their questions and concerns about this innovation that may become a school-wide program at a later date. We would also like to continue to monitor the program in the pilot classes to establish a pattern of maintenance of the integrity of the strategy program. The administration will be encouraged to provide professional days for those involved in the program — days set aside for retreats for reflecting and renewal.

Guidelines for Administrators (Supervisors, Coordinators, etc.)

If you are an administrator eager to try your hand at implementing a program similar to the one described in this book, you might want to begin with the ten guidelines listed below. Following those guidelines are guidelines for teachers who would like to act as change-masters and begin a strategy program. Further guidelines can be found in the 1990 Yearbook of the Association for Supervision and Curriculum Development (Joyce, 1990).

1. Schedule a series of meetings to discuss teacher concerns about the academic needs of their students.

2. Read articles and chapters in professional journals and books that suggest remedies for the concerns addressed by the teachers.

3. Supply teachers with professional journals and books (or photocopies of text from them) that address their concerns and invite the teachers to discuss their reading with you as well as to share the results of their reading with other teachers at a future meeting.

4. Observe in a few classrooms over a period of days to see instruction in the same area of the curriculum that relates to teachers' areas of concern.

5. Write notes to teachers regarding observations in specific classrooms, making sure to acknowledge each teacher's area of concern(s) and the positive steps which are being taken to address the student need that is a concern.

6. Invite experts in cognitive psychology and education to present

inservice programs for the faculty regarding their concerns and follow-up these inservice meetings with meetings to discuss implementation of the experts' ideas. If budgetary or other constraints prohibit the experts' presenting in person, rent videotaped lectures by these experts.

7. Send several potential change-master teachers to conferences where methods of addressing their concerns about students will be addressed.

8. Hold sharing meetings for teachers who are struggling with the same student concerns and who are experimenting with methods to address these concerns.

9. Form a committee of teachers to assist you in developing a pilot program for teaching students strategies to cope with the areas which concern teachers.

10. Have the committee jointly write and field test a strategy program using the ideas presented in this text.

Guidelines for Teachers as Change-masters

1. Assess your students' academic needs.

2. Select the most common, yet critical, need among your students.

3. Design and teach a series of strategy lessons (based on this text) to address the common need.

4. Discuss your project with colleagues who also teach your students and solicit their support.

5. Invite your supervisor to observe your lessons and collaborate with you in developing strategy lessons.

6. Encourage someone in your school's administrative hierarchy to implement the Guidelines for Administrators (or, if this approach is not successful, begin to assume the role of teacher-leader and put in place as many of the Guidelines for Administrators as possible).

FINAL WORDS

Though efforts to improve and change our program are always in process, we have never before undertaken an innovation of the magnitude of our strategies project. This project requires the commitment and understanding of the entire faculty, and the professional-support staff — 57 people in all. In the past, when one area of the curriculum (for example, reading or writing) was in the throes of change, other departments were little affected and provided a calming balance to the anxiety and uncertainty of the change process.

This time, when it is necessary to the success of the project that many staff members (with a variety of specialties and varying degrees of experience with change projects) be involved, reactions have varied from exhilaration to panic. Even the most secure have confided that change is threatening. Some faculty members respond with anxiety, others with feelings of stress, loss, or ambivalence. For all, there is some kind of struggle involved. In response to their struggle, the faculty has appreciated the availability of the school's director, supervisors, and psychological services staff members, as well as peers, to help them work through the specifics of implementing a strategy program in their classrooms.

We are discovering that each teacher seems to need time to work through the process of making meaning out of the change and reformulating his or her program to accommodate the change. Patience, a receptive ear, and a problem-solving attitude are proving to be valuable characteristics of both the innovators and the other members of the faculty. We are discovering once again that "the psychological process of learning and understanding something new does not happen in a flash" (Fullan, 1982, p. 38).

The cost in time and energy to develop the content-process program is great, but the cost to our students to not attempt it would be even greater. Concerns and resistance are inherent in change, but the results, in terms of professional excitement and growth and the increased success of our students, make it a struggle we would not miss.

References

Anderson, R.C. & Pearson, P.D. (1984). A schema-theoretic view of basic processes in reading comprehension. In P.D. Pearson (Ed.), *Handbook of reading research* (pp. 255-291). New York: Longman.

Au, K.H. (1988, April). *The staff development of novice and expert teachers of reading.* Presentation to the Conference on Reading Research, Anaheim, CA.

Barell, J., Liebmann, R., & Sigel, I. (1988). Fostering thoughtful self-direction in students. *Educational Leadership, 45* (7), 14-17.

Baron, J., Badgio, P.C., & Gaskins, I.W. (1986). Cognitive style and its improvement: A normative approach. In R.J. Sternberg (Ed.), *Advances in the psychology of human intelligence* (Vol. 3, pp. 173-220). Hillsdale, NJ: Lawrence Erlbaum.

Barrett, S.L. (1985). *It's all in your head: A guide to understanding your brain and boosting your brain power.* Minneapolis: Free Spirit Publishing Co.

Bereiter, C. & Scardamalia, M. (1985). Cognitive coping strategies and the problem of "inert knowledge." In S.F. Chipman, J.W. Segal, & R. Glaser (Eds.), *Thinking and learning skills, Vol. 2: Research and open questions* (pp. 65-80). Hillsdale, NJ: Lawrence Erlbaum.

Beyer, B. K. (1988a). Developing a scope and sequence for thinking skills instruction. *Educational Leadership, 45* (7), 26-30.

Beyer, B.K. (1988b). *Developing a thinking skills program.* Boston: Allyn & Bacon.

Borkowski, J.G., Estrada, M. T., Milstead, M., & Hale, C.A. (1989). General problem-solving skills: Relations between metacognition and strategic processing. *Learning Disability Quarterly, 12,* 57-70.

Brady, M. (1989). *What's worth teaching? Selecting, organizing, and integrating knowledge.* Albany, NY: State University of New York Press.

Brandt, R. (1988-89). On learning research: A conversation with Lauren Resnick. *Educational Leadership, 46* (4), 12-16.

Brandt, R. (1988). On teaching thinking: A conversation with Art Costa. *Educational Leadership, 45* (7), 10-13.

Bransford, J.D. & Stein, B.S. (1984). *The ideal problem solver*. New York: W.H. Freeman.

Bransford, J.D. & Vye, N.J. (1989). A perspective on cognitive research and its implications for instruction. In L.B. Resnick & L.D. Klopfer (Eds), *Toward the thinking curriculum: Current cognitive research* (pp. 173-203). Alexandria, VA: Association for Supervision and Curriculum Development.

Brophy, J. (1990). Teaching social studies for understanding and higher-order applications. *The Elementary School Journal, 90,* 351-417.

Brown, A.L. (1978). Knowing when, where, and how to remember: A problem of metacognition. In R. Glaser (Ed.), *Advances in instructional psychology* (Vol 1). Hillsdale, NJ: Lawrence Erlbaum.

Brown, A.L. (1985). Teaching students to think as they read: Implications for curriculum reform (Reading Ed. Rep. No. 58). Urbana-Champaign: University of Illinois, Center for the Study of Reading.

Brown, A.L., Palincsar, A.S., & Armbruster, B.B. (1984). Inducing comprehension-fostering activities in interactive learning situations. In H. Mandl, N. Stein, & T. Trabasso (Eds.), *Learning and comprehension of texts* (pp 255-286). Hillsdale, NJ: Lawrence Erlbaum.

Brown, J.S., Collins, A., & Duguid, P. (1989). Situated cognition and the culture of learning. *Educational Researcher*, 18 (1), 32-42.

Bruner, J. (1985). On teaching thinking: An afterthought. In S.F. Chipman, J.W. Segal, & R. Glaser (Eds.), *Thinking and learning skills, Vol. 2: Research and open questions* (pp. 597-607). Hillsdale, NJ: Lawrence Erlbaum.

Chambers, J.H. (1988). Teaching thinking throughout the curriculum —Where else? *Educational Leadership*, 45 (7), 4-6.

Chan, L.K.S. & Cole, P.G. (1986). The effects of comprehension monitoring training on the reading competence of learning disabled and regular class students. *Remedial and Special Education, 7,* 33-40.

Chance, P. (1986). *Thinking in the classroom*. New York: Teachers College Press.

Chomsky, C. (1972). Stages in language development and reading exposure. *Harvard Educational Review, 42,* 1-33.

Costa, A.L. (1987). Thinking skills: Neither an add-on nor a quick fix. In M. Heiman & J. Slomianko (Eds.), *Thinking skills instruction:*

Concepts and techniques (pp. 16-23). Washington, D.C.: National Education Association.

Cunningham, P.M. (1975-76). Investigating a synthesized theory of mediated word identification. *Reading Research Quarterly, 11,* 127-143.

Cunningham, P.M., Moore, S.A., Cunningham, J.W., & Moore, D.W. (1983). *Reading in elementary classrooms.* New York: Longman.

Day, M.C. (1985). On meeting the challenge. In S.F. Chipman, J.W. Segal, & R. Glaser (Eds.). *Thinking and learning skills, Vol. 2: Research and open questions* (pp. 587-596). Hillsdale, NJ: Lawrence Erlbaum.

Derry, S. J. (1988-89). Putting learning strategies to work. *Educational Leadership, 46* (4), 4-10.

Derry, S.J. & Murphy, D.A. (1986). Designing systems that train learning ability: From theory to practice. *Review of Educational Research, 56,* 1-39.

Dewey, J. (1933). *How we think: A restatement of the relation of reflective thinking to the educative process.* Boston: Heath.

Duffy, Gerald G. & Roehler, Laura R. (1986). *Improving classroom reading instruction.* NY: Random House.

Duffy, G.G. & Roehler, L.R. (1987). Teaching reading skills as strategies. *The Reading Teacher, 40,* 414-418.

Flavell, J.H. (1985). *Cognitive development* (2nd ed.). Englewood Cliffs, NJ: Prentice-Hall.

Frederiksen, N. (1984). Implications of cognitive theory for instruction in problem solving. *Review of Educational Research, 54* (3), 363-407.

Fullan, M. (1982). *The meaning of educational change.* New York: Teachers' College Press.

Gaskins, I.W. (1980). *The Benchmark story.* Media, PA: Benchmark Press.

Gaskins, I.W. (1981). Reading for learning: Going beyond basals in the elementary grades. *The Reading Teacher, 35,* 323-328.

Gaskins, I.W. (1982). A writing program for poor readers and writers and the rest of the class, too. *Language Arts, 59,* 854-861.

Gaskins, I.W. (1984). There's more to a reading problem than poor reading. *Journal of Learning Disabilities, 17,* 467-71.

Gaskins, I.W. (1988a). Helping teachers adapt to the needs of students with learning problems. In S.J. Samuels & P.D. Pearson (Eds.). *Changing school reading programs* (pp. 143-159). Newark, DE: International Reading Association.

Gaskins, I.W. (1988b). Introduction: A special issue on poor readers in the classroom. *The Reading Teacher, 41*, 748-749.

Gaskins, I.W. (1988c). Teachers as thinking coaches: Creating strategic learners and problem solvers. *Journal of Reading, Writing, and Learning Disabilities, 4*, 35-48.

Gaskins, I.W. (in press). And it works for them, too! In J.T. Feeley, D.S. Strickland, & S.B. Wepner (Eds.), *From writing process to reading process: K-8 teachers share their literacy programs.* New York: Teachers College Press.

Gaskins, I.W. & Baron, J. (1985). Teaching poor readers to cope with maladaptive cognitive styles: A training program. *Journal of Learning Disabilities, 18*, 390-394.

Gaskins, I.W., Downer, M., Anderson, R.C., Cunningham, P.M., Gaskins, R.W., Schommer, M., & the Teachers of Benchmark School (1988). A metacognitive approach to phonics: Using what you know to decode what you don't know. *Remedial and Special Education, 9*, 36-41, 66.

Gaskins, I.W. and Elliot, T.T. (1983). *Teaching for success: Administrative and classroom practices at Benchmark School.* Media, PA: Benchmark Press.

Glaser, R. (1984). Education and thinking: The role of knowledge. *American Psychologist, 39*, 93-104.

Glaser, R. (1987a). Introduction: Further notes toward a psychology of instruction. In R. Glaser, *Advances in instructional psychology* (Vol. 3, pp. vii-xxv). Hillsdale, NJ: Lawrence Erlbaum

Glaser, R. (1987b). Learning theory and theories of knowledge. In E. De Corte, H. Lodewijks, R. Parmentier, & P. Span (Eds.), *Learning and instruction: European research in an international context* (Volume 1, pp. 397-414). New York: Pergamon Press.

Glaser, Robert (1989). To plan for a century. *Educational Researcher, 18* (1), p. 5.

Good, T.L. & Brophy, J. (1989). Teaching the lesson. In R. E. Slavin (Ed.), *School and classroom organization* (pp. 25-68). Hillsdale, NJ: Lawrence Erlbaum.

Graves, D. H. (1975). An examination of the writing processes of seven-year-old children. *Research in the Teaching of English, 9*, 227-241.

Hall, G.E. & Hord, S.M. (1987). *Change in schools*. Albany, NY: State University of New York Press.

Hayes, J.R. (1989). *The complete problem solver* (2nd ed.). Hillsdale, NJ: Lawrence Erlbaum.

Hirsch, E.D., Jr. (1987). *Cultural literacy*. Boston: Houghton Mifflin.

Hord S.M., Rutherford, W.L., Huling-Austin, L. & Hall, G.E. (1987). *Taking charge of change*. Alexandria, VA: Association for Supervision and Curriculum Development.

Johnston, P. (1985). Teaching students to apply strategies that improve reading comprehension. *The Elementary School Journal, 85*, 635-645.

Jones, B.F., Palincsar, A.S., Ogle, D.S., & Carr, E.G. (1987). *Strategic teaching and learning: Cognitive instruction in the content areas*. Alexandria, VA: Association for Supervision and Curriculum Development.

Joyce, B. (Ed.), (1990). *Changing school culture through staff development*. Alexandria, VA: Association for Supervision and Curriculum Development.

Joyce, B. (1985). Models for teaching thinking. *Educational Leadership, 42*, 4-7.

Joyce, B. & Weil, M. (1986). *Models of teaching* (3rd ed.). Englewood Cliffs, NJ: Prentice-Hall.

Kirby, J.R. (1988). Style, strategy, and skill in reading. In R.R. Schmeck (Ed.), *Learning strategies and learning styles* (pp. 229-274). New York: Plenum Press.

Klein, M Frances (1989). *Curriculum reform in the elementary school: Creating your own agenda*. New York: Teachers College Press.

Lieberman, A. & Rosenholtz, S. (1987). The road to school improvement: Barriers and bridges. In J.I. Goodlad (Ed.), *The ecology of school renewal: NSSE yearbook* (pp. 79-98). Chicago: University of Chicago Press.

Levine, S.L. (1989). *Promoting adult growth in schools: The promise of professional development*. Boston: Allyn and Bacon.

Manolakes, G. (1988). Comprehension: A personal experience in content area reading. *The Reading Teacher, 42*, 200-202.

Marzano, R.J., Brandt, R.S., Hughes, C.S., Jones, B.F., Presseisen, B.Z., Rankin, S.C., & Suhor, C. (1988). *Dimensions of thinking: A framework for curriculum and instruction*. Alexandria, VA: Association for Supervision and Curriculum Development.

Newman, D., Griffin, P. & Cole, M. (1989). *The construction zone: Working for cognitive change in school*. New York: Cambridge University Press.

Nickerson, R.S. (1988). On improving thinking through instruction. In E.Z. Rothkopf (Ed.), *Review of Educational Research, 15* (pp. 3-57). Washington, D.C.: AERA.

Nickerson, R.S., Perkins, D.N., & Smith E.E. (1985). *The teaching of thinking*. Hillside, NJ: Lawrence Erlbaum.

Palincsar, A.S. & Brown, A.L. (1989). Instruction for self-regulated reading. In L.B. Resnick & L.E. Klopfer (Eds.), *Toward the thinking curriculum: Current cognitive research* (pp. 19-39). Alexanderia, VA: Association for Supervision and Curriculum Development.

Paris, S.G. (1989, January). Creating strategic readers. Talk given at the Delaware Valley Reading Association meeting, Philadelphia, PA.

Paris, S.G., Lipson, M.Y., & Wixson, K.K. (1983). Becoming a strategic reader. *Contemporary Educational Psychology, 8*, 293-316.

Paris, S.G. & Oka, E.R. (1989). Strategies for comprehending text and coping with reading difficulties. *Learning Disability Quarterly, 12*, 32-42.

Pearson, P.D. (1985). Changing the face of reading comprehension instruction. *The Reading Teacher, 38*, 724-738.

Perkins, D.N. & Salomon, Gavriel (1989). Are cognitive skills context-bound? *Educational Researcher, 18* (1), 16-25.

Peterson, P.L., Fennema, E., & Carpenter, T. (1988-89). Using knowledge of how students think about mathematics. *Educational Leadership, 46*, 42-46.

Pogrow, S. (1988). Teaching thinking to at-risk elementary students. *Educational Leadership, 45* (7), 79-85.

Prawat, R.S. (1989). Promoting access to knowledge, strategy, and disposition in students: A research synthesis. *Review of Educational Research, 59*, 1-41.

Presseisen, B. (1988). Avoiding battle at curriculum gulch: Teaching thinking and content. *Educational Leadership, 45* (7), 7 & 8.

Pressley, M., Gaskins, I.W., Cunicelli, E.A., Burdick, N.A., Schaub-Matt, M. Lee, D.S., & Powell, N. (in press). Perceptions of Benchmark School's experienced strategy teachers and strategy researchers about the nature of effective long-term strategy instruction. *Learning Disabilities Quarterly*.

Pressley, M., Goodchild, F., Fleet, J., Zajchowski, R., & Evans, E.D. (1989). The challenges of classroom strategy instruction. *The Elementary School Journal, 89*, 301-342.

Raths, L.E., Wassermann, S., Jonas, A., & Rothstein, A. (1986). *Teaching for thinking: Theories, strategies, and activities for the classroom* (2nd ed). New York: Teachers College Press.

Resnick, L.B. (1987). *Education and learning to think.* Washington, D.C.: National Academy Press.

Resnick, L.B. & Klopfer, L.E. (1989). Toward the thinking curriculum: An overview. In L.B. Resnick & L.E. Klopfer (Eds.), *Toward the thinking curriculum: Current cognitive research* (pp. 1-18). Alexandria, VA: Association for Supervision and Curriculum Development.

Schmeck, R.R. (1988a). Individual differences and learning strategies. In C.E. Weinstein, E.T. Goetz, & P.A. Alexander (Eds.), *Learning and study strategies: Issues in assessment, instruction, and evaluation* (pp. 171-191). San Diego: Academic Press.

Schmeck, R.R. (1988b). An introduction to strategies and styles of learning. In R.R. Schmeck (Ed.), *Learning strategies and learning styles* (pp. 3-12). New York: Plenum Press.

Schon, D.A. (1983). *The reflective practitioner: How professionals think in action.* New York: Basic Books.

Shuell, T.J. (1986). Cognitive conceptions of learning. *Review of Educational Research, 56*, 411-436.

Slavin, R.E. (1983). *Cooperative learning.* New York: Longman.

Slavin, R.E. (Ed.) (1989). *School and classroom organization.* Hillsdale, NJ: Lawrence Erlbaum.

Snowman, J. (1986). Learning tactics and strategies. In G.D. Phye & T. Andre (Eds.), *Cognitive classroom learning: Understanding, thinking, and problem solving* (pp. 243-275). Orlando: Academic Press.

Stodolsky, S.S. (1988). *The subject matters.* Chicago: University of Chicago Press.

Thomas, J.W., Strange, A., & Curley, R. (1988). Improving students' self-directed learning: Issues and guidelines. *The Elementary School Journal, 88*, 313-326.

Vosniadou, S. & Brewer, W.F. (1987). Theories of knowledge restructuring in development. *Review of Educational Research, 57*, 51-67.

Weinert, F.E. & Kluwe, R.H. (Eds.) (1987). *Metacognition, motivation, and understanding.* Hillsdale, NJ: Lawrence Erlbaum.

Weinstein, C.F. & Mayer, R.F. (1986). The teaching of learning strategies. In M.W. Wittrock (Ed.), *Handbook of research on teaching* (pp. 315-327). New York: Macmillan.

Wittrock, M.C. (1986). Students' thought processes. In M.C. Wittrock (Ed.), *Handbook on research on teaching* (pp. 297-314). New York: Macmillan.

Wolman, B.B. (Ed.) (1989). *Dictionary of behavioral science* (2nd ed.). San Diego: Academic press.

Wong, B.Y.L. (1985). Self-questioning instruction research: A review. *Review of Educational Research, 55,* 227-268.

About the Authors

IRENE W. GASKINS

Irene W. Gaskins is an educational psychologist who is founder and director of Benchmark School in Media, Pennsylvania. She received her Ed.D. at the University of Pennsylvania where she taught graduate and undergraduate courses in reading for 15 years. While earning her advanced degrees, she taught in both elementary and secondary schools and served as a reading specialist and district reading coordinator. Her publications include research and applied articles concerning learning problems, cognitive style, and instructional procedures for teaching children with reading problems. She was the guest editor of the April, 1988, issue of *The Reading Teacher*, Teaching Poor Readers: What Works? With Richard Anderson, Patricia Cunningham, Marjorie Downer, and the teachers of Benchmark School, she developed a decoding program which features using known words to decode unknown words. She is a principal investigator in the James S. McDonnell Foundation Program in Cognitive Studies for Educational Practice.

THORNE T. ELLIOT

Thorne T. Elliot has spent her entire 19-year teaching career at Benchmark School. A student in Dr. Gaskins' reading methods courses at the University of Pennsylvania, Mrs. Elliot volunteered to work as a teaching assistant at Benchmark School during the summer of 1971. She continued at Benchmark as a teaching assistant while attending graduate courses to earn her master's degree in reading. Upon completion of those courses she began teaching full time at Benchmark School. At present, in addition to her classroom duties as a language arts teacher, Mrs. Elliot is supervisor of the art and music programs at Benchmark, as well as the editor of all publications.

JAMES E. BENEDICT

James E. Benedict graduated from the University of Virginia in 1986 with a B.A. in history. The following year he attended Rutgers University in pursuit of a graduate degree in history. During the summer of 1987 Mr. Benedict worked at Benchmark School as a summer school teaching assistant, a job that led to his remaining at Benchmark for three years as a research assistant and history teacher in the James S. McDonnell research and development project to develop strategic learners, thinkers, and problem solvers. Currently Mr. Benedict is a graduate student in the Divinity School of Harvard University.

Index